THE ARABS
in the Mind of

In Memory of my brother

Hanna Wadie Suleiman
(1931–1986)

who dedicated his life to
the service of his people

CONTENTS

FIGURES AND TABLES

Figures

Tables

PREFACE

This book constitutes a multi-faceted look at American perceptions of the Middle East and the peoples of the region, particularly the Arabs. Although our focus will be on American attitudes toward Arabs, it should be obvious that American attitudes toward any particular Middle Eastern group are better understood and more clearly illustrated through the presentation of their views of other peoples of the region. This is particularly the case since American perceptions of Zionism/Israel, for instance, very much affect their attitudes toward Arabs, who are in conflict with Israel. Furthermore, as most Americans cannot distinguish between Arabs, Turks, and Iranians, lumping them all together as Muslims, it is necessary to discuss American attitudes toward Islam as well as the non-Arab Muslim peoples of the region.

Chapter one discusses the interaction between the United States and the Middle East as well as the factors affecting their relationship, e.g. Muslim-Western contacts and perceptions, Zionism, the Palestine question, Arab nationalism, etc. Chapters two, three, and four provide a systematic and longitudinal study of American press coverage of Middle East news during the 1956, 1967 and 1973 wars. These give us a clear picture of the atmosphere and the "state of mind" of Americans (as represented by the reports in the main newspapers and magazines here studied) during each one of these Arab-Israeli confrontations. They also enable us to compare and contrast the public and official American views and policies at these critical junctures in the fortunes of the peoples of the Middle East. This excercise is carried out in chapter five, where I also argue that stereotypes, especially negative ones of Arabs, have been used as a weapon that has proved to be as effective as some of the military, economic, or political weapons.

Chapter six presents the results of a survey of American high school teachers and their views of Arabs, Muslims, Palestinians, Israelis, etc. Because of the importance of schools in inculcating values, attitudes, and stereotypes about other peoples and countries, this study attempts to gauge the impact which high schools have on Americans in the development of specific orientations toward the Middle East and its peoples. Unfortunately, ignorance about, and some prejudice against, Arabs and Muslims are detected here also, particularly where social studies teachers have had little or no university courses dealing with the Middle East or the Arab world.

Chapter seven presents a thorough survey of American attitudes on the Middle East as reflected in hundreds of public opinion surveys over a period of a half-century, beginning in 1939. The issues discussed here include the American public's views on Arabs, Israelis, Palestinians, the Palestine Liberation Organization, oil and the oil boycott, the Palestine and Arab-Israeli conflicts, sympathy for the protagonists, as well as what specific policies should be adopted by American decision-makers. In addition, a comparative study of the polling agencies is presented and the various biasing tactics of some pollsters, especially Harris, are clearly delineated.

Chapter eight discusses the impact of American attitudes and stereotypes on American-Arab relations. This includes the pressures on news reporters, the self-censorship exercised by writers on the Middle East, the lack of sensitivity to Arab concerns, the harassment of the Arab-American community, and the pressures on political decisionmakers and aspirants for high political office. It is further argued that American government officials, basing their decisions on erroneous assumptions and negative stereotypes of Arabs, followed policies which contributed to the 1973 war—a war which could have been avoided if American leaders had more accurate and objective views and attitudes toward the Arabs and Israelis.

Chapter nine presents a clear and much-needed critique of the Arab information effort or campaign in North America. First, a thorough review of the discussions, reports and decisions of the Arab Ministers of Information as well as the pertinent agencies of the League of Arab States is presented. Then a constructive but critical assessment of these reports and activities is provided. This is followed by a set of suggestions and recommendations setting out what is needed to improve the Arab information (not propaganda) effort in America.

Chapter ten provides a brief summary of the main conclusions to be drawn from these studies. It also addresses the issue of whether or not an Arab-American dialogue is feasible and/or desirable.

The study presented as an Appendix (which is co-authored with Professor Shanto Iyengar) is rather technical and examines American public support for Egypt and Israel in relation to changes in United States policy toward the Middle East. The results indicate that changes in public images tend to follow, rather than precede, official policy.

Finally, a fairly comprehensive and up-to-date bibliography of writings in English and Arabic on American attitudes toward the Middle East is provided. It should prove most helpful to anyone interested in this topic or in Arab-American relations.

My interest, study and research on the issues raised here began in 1961, when I worked on my M.A. thesis at the University of Wisconsin, Madison, U.S.A. Over the years, my focus broadened to include studies on attitudes and stereotypes manifested in other aspects of the print media. As a member and later Chairman of the Middle East Studies Association of North America (MESA) Committee on the Image of the Middle East in Secondary Education, I worked to analyze some of the Social Science and World History books used in American schools. Also, and under the auspices of the "Images Committee," I conducted a survey of high school teachers in New York, Pennsylvania, Indiana, Kansas, Colorado, and California. In the process, I benefited much from the insights and comments of the other committee members, namely Ayad Al-Qazzaz, William Griswold, John Joseph, Lorne Kenny, Don Peretz, Glenn Perry, and Farhat Ziadeh. Two colleagues in particular have shared their expertise and their research with me over many years, to whom I am grateful. These are Professors Janice J. Terry at Eastern Michigan University and Ayad Al-Qazzaz at California State University, Sacramento. Also, I have had numerous and long discussions on the media, attitudes and stereotypes with Sayed Yassin, Director of the Center for Political and Strategic Studies at *Al-Ahram* in Cairo, Egypt. It was Sayed who suggested that I write a book on the subject which would incorporate my various studies and present the material and arguments in a more integrated and accessible form. I am grateful for his interest and suggestion. In addition, I want to thank four anonymous readers of the original manuscript who offered excellent suggestions for changes, additions and up-dating. This necessitated additional research and writing but it has much improved the final product.

Also, I am most grateful to my wife for her insights, many stimulating discussions, and the numerous critiques and suggestions she appends to the manuscript as she types—and retypes—along. Finally, my children, Suad and Gibran, deserve special thanks for their patience and understanding throughout much of the research and writing of this book.

Grateful acknowledgement is made to the following for permission to reprint previously published material:

Association of Arab-American University Graduates: "Perceptions of the Middle East in American Newsmagazines," in Baha Abu-Laban and Faith T. Zeadey, eds. *Arabs in America: Myths and Realities*, 1975; and "The Arab Information Effort in North America: An Assessment," *Arab Studies Quarterly* (Summer, 1986). *Journal of Palestine Studies*: "National Stereotypes as Weapons in the Arab-Israeli Conflict." (Spring, 1974). Middle East Research Group: "Stereotypes, Public Opinion and Foreign Policy: The Impact on American-Arab Relations," *Journal of Arab Affairs* (1982). Center for Contemporary Arab Studies, Georgetown University: "American Public Support of Middle Eastern Countries: 1939–1979," in Michael C. Hudson and Ronald G. Wolfe, eds., *The American Media and the Arabs* (1980). Middle East Studies Association of North America: *American Images of Middle East Peoples: Impact of the High School* (1977). Northwestern University Press: "American Mass Media and the June Conflict," in Ibrahim Abu-Lughod, ed., *The Arab-Israeli Confrontation of June 1967* (1970). Shanto Iyengar, co-author of Chapter 8, and Sage Publications: "Trends in Public Support for Egypt and Israel, 1956–1978," *American Politics Quarterly* (January, 1980).

Finally, I would like to thank Ms. Jean Adam for her help in preparing the Index.

C H A P T E R 1

America and the Arabs:
The Making of an Image

This introductory essay will sketch the American views of Middle Easterners, especially Arabs, review the main factors contributing to these views, and then discuss the inter-play of relationships between attitudes and policy-making.

Attitudes toward Iran under the Shah were rather vague and uninformed, even among educated Americans. Thus, one survey found that school teachers generally approved of the pro-Western stance of the country but knew little about the people. Their image was of an ancient civilization, of Persian rugs, oil and the Shah.[1] After the ouster of the Shah and the confrontation between the Khomeini regime and the United States, Americans began to view Iranians as Islamic fanatics, cruel and uncivilized.[2]

In the mind of Americans, Turkey is not unlike pre-Khomeini Iran, an ancient country, friendly to, and an ally of, the West. Turks, however, are also recognized as tough fighters and are associated with the Crusades.[3]

Americans view Israel and Israelis in quite positive terms — certainly more positive than those of any other people in the Middle East. They are seen as Jews who are determined to establish a state of their own. While generally viewed as tough good fighters, they are also seen by some as aggressive and "insufferable."[4]

Americans hold generally negative views of Arabs and of specific Arab peoples, such as Palestinians, Lebanese, etc., although "the Arabs" are viewed more negatively than any of the countries or peoples constituting the Arab world. Of all Middle Easterners, with the exception of Khomeini's Iran, Arabs are viewed most negatively. Thus, in a recent survey,

1

they were seen as simultaneously rich and "backward, primitive, un-civilized" people who dressed strangely, mistreated women, and ap-peared to be "warlike, bloodthirsty," "treacherous, cunning," "strong, powerful," and "barbaric, cruel."[5] Obviously, not all, or even most, Americans have such views nor, for that matter, do all Americans in-ternalize even most of these views. However, there is no question that, among Americans, there is a "mind-set," a general picture of Arabs which, though vague, is distorted and incorrect and almost invariably negative, at times bordering on racism.[6] Consequently, when the "appropriate" situation presents itself, such stereotypes are easily con-jured up, and Arabs, or some Arab people or country, become easy, convenient, or "useful" targets. In the 1950's, for instance, President Gamal Abdel-Nasser of Egypt became the focus of an aggressive and vindictive campaign which characterized him as "Hitler on the Nile" and "crypto-communist" at the same time. Also, the Palestine Libera-tion Organization (PLO) and even the Palestinian people as a whole are smeared as a bunch of terrorists, especially when an act of terrorism captures the headlines — and regardless of whether or not the PLO de-nounced the action. Most recently, the Libyan leader, Moammar Qad-dafi, was identified by the United States government as practically the sole instigator of international terrorism and his human identity was stripped from him as he was designated a "mad dog."

We are not here discussing the merits of any of these cases. What we are saying is that the negative image Americans have of Arabs and Muslims makes it easy for anyone hostile to the Arabs to whip up public sentiment against them or against any Arab leader, country, or people. The Zionists certainly exploit this situation; so do American politicians, political aspirants, and American presidents in pursuit of specific policies.[7]

But why do Americans have negative stereotypes of Middle Easterners and Arabs in particular? Many have blamed the situation on Zionists and their supporters who are interested in defending Israel and advan-cing her cause at the expense of the Arabs. If it were not for that, the argument goes, Americans would clearly see that it is in their interest to befriend the Arabs and support their causes, including Palestine.[8] Another argument suggests that countries determine what their national interests are and which states are likely allies and which ones are likely or real enemies constituting a definite or potential threat to their in-terests. Once a country identifies and categorizes other states on this basis, then its leaders develop a basic orientation of friendliness or hostility toward the countries so identified. Friends are then perceived as having generally positive and favorable characteristics whereas enemies are assigned negative stereotypes.[9] One may conclude from this argument, therefore, that Arabs and Arabism are viewed by the United States as a clear and definite threat to its interests in the Middle East — hence the negative reporting and resultant distortion of information and stereotyping.[10]

The above two arguments are not necessarily mutually exclusive and there is definitely a feedback process where a change in perception, for instance, might also influence policy to some extent.[11] Also, in a democracy the policymaking process allows for potential change as a result of popular outcry or pressure by a determined and well-organized minority.[12] Nevertheless, while both arguments are viable, there is substantial evidence that the national interest argument is more valid and has been the over-all basis for U.S. policy — at least since the establishment of the state of Israel.[13] If that is the case, why and in what way would America and the Arab world be enemies? It is important to clarify that Arabs and Americans, as peoples, are not necessarily, nor are they in fact, antagonistic to each other. If any gap separates them, it is a cultural/religious one, which will be discussed later. The clash between the two sides has been on the level of national interests as perceived by successive governments in the United States on one side and advocates of Arab nationalism and radical Muslim fundamentalism on the other. Specific Arab leaders have attempted to advance these causes, such as Gamal Abdel-Nasser and Muammar Qaddafi, as well as various anti-establishment radical Islamic movements.

The first major conflict between the two sides occurred in the 1950's. At that time, the United States was just beginning its role as the major Western power in the Middle East and the foremost defender of a strategic region made enormously more important with the discovery of the largest reserves of oil and gas in the world. Simultaneously, the rulers of the various Arab states were being challenged by a new and major force demanding sweeping and revolutionary change (*inqilab*). The rising tide of revolutionary Arab nationalism sought and occasionally brought about the overthrow of regimes and rulers viewed to be corrupt, inept, or anachronistic — and which had to be removed if the dream of a resurgent and united Arab nation was to be realized. The intellectuals who led the Arab nationalist movement claimed to speak in the name, and on behalf, of the whole Arab nation and therefore directly challenged any and all Arab rulers who were seeking to maintain and strengthen their own legitimacy in their newly-established states.

In addition to threatening specific Arab rulers and regimes, Arab nationalism and its proponents challenged the United States and its Western allies by the demand for a complete and sweeping break with the ex-colonial powers. Such a move also carried the corresponding call for Arab nationalists to seize, and excercise complete control over, the resources of the Arab world, especially oil. The challenge was clear to all sides, the Arab nationalists, the Arab rulers and their local supporters, as well as the Western powers, including the United States. When President Nasser of Egypt took up the Arab nationalist cause, the threat to several Arab regimes greatly intensified. Successive American administrations, while at times considering the possibility of siding with the Arab nationalist tide, usually decided that American interests were better served by supporting the local rulers, especially as Nasser and other Arab nationalists began to turn to the Soviet Union for help in their quest for sweeping change in the status quo.

Another complicating factor in the relationship between Arabs and Americans was (and is) the question of Palestine/Israel. Up to 1948, most American leaders, in and out of government, were of the opinion that it was not in America's interest to antagonize the Arab or Muslim worlds — and that the establishment of a Jewish state in Palestine would do just that. Nevertheless, the Middle East did not, at the time, constitute an area of major strategic concern to the United States, In any case, to the extent that Americans viewed the area in such terms, they still thought of it as being under a European, especially British, sphere of influence. Under such circumstances, therefore, it was possible — and indeed became feasible — for a determined, well-organized and well-financed interest group within the American body politic, namely the Zionist movement, to utilize the regular mechanisms of a democratic government and society in order to have its own partisan interests accepted as national policy. How this was done has been detailed in many accounts of that critical period for the Middle East and for the Arab world in particular. Very briefly, the following activities were initiated or intensified. A major media campaign was launched to persuade the public that Palestine was the last — and only — haven for Europe's destitute Jewish refugees and displaced persons, the survivors of the Nazi extermination camps. In the process, ignorance of and indifference toward Arabs, including the Palestinians, made it easy to treat Arabs and their arguments as insignificant. The press and electronic media were employed, as were the movies. Furthermore, tremendous pressure was applied to get political leaders to espouse the Zionist program and support its adoption as policy. The Democratic and Republican parties, hoping to capitalize on the issue in order to advance their own fortunes, began to out-bid each other both in being the first to announce their support, and in offering more support, for the Zionist cause. Congressmen as well as those aspiring to political office suddenly found a useful and safe issue to exploit in their campaigns. Pressure was applied on the State Department, the War Department and every government agency involved in policy-making on this issue. Finally, the most intense pressure was focused on President Harry S. Truman as the key foreign policy maker.[14]

Success of the Zionist campaign in the United States in 1948 was facilitated by other factors, which continue to operate today and should, therefore, be discussed. In addition to operating in a democratic system in the United States, the Zionists had the advantage of working in a society in which there was no equivalent countervailing pressure group. Thus, especially in 1948, but even today to a great extent, the absence of effective Arab associations working for Arab causes in the United States has made the Zionist task easier and the results of its efforts much greater. The Arab effort in the United States has also been handicapped by the fact that Arab-Americans are relatively small in number, not well-organized, tend to be non-political, and are fractionalized into numerous sectarian and "ethnic" groupings based on their country of origin.[15]

Another factor contributing to the success of Zionism in America is the fact that most Arabs are Muslims, when Islam has not been well-known in the United States and where antipathy to Muslims is not uncommon. Historically, the Christian West has viewed Islam with suspicion and fear. For over a thousand years, Islam presented a serious threat to Christianity, both as a religious institution and as an ideology—and the memory of that threat has apparently lingered on. Part of the Western response to this fear of Islam has been expressed in antagonistic and unfavorable writings about Islam and the Muslims, including the Arabs. In the process, western writers on Islam, including Orientalists and contemporary textbook writers and journalists, have often presented Islam and Muslims in an unfavorable light.[16] Since most Americans do not distinguish between Arabs and Muslims and think that the two terms are synonymous, negative reporting about Islam automatically tarnishes the Arabs. This problem is greatly magnified when another misperception is added to the formula, namely the fact that Americans generally do not distinguish between Arabs, Turks, and Iranians. Thus, when America is at odds with any Middle Eastern Muslim country, the resultant antagonism and negative stereotyping are quickly transferred to the Arabs as well. A recent example is the conflict between the United States and the Khomeini regime in Iran, especially during the hostage crisis, which also saw an increased anti-Arab hostility.

To sum up, when Zionism was attempting to make inroads in the United States, it found an atmosphere that was conducive to its purpose, almost as much as it was hostile to the proponents of Arab nationalism. Support of the Zionist enterprise was also made more acceptable to the public since it was presented as a humanitarian project to aid destitute refugees and displaced persons — the remnants of European Jewry which had suffered persecution over the centuries at the hands of Christian nations. It was easy, convenient and indeed psychologically appealing for many people in the West, including the United States, therefore, to rid themselves of the guilt feeling for the previous ill-treatment of Jews by lending a helping hand in the establishment of a Jewish state — especially since it was to be set up far away and on territory which did not belong to them.

For many years after the establishment of Israel, American orientations toward that state were primarily influenced by cultural and internal structural factors. In other words, and more specifically, United States governments under Dwight Eisenhower and John Kennedy were still seeking a *modus vivendi* with the Arab nationalist movement and avoided, therefore, a complete identification with the state of Israel or a complete break with President Nasser and his Arab followers.[17] However, beginning with the Lyndon Johnson administration, and especially the 1967 war, Arab nationalism and its advocates became a primary target, and United States policy became more clearly committed to a strong Israel, to be employed in the defense of American interests in the Middle East.[18] As the Israeli-American "alliance" strengthened, major differences between the two countries have arisen in two main areas in which perceptions of their respective national interests have diverged. The first and minor difference pertains to American arms sales to specific Arab countries friendly to the United States, such as Jordan, Saudi Arabia, and Egypt. The other and more serious difference pertains to the Carter Administration's attempt at a comprehensive settlement of the Palestine and Arab-Israeli conflicts.[19]

During such differences, cultural and domestic political factors are utilized fully by the Israelis and their supporters in the United States, the committed Zionists as well as those who strongly believe that Israel is America's best ally and the most effective defender of U.S. interests in the region.

Cultural similarities or differences do not, in and of themselves, determine the foreign policies of sovereign states. They do, however, have an impact on the policy-making process. Thus, with two friendly states whose peoples have the same or similar cultural backgrounds, communication is much facilitated and good rapport is more easily attained. On the other hand, the leaders of any two states having different cultures who determine that they have mutual interests will have to work harder to achieve better communication and greater rapport between their peoples. In situations where two peoples or nations pursue antagonistic goals *and* simultaneously belong to two quite different cultural heritages, the antagonism is likely to be intensified and more quickly generated. Furthermore, even when some mutual interests are identified by the respective leaders, attempts at rapprochement will be more difficult to accomplish. This is particularly the case when important elements within either or both groupings are determined, for their own ends, to keep the antagonism in place and intact. This latter situation is the one in which the Arabs/Muslims and the West, especially the United States, have found themselves throughout much of their contact and many of their encounters, as will be discussed below.

Historical Background

Before the rise of Islam, the Byzantines expressed little interest in the Arab tribes — except when they needed and used them as military allies against the Persians. Even then, the interest was not in the sedentary or urban Arab communities but in the nomadic tribes. These were represented as living an austere and simple life. They were excellent warriors but they basically pillaged for ransom or exacted tribute. The Byzantines viewed these Arab tribes negatively and identified them as *barbaroi*, except when some of them were Christianized or became military allies. However, they were viewed as unreliable allies and inept in fighting pitched battles. Also, their pagan gods were attacked, and the practice of human sacrifice was falsely attributed to them. Their dress and way of life were viewed as primitive and their morals, especially in sexual matters, were condemned.[20]

The Byzantines' views of the Arabs filtered through to Europe and constituted part of the Western image of Arabs at the time of the rise of Islam. To this picture were added many others as the Islamic empire expanded. In a study of Western attitudes toward Muslims before the Crusades, James Waltz enumerates six different orientations, shading into one another, with specific individuals sometimes holding several of them. These attitudes were indifference, coexistence, political hostility, military hostility, academic hostility and religious hostility. In fact, indifference and ignorance might have been dominant throughout, but certainly those were the attitudes at the beginning of Islam (622–710), changing to political hostility (710–1000) which then was transformed into religious hostility (1000–1216) — and war. Nevertheless, while there was much ignorance, indifference, and some prejudice, the major change in Western attitudes toward Arabs and Muslims came when the church hierarchy (i.e. popes) took over political leadership and power from inept secular authorities, called for peace among warring Christian nations, *and* sought to direct that antagonism and war against the Muslim outsiders. When the erstwhile attitude of co-existence between Muslim and Christian communities turned into confrontation, an anti-Muslim ideology was developed which painted a dark and evil picture of Islam, the Prophet, and Muslims in general, including, of course, the Arabs (Saracens, Ishmaelites, etc.).[21] It was this picture which then came to dominate Western European attitudes for hundreds of years — even up to this century, at least in some respects.[22]

This Medieval Western picture of the Muslims and Arabs was later inherited by the inhabitants of the American colonies. In formulating these negative views, an attempt was made to discredit Islam by trying to discredit its founder. Arabs and Muslims were viewed as pagans, worshipping Mohammed as well as other gods. Exceptional cruelty and savagery were traits attributed to them. In fact, Western literature reflected such attitudes. For example, the main themes represented in Elizabethan literature about the Orient were war, conquest, fratricide, treachery, and lust.[23]

These and similar themes were propagated in most of the reports by Western merchants and travellers who visited the Middle East in the sixteenth and seventeenth centuries. In fact, no distinction was made between Arabs and other residents of the area under Ottoman rule. Arabs were referred to by different names and were given slightly different attributes depending on where they live: for instance, desert

(Arabs) Levant (Saracens), North Africa (Moors) or Egypt (Mamelukes). They were all viewed as wild, cruel, savage or robbers, in greater or lesser degree.[24] Also, once the *Arabian Nights* was translated into Western languages, in the eighteenth century, Arabs became identified with the book, and the traits and life-styles of the characters in these tales were automatically and repeatedly transferred to "the Arabs". To Westerners, the Arabs were now viewed as "very superstitious . . . indolent, excessively obstinate, submissive to authority, and sensual."[25] Other travellers and scholars in the nineteenth century amplified these themes and began to make a distinction between the bedouin (sometimes identified as a noble savage) and the city-dweller. The desert Arab had a more favorable and romantic image as independent, simple, free, struggling against great odds, hospitable, brave, and a good fighter. By contrast, city Arabs were viewed as untrustworthy, unattractive, rancourous, and revengeful.[26]

While Americans inherited this image of Arabs and Muslims from the West, they added other specifically American ingredients — influenced by distinctly American factors. These included a greater emphasis on the Bible as a literal representation of what happened in the Middle East. In the Bible, the Arabs are portrayed as nomadic bedouins, wily politicians, and "lurking" mercenaries.[27] Also, they were seen as a continual threat to the Hebrews in the Old Testament accounts and were, at times, presented as "God's agents of retribution and temptation." Other images were related to violence, sensuality, and extreme wealth.[28]

Three other distinctly American factors which add to the European image of Arabs are: The American tendency to identify with the Ancient Hebrews; the ideology of Savagism; and the ideology of Mission. It was particularly true of the Puritans of New England to see themselves metaphorically, as Israelites. Some, like Cotton Mather, even believed that the American Indians were the descendants of the Scythians or Canaanites. The analogy of the Arabs with American Indians was established early — and persisted. Thus, "where the earliest American settlers saw themselves as ancient Israelites, twentieth century Americans frequently compared the modern Israelis to the American pioneers."[29]

The ideology of Savagism was developed by the early American pioneers primarily to protect themselves, as the civilized people, from the "noncivilized" Indians. The America they discovered was a terrifying wilderness, a wild country, "a moral vacuum, a cursed and chaotic wasteland."[30] In this wilderness, the Indians lived as savages. They had to be Christianized or eliminated—for fear that the European settlers themselves might otherwise become uncivilized savages.[31] While American attitudes toward Indians changed and much sympathetic writing appeared, beginning late in the nineteenth century, this happened after the Indian ceased to be a physical and moral threat to the colonists.[32] The point, however, is that the ideology of Savagism and the basic orientation toward Indians were then applied to the Arabs, especially Palestinian Arabs, in their conflict with Zionism and Israel.

In the nineteenth century, Americans began to come in contact with Arabs and Muslims on a more personal level, as missionaries found their way to the area to preach the gospel. As is well known, the attempt to convert Muslims to Christianity was not very successful; in fact, it even proved to be difficult to attract other Christians to Protestantism. However, as the American msisionaries lived in the area and mingled among the inhabitants, they began to send reports and write books about the Middle East, Muslims, Turks, Eastern Christians, and Arabs generally. By and large, these reports were quite negative and had a major impact on the public as well as policy-makers.[33] According to Helen M. Kearney, most missionary accounts blurred the distinction between Muslims and Christians in the Middle East and viewed both negatively:

> "[B]oth religious communities were believed to share moral and intellectual deficiencies which locked the Oriental races into a state of semi-barbarism: a rigid dogmatism which stifled intellectuality and science; an ineradicable indolence which inhibited efficient and rational productivity; a staggering illiteracy rate; the paralyzing apathy of fatalism; a universal brutality and oppression without the mitigating compensation of a competent bureaucracy, a judicial system, an educational program or even rudimentary sanitation. Derivative social values and communal attitudes toward truth, individual freedom, the sanctity of human life, slavery, the status of women, technology, reinforced and perpetuated a system inimical to modernity."[34]

The conduct of World War I, the Armenian massacres, and the need for Arab allies temporarily modified the above attitudes. Thus, both Armenians and Arabs were seen in a more positive light, but this transformation "dissolved in the wake of peace and they [Arabs and Armenians] reappeared in the post-war media in the familiar visages of the exotic and alien Levantines."[35]

The romantic image of the Arab gave way to other aspects of Arab characterizaiton more suitable for the needs and political aims of interested parties in the West, including the United States. The communications media, especially films, the entertainment industry and television have generally and repeatedly portrayed the Arab in negative terms. In biblical and political films, Arab and Jew are presented in conflict and the Jew is continually favored over the Arab. Arabs and Muslims are presented as members of the outgroup, Jews and Israelis as part of the ingroup. Sex and violence are dominant themes and Arabs are portrayed as dangerous, and their values viewed as immoral.[36] Similar themes are developed, often with fanciful and fantastic plots, about Arab wealth and petro-dollars endangering Western economies, and about alleged Arab and Islamic schemes to steal, develop or somehow use nuclear weapons to endanger or even destroy Western countries or threaten Western civilization.[37]

The rise of the Zionist movement, the conflict over Palestine and the advancement of imperialist and colonial interests, as well as Arab naivete in both public relations and international politics, contributed to this deleterious development. It was easy, for instance, for Britain and France to use Arab "backwardness" as an excuse to implant themselves as the masters of the region. Furthermore, Zionism could argue that a Jewish state would be a better protector of imperial interests. Arabs were then viewed as both dispensable and disposable nomads.[38] As for Americans, "the Arabs are a people who have lived outside of history."[39] If they register at all in the mind of most Americans, it certainly is not through their major contributions to world civilization. Rather, they are viewed as a Middle East people who have changed little since the time of Christ and who, in the twentieth century, have opposed Western penetration of the area and are locked in mortal combat with Israel, a Western "ally" and, to Christian fundamentalists, a fulfillment of prophecy.[40]

It is clear from the above that the Zionists found it easier to spread their message and advance their cause exactly because the Western image of Arabs/Muslims (i.e. the Zionists' enemy) was already very negative. Within the United States, Zionists were far more successful at first in debunking the Arab case and attacking the Arab/Muslim character than they were in persuading political decision-makers to accept their plan for a Jewish state. However, once that was accomplished, they could also proclaim and demonstrate their usefulness in advancing

American interests in the area.

In addition to the above, the Zionists have shown themselves as great communicators and most adept at presenting their point of view, whereas the Arab side has not been able to do so, at least for much of the time. The consequence has been a continuing media campaign which simultaneously builds a positive image of Israel/Zionism and denigrates Arabs/Muslims through negative stereotypes. The various studies in the book detail these issues and provide specific examples spanning a period of some thirty years.

NOTES

1. Michael W. Suleiman, *American Images of Middle East Peoples: Impact of the High School* (New York: Middle East Studies Association of North America, 1977), pp. 49–50.

2. Edward W. Said, *Covering Islam* (New York: Pantheon Books, 1981).

3. Suleiman, *op. cit.*, p. 50.

4. *Ibid.*, pp. 47–48. See also, Shelley Slade, "The Image of the Arab in America: Analysis of a Poll on American Attitudes," *The Middle East Journal*, Vol. 35, No. 2 (Spring, 1981), p. 147.

5. Slade, *op. cit.*, pp. 147–50.

6. Seymour Martin Lipset and William Schneider, "Carter vs. Israel: What the Polls Reveal," *Commentary*, Vol. 64, No. 5 (Nov., 1977), p. 22; and Michael W. Suleiman, "An Evaluation of Middle East News Coverage in Seven American Newsmagazines, July-December, 1956." (M.A. thesis, University of Wisconsin, Madison, 1961).

7. See Alfred M. Lilienthal, *The Zionist Connection* II (New Brunswick, N.J.: North American, 1982); and Paul Findley, *They Dare to Speak out: People and Institutions Confront Israel's Lobby* (Brattleboro, VT: Amana Books 1985).

8. Most of the literature from the Arab side holds to this view.

9. William Buchanan and Hadley Cantril, *How Nations See Each Other* (Urbana, Ill.: University of Illinois Press, 1953). See also Bernard C. Cohen, *The Press and Foreign Policy* (Princeton University Press, 1963); and *The Public's Impact on Foreign Policy* (Boston: Little, Brown, 1973).

10. Ibrahim I. Ibrahim, "The American-Israeli Alliance: *Raison d'etat* Revisited," *Journal of Palestine Studies*, Vol. 15, No. 3 (Spring, 1986), pp. 17–29.

11. Richard P. Stevens, "Zionism Re-examined: U.S. Tool or Israeli Lobby?" in Margaret Pennar, ed., *The Middle East: Five Perspectives* (North Dartmouth, MA: Association of Arab-American University Graduates, 1974), pp. 29–32

12. For a recent example from the Carter years, see Montague Kern, *Television and Middle East Diplomacy: President Carter's Fall 1977 Peace Initiative* (Washington, D.C.: Center for Contemporary Arab Studies, Georgetown University, 1983). See also Montague Kern, Patricia W. Levering and Ralph B. Levering, *The Kennedy Crises: The Press, the Presidency, and Foreign Policy* (Chapel Hill, NC: University of North Carolina Press, 1983), especially chapter 15.

13. For a recent article and a review of the literature, see Shanto Iyengar and Michael Suleiman, "Trends in Public Support for Egypt and Israel, 1956–1978," *American Politics Quarterly*, Vol. 8, No. 1 (Jan., 1980), pp. 34–60.

14. Among the many books dealing with the subject are the following: Walter Millis, ed., *Forrestal Diaries* (New York: Viking Press, 1951); Harry S. Truman *Memoirs, II Years of Trial and Hope* (New York, Doubleday, 1956); Alfred M. Lilienthal, *What Price Israel?* (Chicago: H. Regnery Co., 1953); Richard P. Stevens, *American Zionism and U.S. Foreign Policy, 1942–1947* (New York: Pageant, 1962); Evan M. Wilson, *Decision on Palestine: How the U.S. Came to Recognize Israel* (Stanford, CA: Hoover Institution Press, 1979); Alan R. Taylor, *Prelude to Israel* (New York: Philosophical Library, 1959); Dean Acheson, *Present at the Creation* (New York: W.W. Norton, 1969).

15. Apart from my own writings on this subject, see Abdulrahman A. Zamil, "The Effectiveness and Credibility of Arab Propaganda in the United States." (Ph.D. dissertation, University of Southern California, 1973).

16. Edward W. Said, *Orientalism* (New York: Vintage Books, 1979); William J. Griswold, *The Image of the Middle East in Secondary School Textbooks* (New York: Middle East Studies Association of North America, 1975); Samir Ahmad Jarrar, "Images of the Arabs in United States Secondary School Social Studies Textbooks." (Ph.D. dissertation, Florida State University, 1976); Ayad Al-Qazzaz, "Images of the Arab in American Social Science Textbooks," in Baha Abu-Laban and Faith T. Zeadey, eds., *Arabs in America: Myths and Realities* (Wilmette, IL: Medina University Press International, 1975), pp. 113–132; and Glenn Perry, "Treatment of the Middle East in American High School Textbooks," *Journal of Palestine Studies*, Vol. 4, No. 3 (Spring, 1975), pp. 46–58.

17. Henry William Brands, Jr., "What Eisenhower and Dulles Saw in Nasser: Personalities and Interests in U.S.-Egyptian Relations," *American-Arab Affairs*, No. 17 (Summer, 1986), pp. 44–54.

18. William B. Quandt, *Decade of Decisions: American Policy Toward the Arab-Israeli Conflict, 1967–1976* (Berkeley, CA: University of California Press, 1977); Donald Neff, *Warriors for Jerusalem: The Six Days That Changed the Middle East* (New York: Linden Press/Simon Schuster, 1984); and Stephen Green, *Taking Sides: America's Secret Relations with a Militant Israel* (New York: Morrow, 1984).

19. William B. Quandt, *Camp David: Peacemaking and Politics* (Washington, D.C.: Brookings, 1986); Jimmy Carter, *Keeping Faith: Memoirs of a President* (New York: Bantam, 1983).

20. Vassilios Christides, "The Image of the Pre-Islamic Arab in the Byzantine Sources." (Ph.D. dissertation, Princeton University, 1970).

21. James Calvin Waltz, "Western European Attitudes Toward the Muslims Before the Crusades." Ph.D. dissertation, Michigan State University, 1963).

22. See, in particular, Norman Daniel, *Islam and the West: The Making of an Image* (Edinburgh: Edinburgh University Press, 1960); *Islam, Europe and Empire* (Edinburgh: Edinburgh University Press, 1966); R.W. Southern, *Western Views of Islam in the Middle Ages* (Cambridge, MA: Harvard University Press, 1962); and Abderrahim Ali Nasralla, "The Enemy Perceived: Christian and Muslim Views of Each Other During the Crusades." (Ph.D. dissertation, New York University, 1980).

23. Louis Wann, "The Oriental in Elizabethan Drama," *Modern Philology*, Vol 12, No. 7 (Jan., 1915), pp. 163–187. See also, Mohammad Hassan Asfour, "The Crescent and the Cross: Islam and the Muslims in English Literature from Johnson to Byron." (Ph.D. dissertation, Indiana University, 1973).

24. Sari J. Nasir, *The Arabs and the English* (London: Longman, 1979). Second edition.

25. *Ibid.*, p. 65.

26. *Ibid.*, p. 71: and Ahmed Mohamed Metwalli, "The Lure of the Levant, The American Literary Experience in Egypt and the Holy Land: A Study in the Literature of Travel, 1800–1865." (Ph.D. dissertation, State University of New York at Albany, 1971).

27. James A. Montgomery, *Arabia and the Bible* (Philadelphia, Pa.: University of Pennsylvania Press, 1934), pp. 27–36.

28. Terry Brooks Hammons, " 'A Wild Ass of a Man': American Images of Arabs to 1948." (Ph.D. dissertation, University of Oklahoma, 1978), pp. 20–22.

29. *Ibid.*, p. 35.

30. Roderick Nash, *Wilderness and the American Mind* (New Haven, CT: Yale University Press, 1967), p. 24.

31. Roy Harvey Pearce, *The Savages of America: A Study of the Indian and the Idea of Civilization* (Baltimore, MD: The Johns Hopkins Press, 1953)., pp. 143–144.

32. Nash, *op. cit.*, pp. 143–144.

33. Joseph Leon Grabill, "Missionaries and Conflict: Their Influence Upon American Relations with the Near East, 1914–1927." (Ph.D. dissertation, Indiana University, 1964).

34. Helen McCready Kearney, "American Images of the Middle East, 1824–1924: A Century of Antipathy." (Ph.D. dissertation, University of Rochester, 1976), p. 176.

35. *Ibid.*, p. 372.

36. Sari J. Nasir, "The Image of the Arab in American Popular Culture." (Ph.D. dissertation, University of Illinois, 1962); Jack G. Shaheen, *The TV Arab* (Bowling Green, O.: Bowling Green State University Popular Press, 1984); and "The Hollywood Arab: 1984–86," *Mideast Monitor*, Vol. 3, Nos. 1 & 2 (1986), pp. 1–6.

37. Janice J. Terry, *Mistaken Identity: Arab Stereotypes in Popular Writing* (Washington, D.C.: American-Arab Affairs Council, 1985).

38. This is a continuing theme in Zionist writings about Palestinians. Lately, this assertion was resurrected with much fanfare and accorded much publicity and support among Americans in the form of a book by Joan Peters, *From Time Immemorial: The Origins of the Arab-Jewish Conflict Over Palestine* (New York; Harper and Row, 1985). See also the various critiques of the book, including Anthony Lewis, "There Were No Indians," *New York Times*, Jan. 13, 1986, I, p. 15.

39. William E. Leuchtenburg, "The American Perception of the Arab World," in George N. Atiyeh, ed., *Arab and American Cultures* (Washington, D.C.: American Enterprise Institute, 1977), p. 15.

40. Ruth W. Mouly, *U.S.-Arab Relations: The Evangelical Dimension* (Washington, D.C.: National Council on U.S.-Arab Relations, 1985); *The Religious Right and Israel: The Politics of Armageddon* (Chicago: Midwest Research, 1985); Wesley Granberg-Michaelson, *The Evangelical Right and Israel: What Place for the Arabs?* (Washington, D.C.: American-Arab Anti-Discrimination Committee, n.d., 1983?, ADC Issues #8); O. Kelley Ingram, "Christian Zionism," *The Link*, Vol. 16, No. 4 (Nov., 1983), pp. 1–13; and Grace Halsell, *Prophecy and Politics: Militant Evangelists on the Road to Nuclear War* (New York: Lawrence Hill, 1986).

CHAPTER 2

An Evaluation of Middle East News Coverage
in Seven American Newsmagazines
July–December, 1956

Arabs often point to Israel as the cause of their alienation from the
United States and the cause of their suspicion of American Middle East
policy, and frankly accuse the United States Government and press of
complete subservience to the will of the Zionists who set up the state
of Israel and continue to supply it with hundreds of millions of dollars
every year. They also charge that no impartial account of any Middle
East problems could be stated in the American press where, on the contrary, the Israeli-Zionist points of view prevail and predominate. These
are very serious charges indeed and should not be taken lightly. This
study was designed to test the validity of the last charge above, concerning the American press.

It may be useful to state at the outset what the study is not supposed
to show. It will not tell us whether or not United States policy towards
the Middle East is affected by the manner in which the press will treat
Arab-Israeli relationships. Rather, it will be assumed along with Louis
Lyons in his introduction to Wilton Wynn's *Nasser of Egypt, The Search
for Dignity* that "the quality of the information we have on other peoples
determines the images of them we have in our heads." If it is further
assumed that a country can act on and is only what it knows and that
the press, the purveyor of that knowledge, acts as a policymaker at times,
it becomes obvious how important it is that the press be "neutral" or
at least balanced in its reporting or interpretation of news concerning
a foreign policy issue. In other words, the study subsumes an implicit
comparison of the press content with a standard of balance or fairness
which is necessary if policymakers are to formulate policies deemed in
the best interest of the United States.

Problem and Method

The problem, then, is to objectively describe the treatment given in the American press to Arabs and Israelis (Zionists) and to their respective causes. Content analysis (a research technique for the objective, systematic, and quantitative description of the manifest content of communication) is the tool utilized here to determine whether or not and how much the American press has been partial in its portrayal of Arab-Israeli issues. In order to avoid a haphazard approach to the problem, a certain time period had to be chosen. The Suez crisis, July-December, 1956, provided a manageable span of time (six months) during an interval of "active hostility" between an Arab country, Egypt, and the state of Israel, in addition to the many border incidents on the Israeli-Jordan frontier.

Since it is obviously not possible to study all newspapers and magazines in the United States, some selection was necessary. The question of what is a representative sample is very difficult to determine. Thus, the choice, to a great extent, was arbitrarily made. Weekly newsmagazines were thought to provide a somewhat fair sample of the kind of news reporting and interpretation with which the American reading public is provided. Though not a magazine in the proper sense, the *New York Times* "News of the Week in Review" was also included in the study since it is generally considered the "newsbible" of the intellectuals and government officials in the United States. The others were: *U.S. News and World Report, Newsweek, Time, Life, The Nation,* and *The New Republic.* In 1956 during the Suez crisis, about eleven million copies of these magazines were sold every week.[1]

For the sake of comprehensiveness, painstaking efforts were made to study every item relating to the Arabs, the Jews, the Arab states, or Israel. Once the problem was clearly defined and the magazines were selected, the next step became one of refining the problem at hand and putting substance into it by formulating appropriate hypotheses for investigation. This was done partly through reading some reports and articles in these magazines, and partly through a study of the Arab-Israeli problem. Only two hypotheses will be discussed in this chapter. In their final form, the hypotheses read as follows:

Hypothesis I

Most news reporters and correspondents present an image of the Arab which has been perpetrated in Hollywood movies: a bedouin, perhaps a nomad, having a low standard of living, low level of education, a harem where the women have very few rights and privileges, if any. He is undemocratic, living in squalor, under a tyranny of group or tribal loyalty and submission. On the other hand, the Israelis are praised for being "democratic" and "like the West."

Hypothesis II

There is frequent mentioning of the previous ill-treatment of Jews, and emphasis on Israel's desire for "peace" and "security" as well as Israel's achievements. Little mention is made of the plight of the Arabs of Palestine. On the contrary, in the Arab-Israeli conflict the Arabs are presented as the aggressors, the "bad guys", the "hostile" nations surrounding the under-dog Israel, and intent upon its destruction.

The next step involved translating the hypotheses into categories which adequately expressed them. Thus, out of Hypothesis I, for instance, emerged such categories as "the Arab is portrayed as a bedouin;" "the Israeli has a high standard of living;" "the Israeli has good qualities," etc. But these and other categories were still too generalized to serve as adequate tools of analysis. Hence, specific and concrete indicators were required which, while representing the categories, referred directly to the text or content being studied. The categories could, of course, be represented by innumerable items. The indicators, however, were only a representative sample of such items. Thus, under the category "the Arab has a low standard of living," the following would be appropriate indicators: indigent (ce), poverty, pauperism, destitute (ion), want, lack, etc. The frequency of occurrence of each of such symbols or indicators was recorded for each of the categories under the two hypotheses. Then tables were set up to compare (1) the intra-content (for each magazine) treatment of Arabs and Jews, and (2) the different treatments of the subject matter by the various newsmagazines studied.

Once an article, column, or editorial was read through and all the appropriate indicators were recorded the item as a whole was judged as to whether it was pro Arab, pro Israel, con Arab, con Egypt, con Israel, etc. Quite often, an item was both pro one side and con another. It may be noted that this last process is neither as valid nor as reliable as the other, where mere symbols are counted and recorded. In other words, there is more room for subjective reporting here. However, every attempt was made to be objective, and any time there was any doubt as to whether an article was on the whole anti-Arab or balanced, for instance, the article was placed in the latter category.

Hypothesis I

It is a common charge made by the Arabs that the American press almost always portrays them as a backward, desert-roaming, harem-breeding, undemocratic lot whereas the Israelis are pictured as Western-like and democratic. The charge, if true, is particularly unpleasant to the town and city Arabs in general and to the educated ones in particular. It is not surprising, therefore, to find the reading public of the Arab world, predominantly composed of city and town-dwellers, outraged when they are equated or even associated with the wandering bedouin of the desert. The pertinent question is, are they so equated or associated by the magazines under study? The somewhat unexpected answer is a definite "no"! What happens is the following: The American public is understandably more interested in reading about a "different" way of life. It is admittedly "quaint" to see a picture of a person in flowing robes with a *kaffieh* on his head, riding a camel in the desert. Thus, reports about tribes and tribesmen are fairly frequent. The reports and pictures are true and not fabricated. However, they represent one minor facet of Arab life; for less than ten per cent of all Arabs are still either nomad or semi-nomad.[2] Furthermore, these reports partially reinforce the image of the Arabs which Hollywood once represented and still represents in its search for variety, drama, romance, and wild imagination.[3]

The other alleged attributes in Table I are perhaps true to a large extent. Standards of living and education are low for most people, dishonesty and unreliability, especially among some government officials may still be found; and Arab women still do not occupy the high position of their Western counterparts. Disunity and rivalry are still the stumbling blocks to the cherished goal of Arab unity. If the above is true, then what is the hue and cry all about when these facts are reported? The answer is simple, though not too obvious. Most people do not like to be told the truth if it hurts. The Arabs are no exception. Furthermore, Arab intelligentsia, seeking to escape the unpleasant reality, have taken up the habit of thinking in terms of the ideal-self of the future.

TABLE 1

HYPOTHESIS I

ARAB AND ISRAELI CHARACTERISTICS IN PRESS

Name of Magazine	ARAB CHARACTER								ISRAELI CHARACTER				
	Nomadic Living	Low Standard of Living	Low Standard of Education	Women Few Rights	Undemocratic Orientation	Dishonesty, Unreliability	Disunity and Rivalry	"Good" Qualities	High Standard of Education	High Standard of Living	Democratic and Western-like	"Good" Qualities	"Bad" Qualities
New York Times	12	17	5	0	2	0	12	4	0	0	1	1	0
U.S. News & World Report	41	42	31	0	10	16	20	0	0	0	0	0	0
The Nation	3	10	7	1	6	4	1	8	1	1	6	2	0
The New Republic	0	9	4	0	5	8	5	0	4	1	3	18	0
Life	21	1	1	1	0	0	4	0	2	0	0	0	0
Newsweek	24	15	1	1	2	0	2	0	0	0	0	0	0
Time	18	15	2	9	1	10	18	5	0	0	0	8	0
Total	119	1C1	51	12	26	38	62	17	7	2	10	29	0

Numerals indicate the number of times the particular characteristic is mentioned.

They look upon the modernizing efforts that are being expended as harbingers of things to come. The Western press, however, has not been very compromising on this score. Only very few reports alluded to the reforms and attempts made by the Arab countries to improve the lot of their people. Also, most of such reports concerned the then strongly pro-Western countries of Tunisia, Morocco and Lebanon. Other Arab countries and in particular Egypt, which was in the news then, had made many advances in various educational, commercial and industrial fields. Hardly any reports gave extensive coverage to this progress.

As for the Israelis, there was no strong attempt to present them as democratic and Western-like, having high standards of living and education, every time they were mentioned. On the whole, these things were taken for granted. Only when there was a special report on Israel were the above qualities stressed. What is more significant here is the fact that no unfavourable attribute was assigned to them.

Hypothesis II

Unless one is acquainted with the happenings in the Middle East and has had a first-hand study of the many problems of that area, one is incapable of detecting any misinformation or slanting of the news in the American press. In 1954, the International Press Institute at Zurich, Switzerland, published a pamphlet entitled "The News from the Middle East." The reporters, whose opinions were quoted in the Zurich survey, made it very clear that the Arabs were the greatest "sufferers" from the reporting on Middle East news, as a combination of factors worked against them: stereotype, pro-Israel and Zionist pressure in the United States, and fear of the "anti-Semitic" label.[4] Some reporters also stated that the "restrictive practice" existed mainly in the United States (not in the Middle East) where "American editors are nearly all afraid to tell the truth about the Arab-Israeli controversy because of the Zionist lobby."[5] United Nations Truce Supervision Organization (UNTSO) officials seem to support the reporters' contentions. Colonel W.T. McAninch, Military Observer (UNTSO), (1952–54) wrote bluntly:

"Zionism has seemingly blinded large numbers of . . . American Jews and exploited the ignorance and apathy of the majority of Americans. Today, United States relations with the Middle East are in grave jeopardy as a result."[6]

Commander E.H. Hutchison, Military Observer and Chairman of the Jordan-Israel Mixed Armistice Commission, 1951–54, wrote in the introduction to his own book, *Violent Truce*, published in 1956; that

> "although many unbiased articles were being published the bulk of the news was still geared primarily to the desires of those who can find no wrong in Israeli actions."[7]

Our present survey substantiates the verity of the preceding contentions. Israel, throughout these national magazines, was presented as being without wrong and having all the right and virtue on its side. The Arabs appeared to be constantly blamed, often seemingly for the simple reason that they happened to be at odds with Israel.

As Tables II and III show, most editorials were anti-Arab and/or pro-Israeli. The few editorials which were sympathetic to the Arabs concerned one or the other of the then pro-Western Iraqi, Lebanese, Moroccan, and Tunisian governments. During this eventful period, marked by a belligerent attitude on the part of Israel, and later France and the United Kingdom, no front-page headline portrayed Israel or the West as aggressors.[8] When they did not display a detached attitude (e.g. "Swords' Point: The Struggle over Suez");[9] the newsmagazines attempted to justify the action (e.g. "What Led the Israelis to Strike").[10] *Life* ran a front-page picture of a wounded Egyptian soldier receiving a drink of water from his Israeli captor.[11] *U.S. News and World Report* had a big tabloid with the catchy phrase "Moscow's Game in Egypt",[12] the title of a lengthy chapter which the magazine extracted from Walter Z. Laqueur's book: *Communism and Nationalism in the Middle East*.

All told, the editorial attacks on the Arabs amounted to 38.6 per cent ($\frac{164 + 29}{500}$ x 100), Table II, compared to *none* against Israel. On the other hand, Israel had 15.6 per cent ($\frac{78}{500}$ x 100), Table II, of the editorials in its favour, compared to the 0.6 per cent ($\frac{3}{500}$ x 100) on the Arab side.[13] Thus, Israel was overwhelmingly exculpated and exonerated whereas the Arabs were incriminated.

A pertinent question presents itself at this time: Was Israel the victim, and the Arabs the aggressors during the period under study? The evidence indicates that Israel was more often the aggressor than the victim. According to the *New York Times*:

> "During the period between last July 29 and Sept. 25, 1956, for example, Israel suffered casualties of nineteen dead and twenty-

TABLE 2

HYPOTHESIS II

SPACE PERCENTAGE OF EDITORIALS ON M.E.*
JULY-DECEMBER, 1956

Name of Magazine	con Nasser	con Egypt	con Arabs	pro Nasser	pro Arabs	pro Israel	pro G.B.	pro France	pro U.S.A	con Israel	con G.B.	con France	con U.S.A	Balanced	Neutral	Total Number of Pages
New York Times	40	0	0	0	3	6	12	12	0	0	0	0	0	15	42	2.3
U.S.News & World Report	81	0	0	0	0	19	19	19	†	0	0	0	†	0	19	5.25
The Nation	0	0	29	0	0	21	0	0	35	0	35	40	9	3	12	9.33
The New Republic	14	0	0	0	0	32	0	0	7	0	0	0	0	100	81	7.00
Life	29	0	0	0	0	0	20	0	45	0	26	7	0	32	13	5.16
Total	164	0	29	0	3	78	51	31	87	0	61	47	9	150	167	29.04

* Except for the column on the extreme right all numbers indicate the percentage (in pages) of editorials under each category.

† Not reported.

If added horizontally, total exceeds 100 per cent because the same editorial can be and often is pro one party and con another.

TABLE 3

HYPOTHESIS II

ITEM PERCENTAGE OF EDITORIALS ON M.E.*
JULY-DECEMBER, 1956

Name of Magazine	con Nasser	con Egypt	con Arabs	pro Nasser	pro Arabs	pro Israel	pro G.B.	pro France	pro U.S.A.	con Israel	con G.B.	con France	con U.S.A.	Balanced	Neutral	Total Number of Items
New York Times	37.5	0	0	0	4	4	12.5	12.5	0	0	0	0	0	12.5	46	24
U.S.News & World Report	83	0	0	0	0	17	17	17	†	0	0	0	†	0	17	6
The Nation	0	0	0	0	0	8	0	0	23	0	23	23	23	8	15	13
The New Republic	4	0	12.5	0	0	12.5	0	0	4	0	0	0	0	39	39	24
Life	29	0	0	0	0	0	14	0	43	0	29	14	0	29	14	7
Total	153.5	0	12.5	0	4	41.5	43.5	29.5	70	0	52	37	23	88.5	131	74

* Except for the column on the extreme right all numbers indicate the percentage (in number of items) of editorials under each category.

† Not reported.

If added horizontally, total exceeds 100 per cent because the same editorial can be and often is pro one party and con another.

eight wounded, and lodged fifty-nine complaints, according to
Brig. Gen. E.L.M. Burns, the U.N.'s ranking officer in the area.
In the same period Jordan lost seventy-two killed and twenty-four
wounded, and filed 210 complaints."[14]

Excluding the casualties which ran into the hundreds as a result of
the combined Israeli-British-French armed attack against Egypt, how
did Israel, the country which the American press presented as the victim, fare in the bloody count-down? The figures speak for themselves:

Israel			Jordan		
Dead	Wounded	Complaints	Dead	Wounded	Complaints
34	57	9	159	24	210

Yet one might ask if these figures are not lopsided because they cover
a short period of time in which Israel might have been overly aggressive.
United Nations Mixed Armistice Commission statistics show, however,
that the above were no isolated or exceptional incidents. From June,
1949, to October 15, 1954, Israel was condemned for 95 violations of
the Armistice; Jordan was condemened for 60.[15] During the same
period:[16]

Israel		Jordan	
Killed	Wounded	Killed	Wounded
34	57	127	118

But if the record condemns Israel so conclusively, how is the American
press able to "hide" the facts and, indeed, often make the victim appear
as an aggressor? Part of the answer has already been given: the overwhelming majority of all editorials written were in defence of, in sympathy with, or in admiration of Israel, often attacking the Arabs at the
same time.

What is more alarming, perhaps, is that no one seemed to dare condemn Israel or treat it harshly. Of all the reporting on the Middle East,
covering the eventful period only scantily described above, slightly over
0.5 per cent ($\frac{4}{700}$ x 100), Table IV, was anti-Israeli. This 0.5 per cent
was composed of texts of speeches of, or straight interviews with, Arab
leaders who attacked Israel in the process. The only condemnation of
Israel, if it could be called a condemnation, was a one and one-third
page article which appeared in *Time* attempting to establish collusion

TABLE 4

HYPOTHESIS II

SPACE PERCENTAGE OF ALL REPORTING ON M.E. *
JULY-DECEMBER 1956

Name of Magazine	con Nasser	con Egypt	con Arabs	pro Nasser	pro Arabs	pro Israel	pro G.B.	pro France	pro U.S.A.	con Israel	con G.B.	con France	con U.S.A.	Balanced	Neutral	Total Number of Pages
New York Times	10	0	1	0	0.7	6.5	5	3	0	0	0	0	0	67	18	46.25
U.S. News & World Report	44	2	5	0.6	2	20	11	9	†	2	2	2	†	19	16	202.70
The Nation	2	0	8	0	11	30	1	1	8	0	14	14	1	22	13	42.00
The New Republic	12	0	20	0	13	22	0	0	1	0	3	0	3	26	23	45.16
Life	13	3	1	3.5	0	24	8	3.5	8	0	18	.5	0	39	11	57.19
Newsweek	29	0	2.5	0	1.3	6.5	15.8	6.5	2.8	0	0	0	1.3	30	30.2	100.00
Time	17	1	3	.5	0	1	6	6	3	2	6	1.4	0	42	14	73.99
Total	127	6	40.5	4.6	28	110	46.8	29	22.8	4	43	17.9	5.3	245	125.2	567.29

* Except for the column on the extreme right all numbers indicate the percentage (in pages) of press coverage under each category.

† Not reported.

If added horizontally, total exceeds 100 per cent because the same can be and often is pro one party and con another.

TABLE 5

HYPOTHESIS II

ITEM PERCENTAGE OF REPORTING ON M.E.*
JULY-DECEMBER, 1956

Name of Magazine	con Nasser	con Egypt	con Arabs	pro Nasser	pro Arabs	pro Israel	pro G.B.	pro France	pro U.S.A.	con Israel	con G.B.	con France	con U.S.A.	Balanced	Neutral	Total Number of Items
New York Times	12	0	1	0	1	8	4	2	0	0	0	0	0	57	23	187
U.S. News & World Report	44	3	5	2	3	16	10	8	†	3	3	3	†	17	28	100
The Nation	6	0	3	0	6	22	3	3	12	0	12	12	9	19	16	31
The New Republic	11	0	15	0	6	15	0	0	2	0	2	0	2	26	26	41
Life	16	3	3	3	1	16	8	5	16	0	12	3	0	32	19	31
Newsweek	20	0	3	0	0	8	3	3	4	1	0	0	2	31	42	103
Time	9	2	3	1	0	1	3	3	4	1	4	1	0	46	24	95
Total	118	8	33	6	17	86	37	24	35	4	33	19	13	228	178	588

* Except for the column on the extreme right all numbers indicate the percentage (in number of items) of coverage under each category.

† Not reported.

If added horizontally, total exceeds 100 per cent because the same item can be and often is pro one party and con another.

in the combined Israeli-British-French attack on Egypt.[17]

Whenever Israel committed an aggressive act, the press came to its defense, describing the act as a reprisal raid. Almost in every instance, in reporting Israeli military actions the American press emphasized the contention that Israel had been driven to an act of desperation. Israel's condemnation by the United Nations was either ignored or barely mentioned. Yet U.N. condemnation of either side is a serious matter and takes place only after detailed investigation of all the issues, including provocation, is made. As Commander Hutchison wrote on the Israeli attack on the Gaza Strip:

"People seem to forget, under the steady barrage of propaganda in favour of Israel, that a careful study of all facts concerning an incident is made before the Security Council adopts a resolution of condemnation. If the happenings preceding the Israeli attack had warranted such severe action then both Egypt and Israel would have been condemned."[18]

Table VI shows a definite partiality on the part of these national magazines toward Israel. The Arabs were pegged as idle and poor, incapable of achieving much, though a few kind remarks were made about the modernization attempts in Tunisia and Morocco. Israel, on the other hand, was presented as a miracle-worker, turning the desert into a paradise on earth. Also, throughout the magazines, there were articles or comments about the World War II Nazi massacres and horrible treatment of the Jews. Those were terrible deeds which should long be a reminder of man's insane inhumanity to man. One might expect that a similar treatment would be accorded all equally sordid and inhuman tragedies. This was not the case, however. The almost one million Palestinian Arabs who became refugees when the Israeli state was founded hardly received a mention, let alone a report of their plight. Reference to them was made only when an editor wrote that the "refugee problem should be solved."

Why is it that Israel's actions are so thoroughly and quickly justified, and no "bad" thing is said about the Israeli state when even the staunchest 110 per cent American editors and reporters occasionally condemn the actions of the United States Government?[19] Dean Virginia Gildersleeve asked the same question in different words:

"As a good American I freely and publicly condemn acts of my

TABLE 6

HYPOTHESIS II

TREATMENT OF ISRAELIS AND ARABS IN THE PRESS
JULY-DECEMBER, 1956

Name of Magazine	Previous Ill-treatment of Jews	Longing for Peace & Security	Achievements	Among Hostile Neighbors	Arabs' Intent to Destroy Israel	Justifying Israel's Actions	Arabs "Mistreat" Israel	Explaining Away "Good" Acts of Arabs	Mention of Arab Refugees	Arabs' Longing for Peace and Security	Achievements of Arabs	Justifying Actions of Arabs	Israel "Mistreats" Arabs	Explaining Away "Good" Acts of Israel
New York Times	3	32	15	3	24	36	137	2	5	0	2	9	36	0
U.S.News & World Report	1	21	24	19	50	60	64	0	1	0	0	0	0	0
The Nation	12	15	9	4	8	23	25	0	3	0	5	0	4	0
The New Republic	0	13	1	4	24	18	49	4	2	0	0	2	3	0
Life	0	5	10	0	1	1	15	0	2	0	0	0	6	0
Newsweek	15	3	1	0	2	4	11	0	2	0	0	0	6	0
Time	3	11	9	0	9	18	10	0	1	0	4	3	17	0
Total	34	100	69	30	118	162	311	6	16	0	11	14	72	0

Numerals indicate the number of times the particular characteristic is mentioned.

own country which I think wrong. I also condemn at times acts of the long ago homes of my ancestors, England and France. "Why should I not be free to condemn in the same way acts of Israel? Why should that state and that people alone among nations on earth be sacrosanct and untouchable?"[20]

These are cogent questions. Though no simple answer can be given, several possible reasons may be advanced to explain the phenomenon. The fact that the Israelis are much closer culturally to the West than are the Arabs makes their actions easier to comprehend and more readily acceptable. Also, there are many more vocal and/or influential Jews in the United States than there are Arabs.[21] Perhaps what should be stressed here is the fact that the Arabs, even when they have remained as a constellation in a defined area, have overwhelmingly acted as American citizens who are almost completely oblivious of the Arab-Israeli strife in the Middle East. The American Jewish community, on the other hand, has played a much more active role in attempting to further the cause of the Jews in Palestine and to help create and strengthen the state of Israel.[22]

Another explanation for the reluctance to print unfavourable information concerning Israel may be the desire on the part of the American press not to displease and, consequently, alienate its Jewish reading and advertising public.[23]

It may also be a reaction to the long and dismal record of persecution which the predominantly Christian world inflicted upon the Jews throughout history. Another possible contributing factor to the favourable press coverage which Israel (together with Britain and France) received in the United States during the Suez crisis is the origin of the "news" reports.[24]

Tables VII and VIII show both space and item percentages of all the material which was written from or about the Middle East from July to December, 1956. Apart from the United States, Great Britain was the leading "foreign" source of news and information for these American magazines. News from and about the United Kingdom amounted to almost twice that emanating from its then principal antagonist, Egypt. As a matter of fact, though Egypt was a news-maker from late July to the end of our study, it led Israel by a ratio of 3:2 only. Israel, it must be remembered, was in no sense a news-maker during the whole two months of August and September of 1956.

TABLE 7

SPACE PERCENTAGE OF ORIGIN OF MATERIAL ON M.E.[1]
JULY-DECEMBER, 1956

Magazine	Egypt	Arab States	M.E.	Israel	G.B	France	Europe	U.S.A	U.N.	Other	Total
New York Times	10	4	0	4	13.5	7	2.5	49.5	8	1.5	100
U.S. News & World Report	16	3	0	6	31	9	3	33	2	0	103†
The Nation	0	13.5	0	22.6	17.2	0	0	43.4	3.3	0	100
The New Republic	0	13	0	9	32	0	0	46	0	0	100
Life	21	4	18.5	7	16.5	0	0	29	4	0	100
Newsweek	11	8.4	4.3	3.4	22	4	9	37.6	0	0	99.7*
Time	28	6	6	7	29	8	5	18	5	0	112†
Total	86	51.9	28.8	59	161.2	28	19.5	256.5	22.3	1.5	714.7

[1] All numerals indicate the percentage (in pages) of press coverage originating from or written about the particular country or area.

* Total does not add up to 100 per cent because very short items were not included under any "source." Most of them supposedly originated in Europe.

† Total exceeds 100 per cent because some reports supposedly originated in more than one country.

TABLE 8

ITEM PERCENTAGE OF ORIGIN OF MATERIAL ON M.E.[1]
JULY-DECEMBER, 1956

Magazine	Egypt	Arab States	M.E.	Israel	G.B	France	Europe	U.S.A.	U.N.	Other	Total
New York Times	10	4	0	5	13	6	2	50	8	2	100
U.S. News & World Report	16	3	0	5	21	8	4	42	3	0	102†
The Nation	0	9.5	0	9.5	9.5	0	0	68	3.5	0	100
The New Republic	0	7	0	5	22	0	0	66	0	0	100
Life	16	7	7	7	19	0	0	35	9	0	100
Newsweek	8	14	8	5.5	16	5.5	4	38.5	0	0	99.5*
Time	13	10	9	12	21	6	3	23	7	0	104†
Total	63	32.5	24	49	121.5	25.5	13	322.5	30.5	2	705.5

[1] All numbers indicate the percentage (in number of items) of press coverage originating from or written about the particular country or area.

† Total exceeds 100 per cent because some reports supposedly originated in more than one country.

* Total does not add up to 100 per cent because very short items were not included under any "source." Most of them, however, supposedly originated in Europe.

All in all, the Arab world seems to have provided about 24 per cent ($\frac{86 + 51.9 + 28.8}{700}$ x 100) of the news, Israel 12.6 per cent ($\frac{59 + 28.8}{700}$ x 100) ("M.E." added to both Israel and Arab countries), and Europe a big 30 per cent ($\frac{161.2 + 28 + 19.5}{700}$ x 100), Table VII.[25]

It should be emphasized here that all the parties to the Middle East disputes were actually engaged in propaganda wars before, during, and after any period of active hostility. Each adversary tried to present its side of the story to the peoples and governments of the world. It may be assumed that the correspondents of the American magazines were, initially, fair-minded individuals, unbiased toward either side. It is not, perhaps, unfair to argue, however, that these correspondents — in many instances brought to the scene hurriedly and temporarily — are likely to be influenced and even persuaded by the arguments presented by the government and press of the host country. Consequently, a reporter in the United Kingdom, for instance, may not be taxing his conscience much, if at all, when he sends his magazine an "objective" account that, in fact, reflects the British point of view. The same is true of a correspondent stationed in an Arab country, if he speaks Arabic or if there are English language newspapers published in that Arab country.

This element, then might have been a contributing factor (among many others, it is true) to the favourable press coverage that both Britain and France received in this country, even when the United States Government disapproved of their actions morally, politically, and militarily. The same reasoning may be applied to Israel, where nine American correspondents were stationed, as compared to five in Egypt. Hence, the Arab world was definitely at a disadvantage because of the lopsided distribution of American correspondents among the principal antagonists. There were nine American reporters in Israel, five in Egypt, four in Jordan, three in Lebanon, one in Morocco, one in Tunisia, and one roving reporter. Thus, in the whole Arab world there was a total of fifteen American newsmen compared with ten for Israel alone. The *New York Times* had three correspondents stationed in Israel and only one each in Egypt, Lebanon, and Jordan. It was obvious that the reports which originated in non-Arab countries tended to be more antagonistic toward and critical of the Arabs. To put it differently, the reports emanating from Arab countries were on the whole less anti-Arab and more impartial and/or pro-Arab.

Thus, in terms of total news coverage of the July-December 1956 happenings in the Middle East, the United States aside, Western Europe and Israel were the source or subject of twice as much news coverage in the American magazines than all the Arab countries put together. Apart from Western Europe with its tremendous reservoir of American foreign correspondents, Israel alone was the center for 40 per cent of all American foreign reporters covering the Middle East.

Summary and Conclusions

Six national newsmagazines and the *New York Times'* "News of the Week in Review" were studied for an evaluation of their accounts of and editorial policies on Middle East issues, during the July-December 1956 Suez crisis. Two hypotheses were formulated and tested for their validity. On the whole, though urban and "Westernized" Arabs were mentioned and occasionally discussed, a picture of the typical Arab as a desert-living nomad still persisted. This was thought to be a result of an over-emphasis on the latter "interesting" and "romantic" image. The Israelis were presented as Western-like and democratic. The Arabs were presented as the "bad guys", the aggressors against the "peace-loving" Israelis. Israel's main concern was presented as being her own "security" with no bad intentions on her part. When Israel attacked her Arab neighbours with more than average ferocity, her actions were justified as "reprisal raids."

Not all magazines displayed the same partiality or impartiality. The *New Republic* had by far the largest percentage of balanced or neutral editorials on the Middle East (78 per cent, Table III). The *Times'* "News of the Week in Review," followed by *Time* magazine, had the biggest percentage both in items and space provided, of balanced and neutral overall reporting of Middle East news. With the possible exception of *U.S. News and World Report*, there was more impartial or favorable news coverage of Morocco, Tunisia, Lebanon, and Iraq, all pro-Western then, than of the rest of the Arab world. The *New Republic* and the *Nation* in particular were sympathetic to Tunisia, Morocco and Algerian nationalists. *U.S. News and World Report* gave an extremely simplified, black and white account of all Middle Eastern issues. The other magazines displayed a little more flexibility, except when Israel was involved.

Though the above conclusions are confined primarily to the magazines studied during the Suez crisis, they may be applied in a general sense to the American press coverage of Middle East news since the Palestine issue hit the headlines after World War II. The generalization is believed justified since the magazines have large circulations and in view of the

fact that the *New York Times* is considered an authoritative source of news.
As it is realized by now, the Arabs do not fare very well in the
American press coverage of Middle East news. They seem to be consistently presented as the "villains", with the Israelis as the "heroes" in any
conflict or flare-up. Such a black-and-white picture is hardly a compli-
ment to this great American institution. Unless this unbalanced presentation is corrected or compensated for, no adequate knowledge of Middle East issues can be rendered to the American public and government, on which to base an impartial and just solution for the many problems of that area. As it is, the Arabs point to the United States and
say: "You only know us through Israeli eyes." They seem to be right.

NOTES

1. Figures or estimates supplied by the magazines themselves showed that *Life* had
a circulation of 5,739,000 followed by *Time* with over two million copies sold per week.
The *Times'* Sunday edition, *U.S. News & World Report* and *Newsweek* ranged along the
one million mark. *The Nation*, and *The New Republic* sold 25,000–30,000 copies a week each.

2. Erskine B. Childers, *Common Sense About the Arab World* (New York: Macmillan,
1960), p. 88. In the 1980's, only a tiny number of Arabs are still bedouin.

3. Professor Nabih Faris attributes the distorted image which Americans have of Arabs
to four "basic and conditioning" factors: "the Bible, mutual suspicion arising from long
struggle between the followers of Christianity and the follwers of Islam and the defeat
of Christianity in its very birth place, the missionary tradition and outlook concentrating
on the reclamation of the Muslim world to Christ, and the seemingly disinterested works
of the orientalists which seek to find and bare Islam's Achilles' heel." See his "The United
States' Image of the Near East," *Middle East Forum*. Vol 36, Feb. 1960, p. 16.

4. See Alfred Lilienthal, *There Goes the Middle East* (New York: Devin Adair, 1957),
pp. 217–23.

5. *Ibid.*, p. 220.

6. E.H. Hutchison, *Violent Truce* (New York: Devin Adair, 1956), pp. ix–ixx.

7. *Ibid.*, p. xv.

8. Great importance should be attached to headlines, since "that is all that half the
people read." Bernard C. Cohen, *The Press and Foreign Policy* (Princeton. N.J.: Princeton
University Press, 1963), p. 257. Besides, "it appears that the headline sets the stage, as
it were, for the manner in which the story is read. It establishes the frame of reference
within which the facts of the story are perceived. It creates the first mood or impression
which subtly and perhaps unconsciously dominates the reader's attention as he pursues
the whole story. In a way, it provides a lens through which the remainder of the story
or article is perceived." Percy H. Tannenbaum, "The Effect of Headlines on the Interpretation of News Stories," *Journalism Quarterly*, XXX, No. 2, Spring 1953. p. 197.

9. *Newsweek*, Vol. 46 (Sept. 24, 1956), p. 1.

10. *New Republic*, Vol. 135 (Nov. 5, 1956), p. 1.

11. *Life*, Vol. 41 (Nov. 19, 1956), p. 1.

12. *U.S. News & World Report*, Vol. 41 (Aug. 10, 1956), p. 1.

13. In a brief account of a similar, though less extensive and exhaustive study, Professor Ralp Crow found that, though the facts *clearly condemned Israel* for its massive attack on the Jordanian village of Qibya on Oct. 14, 1953, 81 per cent of the editorials in five national American newspapers reported pro-Israel arguments, and only 19 per cent pro-Arab ones. "Is There Bias?" *Middle East Forum.* Vol. 32, March 1957, p. 14.

14. *New York Times,* Oct. 7, 1956; E 2.

15. Hutchison, *op. cit.,* p. 91.

16. *Ibid.,* p. 92.

17. *Time,* Nov. 12, 1956, pp. 32-3.

18. Hutchison, *op. cit.,* p. xvi.

19. As Tables II and III show, at least *some* criticism of France and England was voiced. Even the U.S. was accorded some blame. Yet, the only condemnation of Israel appeared in the letters section: five in *Time* and one each in the *New Republic* and *Newsweek.*

20. Gildersleeve, as quoted in Lilienthal, *op. cit.,* p. 246.

21. See Harry S. Truman, *Years of Trial and Hope* (New York: Doubleday, 1956, II, 157-58.

22. Some articles have recently appeared to illustrate and substantiate this point: Joseph S. Roucek, "The American Zionists as a Pressure Group," *Issues,* Summer, 1964, pp. 36-44; Harry N. Howard, "The American Tradition and U.S. Policy in the Middle East" *Middle East Forum,* April, 1964, pp. 10-22. See also the hearings before the Committee on Foreign Relations of the U.S. Senate, cited in *Ibid,* p. 22. Richard P. Stevens, *American Zionism and U.S. Foreign Policy* (1942-47) (New York: Pageant, 1962).

23. This is true of any newspaper since every newspaper and magazine "is a business enterprise." Cohen, *op. cit.,* p. 66.

24. The correspondent, like the diplomatic official, is influenced by the local press of the host country. See *Ibid.,* p. 66.

25. This compares with 10 per cent Arab, 31 per cent Israeli, 59 per cent neutral sources of news in the reporting of the Qibya incident, cited earlier. Crow, *op. cit.,* p. 13.

CHAPTER 3

American Mass Media
and the June, 1967 Conflict

This analysis follows the same procedure and format as that employed in researching the Suez attack. The results clearly show a significant increase in press bias both in favor of Israel and against the Arab side. In particular, the vilification campaign against President Gamal Abdel-Nasser was most likely intended to undermine his position both within Egypt and as an Arab nationalist leader. American coverage of the 1967 war was clearly among the worst, if not *the* worst, and most biased reporting of any period since WWII.

Future historians studying the events of the summer of 1967 may well conclude that Israel's greatest achievement was not its military victory but rather its success in communicating its point of view. Conversely, the Arabs' major defeat was not on the battlefield but in the competition for men's minds.

As Karl Deutsch put it, "Control of the social institutions of mass communication, and generally of the storage and transmission of information, is an obvious major component of power."[1] The campaign to present the Israeli version, and *only* the Israeli version, of what was happening in the Middle East in the summer of 1967 — a campaign that greatly enhanced Israel's power and bargaining position — was perhaps without comparison in its extent and intensity.

Though no one has yet studied the radio and television coverage of the June War, a few studies have been made of daily newspapers, magazines, and books — "instant potboilers" purporting to tell the latest story of the Arab-Israeli conflict.[2] The American Institute for Political Communication, a nonpartisan, nonprofit organization interested in "improving the flow of government and political affairs information to the American people," found that of eighteen syndicated columnists with

Washington outlets, nine viewed the crisis "chiefly or primarily from the perspective of American foregin policy," six columnists "took a strong, persistent pro-Israeli position," and only one writer did a column which "set out the difficulties, problems and needs of the Arabs."[3] Leslie Farmer, Willard G. Oxtoby, and Harry N. Howard came to similar conclusions in their studies. As Tables 1 and 2 show, my study of the coverage given the June War by American news magazines corroborates this evidence.

In my analysis, I followed the same procedure employed in a previous study of American news reports during the period of the 1956 Suez attack.[4] The same magazines—*U.S. News and World Report, Newsweek, Time, Life, The Nation, New Republic* and the *New York Times'* "The Week in Review"—were used in both studies in order to detect any change in attitude.[5] The overall results of the May-June 1967 study are not much different from those of the July-December 1956 study. However, the *extent* of support for Israel and the antagonism toward the Arabs generally, and toward President Nasser in particular, was significantly greater in 1967. This was true in the editorials as well as the reporting.

The most striking element continues to be the extreme reluctance on the part of the American press to criticize Israel—even on the editorial pages or in feature articles. Very seldom did I come across any reprimand of Israel or the Israelis without an accompanying justification. Only occasionally is the Arab point of view presented, and even then it sounds strange and unconvincing to a reader who has been saturated with the pro-Israeli stance. Sometimes a tactic is employed to discredit the Arab point of view even while presenting it—for instance, to let the Communists speak for the Arabs. The *New York Times* on June 18 reproduced excerpts from an *Izvestia* article attacking the Israelis as aggressors, and *Time* magazine thus dismissed the looting and acts of atrocity by Israeli soldiers as a Communist charge. It also provided Moshe Dayan's explanation: "An army of regulars and reservists of various ages and psychological drives cannot be perfect."[6]

2.

The attitude of the press toward Nasser is illustrated in Table 3. In contrast to Israeli leaders, including Moshe Dayan, the Egyptian president appeared to be the epitome of all that is hateful and bad. There seems to be a strong tendency to blame one man for all the difficulties

TABLE 1

ITEM PERCENTAGE
OF ALL REPORTING ON THE MIDDLE EAST*
MAY-JUNE, 1967

Name of Magazine	con Nasser	con Syria	con Arab	con France	con U.N.	con U.S.A.	con Israel	con Soviet	pro Nasser	pro Syria	pro Arab	pro France	pro U.N.	pro U.S.A.	pro Israel	pro Jordan	Bal-anced	Neutral	Total Number of Items
N.Y.Times	30.8	4.0	8.0	4.0	11.5	—	—	—	—	—	—	—	11.5	11.5	30.8	—	23.0	8.0	26
Life	23.1	—	30.8	—	8.0	—	—	8.0	—	—	—	—	—	8.0	38.5	—	—	—	13
U.S.News & World Report	30.2	4.6	21.0	—	2.3	2.3	2.3	9.3	2.3	—	—	—	—	—	39.5	—	2.3	18.6	43
The Nation	60.0	20.0	—	—	20.0	16.6	—	40.0	—	—	—	—	—	—	—	—	—	20.0	5
New Republic	33.3	—	16.6	16.6	—	16.6	—	16.6	—	—	—	—	—	—	33.3	3.7	—	—	6
Newsweek	44.4	—	7.4	3.7	3.7	—	14.8	14.8	—	—	—	—	—	—	37.0	3.7	—	11.1	27
Time	10.0	—	50.0	10.0	30.0	—	—	10.0	—	—	—	—	—	10.0	50.0	—	—	—	10
Average Percentage	30.2	3.0	17.7	3.0	7.7	1.5	3.8	10.0	0.8	—	—	—	2.3	3.8	36.1	0.8	5.4	10.8	130

* Except for the column on the extreme right and the bottom row, all figures indicate the percentage (in number of items) of press coverage under each category. If added horizontally, total exceeds 100 per cent because the same item can be and often is pro one party and con another.

TABLE 2

ITEM PERCENTAGE OF EDITORIALS
ON THE MIDDLE EAST*
MAY-JUNE, 1967

Name of Magazine	con Nasser	con Syria	con Arab	con France	con U.N.	con U.S.A.	con Israel	con Soviet	pro Nasser	pro Syria	pro Arab	pro France	pro U.N.	pro U.S.A.	pro Israel	pro Soviet	Bal-anced	Neutral	Number of Editorials
N.Y. Times	40	—	20	20	—	—	—	20	—	—	—	—	40	40	20	—	—	20	5
Life	40	—	40	—	20	—	—	—	—	—	—	—	—	20	—	—	—	—	5
The Nation	50	25	—	—	—	25	—	50	—	—	—	—	—	—	—	—	—	25	4
New Republic	20	—	20	20	—	20	—	20	—	—	—	—	—	—	40	—	—	—	5
Time	—	—	100	—	—	—	—	—	—	—	—	—	—	—	100	—	—	—	1
Average percentage	35	5	25	10	5	10	—	20	—	—	—	—	10	15	20	—	—	10	20

Except for the column on the extreme right and bottom row, all figures indicate the percentage (in numbers of items) of editorials under each category. If added horizontally, total exceeds 100 per cent because the same editorial can be and often is pro one party and con another.

of the Middle East. If Nasser is truly *believed* to be the cause of all trouble, then those holding such a view certainly display a good deal of ignorance concerning the Arab world and the region generally. On the other hand, this attitude might be a deliberate attempt on the part of Nasser's enemies to escape the blame for any of the difficulties involved. One wonders, for instance, whether Israeli leaders have so very few faults or if the American press believed these faults were not "news fit to print."

It is interesting to note that the same magazines that described Nasser as cautious and not interested in going to war with Israel switched their stand after the war started and began to condemn Nasser as the cause of all trouble.[7] Furthermore, the picture of Nasser as the master strategist playing the East against the West was dropped in favor of a theory that reached conspiratorial proportions in the hands of C.L. Sulzberger of the *New York Times*. According to Mr. Sulzberger, all the troubles in the Middle East were caused by collaboration between the Soviet masters and the Egyptian client, Nasser. It was charged that Nasser merely followed orders and that he stirred up trouble in the Arab-Israeli conflict in order to divert attention from his difficulties in the Yemen war.[8]

3.

But disparaging remarks were not restricted to Nasser. Hardly any "good" qualities were attributed to the Arabs generally, whereas the Israelis were portrayed as practically without fault. The old romantic stereotype of an Arab as a wandering desert dweller has given way to that of a "dark, shifty-eyed schemer and coward."[9] It is a stereotype that is reinforced by television and the movies. In contrast, the Israelis are pictured as "young, energetic, fun-loving, hard-working, brave, and deeply suntanned."[10]

Table 4 clearly illustrates the reluctance of the American press to portray the Israelis in a bad light, whereas it enumerates the bad qualities of the Arabs without inhibition. As Leslie Farmer summed it up:

> My intention is not to deny that the Arabs have faults; however, putting all the bad or questionable traits of a people — or person — together and reciting them like an indictment can make them look three hundred per cent worse than they are. One could say, with as much truth, "Socrates is ugly, dresses like a disgrace, has a

TABLE 3

CHARACTERISTICS ASCRIBED TO NASSER AND TO ISRAELI LEADERS*
MAY-JUNE, 1967

Name of Magazine	NASSER							ISRAELI LEADERS			
	Dictatorial Attitudes	Cause of all Trouble	Associated with Communism	Anti-Western Attitude	Untrustworthy; Unreliable	Playing East vs. West	Inexperienced; Naive	"Good" Qualities	Hardworking, Tough, Brave	Pro-West	"Bad" Qualities
N.Y. Times	13	41	39	2	3	–	11	11	5	–	2
Life	3	10	10	1	–	–	3	1	–	–	–
U.S. News & World Report	20	43	26	–	11	–	1	21	10	3	–
The Nation	6	4	4	4	–	–	2	–	3	–	–
New Republic	2	4	14	6	2	–	2	–	6	–	1
Newsweek	8	15	10	–	11	–	2	3	17	–	3
Time	–	3	10	–	3	–	2	–	–	–	–
Total	52	120	107	13	30	–	21	36	41	3	6

* Figures indicate number of times a characteristic is mentioned.

TABLE 4

CHARACTERISTICS ASCRIBED TO ARABS AND TO ISRAELIS*
MAY-JUNE, 1967

Name of Magazine	ARAB CHARACTERISTICS							ISRAELI CHARACTERISTICS					
	Nomadic Living	Low Standard of Living	Low Standard of Education	Women: Few Rights	Undemocratic Orientation	Dishonest, Unreliable, Inefficient	Disunited and Contentious	"Good" Qualities	High Standard of Education, Modern	Heroic, Self-Reliant, Hard-working, Efficient	Honest, Self Confident	Democratic and Western Oriented	"Bad" Qualities
N.Y. Times	15	1	1	—	3	18	24	5	—	15	6	—	2
Life	—	—	—	—	2	23	14	4	4	24	9	—	—
U.S. News & World Report	3	15	—	—	—	15	41	5	4	37	2	1	2
The Nation	—	—	—	—	—	—	1	—	—	1	—	—	—
New Republic	—	—	—	—	3	2	3	—	—	7	—	—	—
Newsweek	2	2	—	—	—	11	9	10	5	4	5	3	—
Time	5	0	—	—	—	20	10	12	9	17	4	—	3
Total	25	18	1	—	8	89	102	36	22	105	26	4	7

* Figures indicate number of times a characteristic is mentioned.

dreadful wife but not the sense to divorce her, and spends most of his time talking."[11]

Table 5 shows that the previous ill-treatment and persecution of the Jews were mentioned but not as frequently as had been anticipated. This element was supplied in advertisements in the *New York Times* in which the public was reminded of "the horror and decimation of the European holocaust" from which the people of Israel "are still recovering."[12] The president and the American people were urged to "avoid another Munich" and to act "with other nations if possible — independently if necessary!"[13] Then after the war, Hadassa, the Women's Zionist Organization of America, saluted the "defenders" of Israel.[14]

Israel's alleged interest in peace and security are also emphasized, although it must be added that talk of this nature increased *after* the war in which Israel displayed beyond any doubt that it was in no great danger. The American press began to echo the demands of some Israeli officials that it was not possible to return to the *status quo ante* and that Israel needed to have more "natural" frontiers. This was justified on the basis of "security" and the desire to live "in peace," although it was not immediately obvious to all readers how such an action would make peace more likely between Israel and the Arab countries.

Not only are the Israelis beyond criticism but their achievements, it seems, are beyond compare. One wonders at times how many reporters had visited Palestine before it was taken over by the Israelis in order to speak so authoritatively about how the Israelis "made the desert bloom." And the Israelis are, of course, kind and generous to the Arabs whom "fate" entrusted to their care. Such arguments were presented to justify a possible Israeli takeover of any or all land occupied by Israel in the summer of 1967. The arguments sound much like those of colonialists — arguments that were supposedly rejected by the liberals and intellectuals of the West about twenty years ago.[15]

Despite these achievements, the American leaders were constantly being reminded that the United States had a "moral and legal" commitment to go to Israel's aid. According to the American Institute for Political Communication:

The Johnson Administration . . . was beset by a well-organized domestic pressure campaign in behalf of the Israelis in the two weeks immediately prior to the Arab-Israeli conflict. To retain

TABLE 5

ATTRIBUTES CHARACTERIZING ISRAEL
AND THE ARAB STATES*
MAY-JUNE, 1967

Name of Magazine	Previous Ill-treatment of Jews	Israel's Desire for Peace and Security	Israel's Achievements	Israel strong but small underdog	Arabs intent upon Israel's destruction	Jutifying Israel's Actions	Arabs "mistreat" Israel	Mention of Arab Refugees	Arabs' desire for Peace and Security	Arabs' Achievements	Israel "mistreats" Arabs	Justifying Arabs' Actions	Arabs connected with Soviets	Arabs anti-West
N.Y. Times	—	24	30	11	18	58	47	19	—	—	4	4	18	—
Life	6	10	23	4	24	28	46	11	—	—	6	3	16	—
U.S. News & World Report	1	6	4	34	26	19	29	1	2	—	8	†	91	28
The Nation	—	3	—	1	7	5	9	5	—	—	1	—	10	—
New Republic	—	—	1	1	2	3	4	3	—	—	1	†	5	1
Newsweek	4	8	2	—	5	7	22	13	1	—	7	†	10	9
Time	12	20	11	3	30	30	47	14	—	—	31	8	13	14
Total	23	71	71	54	112	150	204	66	3	—	58	15	163	52

* Figures indicate number of times an attribute is mentioned.

† Not reported

its freedom of diplomatic action and to avoid being pushed into a unilateral approach to the Middle East crisis, the Administration was compelled to wage a defensive communications battle.[16]

4.

The amazing fact is that this campaign continued *after* the war. No presidential hopeful, it seems, can escape making a statement on America's "commitment" to Israel. Political commentators continue to extol Israel's great victory while at the same time expressing disbelief that "tiny" Israel can be a threat to the Arab world. The David and Goliath analogy apparently has not lost its appeal. The public is presented a picture of 2.7 million Israelis squared off against estimates of 60–110 million Arabs.[17] Somehow the writer forgets that he has just described those 60–110 million Arabs as inefficient, divided, weak, and nomadic. Furthermore, the *populations* are compared when the relevant facts concern the *military forces*. Troop strengths in 1967 were estimated at 55,000 Jordanians, 70,000 Syrians, 100,000–150,000 Egyptians, and some 10,000 from the other Arab countries. These several armies *at most* total 285,000, against a total of 300,000 Israeli reservists and regulars under one command.[18] Given the Israeli army's efficiency, excellent training, and up-to-date weaponry, how any reasonable observer can think of the situation as a David-Goliath match is not clear. Reasonable observers, of course, did not. Hugh Sidey reported in *Life*, a report that was also mentioned by Dan Rather of CBS News, that General Earle Wheeler, then chairman of the Joint Chiefs of Staff, had provided capability estimates to President Johnson which showed that the Israeli army would gain victory in three or four days.[19] Arthur Goldberg, then U.S. ambassador to the United Nations, and others were skeptical. Wheeler rechecked with CIA director Richard Helms and then came back with the *same* estimate.[20]

Nonetheless, the hue and cry about Israel's struggle for survival continues. It might be worthwhile to mention that Palestine was struggling for survival when the Zionists succeeded in establishing the state of Israel. After the 1967 war, the United Arab Republic (Egypt) came into that category. Yet James Reston, fully one week after Israel's victory, which he extolled at length, went on to say: "It is not easy to prove that two and a half million Israelis are a dreadful menace to sixty million Arabs!"[21]

Such a stance would seem to create justification for Israel's actions. Thus, news reporters and commentators constantly repeat that the Arabs "threaten" Israel and are intent upon its destruction. Whenever Israel strikes at its Arab neighbors, mistreats its Arab population or annexes new territory, such actions are justified, and Israeli arguments are presented as proof of the logic and rightness of the situation. Furthermore, the Arabs were at the time of the June War frequently and almost indiscriminately associated with the Communist camp. Arab demonstrations against what was believed to be American involvement on the side of Israel were given detailed coverage. Perhaps the worst example was a vituperative anti-Nasser, anti-Egyptian, three-page attack by Thomas Thompson, *Life*'s Paris Bureau chief, entitled "Cairo Diary of U.S. Humiliation."[22]

What of the refugees? Here, the American press accepted the Israeli version of how the Arab leaders allegedly asked the Palestinians to leave their homes until the battle was over, whereas the Zionists supposedly asked them to stay.[23] No effort was ever made to check the veracity of these statements. Some mention of the plight of the Arab refugees at least was made, although the most that any commentator suggested was a token repatriation on the part of Israel (which had ignored repeated U.N. resolutions requesting repatriation of compensation for the refugees). One writer added that all of the refugees could be resettled in "underpopulated Iran and Syria."[24]

5.

It has already been pointed out that the party which succeeds in persuading others of its own version of the conflict has won a major victory. One element which helped Israel in this regard was that most of the "news" came from Israeli or pro-Israeli sources.

Table 6 does not convey a correct picture of the situation *unless* one adds the "U.S.A. or No-Source" column to the "Israel" column. This is not unjustifiable since most of the material with "No Source" indicated came from Israeli sources or sources sympathetic to Israel. *Time* and *Life* provided a listing of their correspondents covering the events in the Middle East. *Time* had one reporter in Beirut who also followed developments in Jordan and Syria, one reporter in the U.A.R., and three in Israel.[25] *Life* had sixteen men in the area, and the locations of nine of these correspondents were indicated. Of the nine, five were in

Israel, two in the U.A.R., one in Jordan, and one with the American
Sixth Fleet in the Mediterranean.[26] If it is assumed that these are not
atypical figures (except for *The Nation* and *New Republic* which are not
news magazines), then it appears that about 60 percent of the reporting
originated in Israel.

The scarcity of reports from the Arab countries involved in the conflict or of accounts portraying the Arab side was attributed in some
quarters to restrictions, harassment, and censorship by the Arabs.[27]
But these should not have proved insurmountable odds to enterprising
correspondents who are supposed to search for a different point of view
or an original story. Besides, it was admitted that the Israelis also applied censorship and travel restrictions.[28] Furthermore, definite attempts were made to present anti-Zionist or pro-Arab positions, but
such attempts were resisted by the news media.[29] What was
demonstrated was a reluctance to present the other side of the coin rather
than a difficulty in obtaining information. A salutary exception was the
Christian Science Monitor which gave fair coverage to both sides. The television networks also deserve praise for their extended coverage of the
United Nations Security Council debates.

6.

It is instructive to follow the developments of the June, 1967, Arab-
Israeli conflict as the American press reported them. In the process,
I will point out the sins of omission and commission as well as the major
themes that emerged from this and other studies of the press during
this period.

Prior to the beginning of the hostilities, the press argued that Nasser
had regained some lost prestige in the Arab world and that he was *not*
interested in a war with Israel, especially since he realized that neither
the U.A.R. alone nor the Arab states together were capable of defeating
the Israelis. Furthermore, the press "laid emphasis on employing the
United Nations to resolve the crisis."[30]

After the start of the war, however, Nasser was branded as the aggressor and the cause of all trouble in the Middle East. The issue of who
actually attacked whom was muddled. Whether or not there was an
intentional attempt to obscure the issue may be judged by the following examples. Hugh Sidey, in his June 16 column in *Life*, first reported
that a CIA monitoring operation told the U.S. government that "the

TABLE 6

ITEM PERCENTAGE OF ORIGIN
OF MATERIAL ON MIDDLE EAST*
MAY-JUNE, 1967

Name of Magazine	U.A.R.	Jordan	Syria	Lebanon	Europe	U.S.A. or No Source	U.N.	Israel	Total Number of Items
N.Y. Times	3.9	—	—	—	—	90.2	—	3.9	26
Life	15.4	7.7	—	—	—	77.0	7.7	46.1	13
U.S. News & World Report	2.3	2.3	—	11.6	16.3	41.8	—	16.3	43
The Nation	—	—	—	—	—	100.0	—	—	5
New Republic	—	—	—	16.6	—	50.0	16.6	16.6	6
Time	20.0	10.0	—	—	10.0	80.0	30.0	40.0	10
Average percentage	5.8	2.9	—	5.8	7.8	66.0	4.9	18.4	103

U.A.R. had launched an attack on Israel" and that later checks confirmed the report. Later in the same article, he writes, "Then secret sources noted that a number of Arab airfields appeared to be inoperative and the pattern of attack began to emerge. The Israelis, *whether first to strike or not*, were moving hard and fast against the U.A.R. Air Force."[31] Another classic example of a most indirect and slanted reporting is Theodore H. White's version of how Israel decided to mount a surprise attack:

> Thus, finally, on Sunday afternoon [June 4, 1967] the Israeli cabinet faced a decision: to wait for diplomatic help, delay which might mean death; or let the army decide time, dimension and method of response to Egyptian attack. Eighteen men met that afternoon and voted yes.[32]

The United Nations suffered in prestige and consequently in effectiveness when a good deal of criticism was directed against Secretary-General U Thant for withdrawing United Nations Emergency Force (UNEF) troops from the Egyptian-Israeli border at the request of President Nasser. However, it occurred to no reporter or commentator to suggest that — if these troops could indeed keep the peace which Israel allegedly was interested in preserving — UNEF be stationed on the Israeli side of the border. Not only was the suggestion not made, but few bothered to mention that Israel had refused since 1956 to station such troops within its borders and that it turned down U Thant's request to move them to the Israeli side after Nasser asked for the "removal of several UNEF posts along the Sinai Line."[33]

The double standard which is displayed in the attitude of some Westerners to the Arabs and the Israelis is illustrated further by the campaign, launched after Israel's victory, to discount the United Nations as an agency capable of helping to resolve the conflict.[34] At the same time, Israel's very existence was upheld by the argument that it had been created by the United Nations.[35] The *New York Times* provided another example of the double standard which was employed. It begins by arguing that "when World War II ended, a Jewish state was ready to be born." While admitting that "in the process nearly a million Palestinian Arabs were dispossessed," the *Times* reprimands the Palestinians and the Arabs generally for "their refusal to come to terms" with Israel. Then it goes on to justify Israel's actions: "Once President Nasser proclaimed the closing of the Strait of Tiran leading into the Gulf of

Aqaba war became a certainty, since the Israelis felt their survival was jeopardized."[36] The reader cannot escape the conclusion that to the *Times'* editor the survival of the Palestinians was not important, whereas that of the Israelis was.

The press employed various tactics to discredit the Arabs or their point of view while helping the Israeli cause. The *New York Times* in late May, for instance, headlined "Egypt's Stand: Nasser's Dangerous Gamble" and "Israel's Stand: A Life and Death Matter."[37] *Life* had a picture of a wounded Arab soldier tended by an Israeli medic.[38] In a background article in the same issue it was mentioned that 90,000 Jews were in Palestine by World War I, but it was not pointed out that this constituted only 10 per cent of the population. The reader is told that by 1947 the Jewish population soared to 600,000 — again not mentioning that the Arabs constituted two-thirds of the total population. While mentioning that the U.N. mediator Count Folke Bernadotte was assassinated by terrorists, the fact that the terrorists happened to be Zionists was conveniently ignored.

Perhaps one of the saddest aspects of American press reporting of the 1967 Middle East war was the presentation of the issue as an Arab-Jewish, or Muslim-Jewish, conflict.[39] Unfortunately, examples abound. C.L. Sulzberger wrote, "France understandably wants to regain a favored place in the Arab world and the easiest way, alas, is by euchring out the English-speakers and ceasing to coddle the Jews."[40] *Time* magazine wrote that Mohammed El-Kony, U.A.R. ambassador to the U.N., "scrapped a 20–page diatribe against the Jews" and gave U Thant a note accepting a cease-fire.[41]

One wonders again if this muddling of the issue is intentional. The conflict is not between Arab and Jew but rather between Arabs, particularly those of Palestine, and the Zionist-Israelis. It is rather ironic that when Arab *secular* nationalism began to emerge late in the nineteenth century, a Jewish nationalism based on *religion* and race also began to gather momentum. The result was the state of Israel. As I.F. Stone, himself an American Jew, put it, " 'It's hard to be a Jew' was the title of Sholom Aleichem's most famous story. Now we see that it's hard to be a goy in Tel Aviv, especially an Arab goy."[42]

The last point that should be mentioned is the dehumanization of the Arab in the American press. This is accomplished by repeatedly reinforcing the stereotype, especially when presenting the "bad" qualities. Marcus Smith observes that "the Arabs are now a prejudice object in the United States."[43] Crude and cruel jokes at the expense of the Arabs appeared in various magazines after the June War. Cartoons, especially those of Bill Mauldin, practically constitute a hate campaign against the Arabs. The various comedy shows on television, especially the "Rowan and Martin Laugh-In," carried the anti-Arab theme further. All this is happening at a time when efforts toward understanding and accommodation among the various racial, ethnic, and religious groups in and outside the United States are gaining momentum.

"The quality of the information we have on other peoples determines the images of them we have in our heads."[44] This survey of American press treatment of Arabs and Israelis shows a definite slighting of the Arabs and their cause. A more responsible press would perform its appointed role in a democracy and help bring about better understanding between Arabs and Americans.

NOTES

1. Karl W. Deutsch, *The Nerves of Government* (New York: Macmillan, the Free Press, 1966), p. 203.

2. American Institute for Political Communication, *Domestic Communications Aspects of the Middle East Crisis* (Washington, D.C.: AIPC, 1967); Leslie Farmer, "All We Know Is What We Read in the Papers," *Middle East Newsletter*, February, 1968, pp.1–5; Willard G. Oxtoby, "The War of Words: A Look at the Literature," in "America and the Middle East," mimeographed (New Haven: New Haven Committee on the Middle East Crisis, 1968), pp. 31–36; Harry N. Howard, "The Instant Potboilers and the 'Blitzkreig War," *Issues*, XXI (Autumn 1967), 48–52.

3. AIPC, *Domestic Communications*, p. 2.

4. See the previous chapter.

5. The period of the study extended from May 11, 1967, the date of the Israeli public statements threatening an "attack" on Syria, to the end of June, 1967.

6. *Time*, June 30, 1967, p. 27.

7. See in particular *Time*, June 2, 1967, p. 21; and *Life*, June 9, 1967, p. 4.

8. *New York Times*, June 25, 1967, p. 8E.

9. Marcus Smith, "Reflections in a Mirror," *Middle East Newsletter*, February, 1968, p. 7.

10. *Ibid.*, p. 6.

11. Farmer, "All We Know Is What We Read in the Papers," p. 5.

12. *New York Times*, June 4, 1967, p. 4E.

13. *Ibid.*, p. 7E.

14. *New York Times*, June 11, 1967, p. 5E.

15. Paul Giniewski, in arguing for apartheid in South Africa and for the establishment of a separate Bantustan, draws upon the Zionist establishment of the state of Israel for illustration. In a nutshell, his case against assimilation and for apartheid is expressed in a rhetorical question: "Did the Jews not learn that the only political rights, the only nationality which could not be contested, the only flag which could not be imputed a crime

were their own, and that instead of being assimilated in foreign nations, instead of being German, English, French, anything but themselves, Hebrew, Palestinian, Israeli?" See his *Two Faces of Apartheid* (Chicago: Henry Regnery, 1961), p. 350.

16. AIPC, *Domestic Communications*, p. 1.

17. *Time*, June 9, 1967. Those were the figures for 1967. In the early 1980's the population of the Arab world was approximately 180 million and Israelis numbered about 4 million. *The Europa Yearbook 1985: A World Survey*, 2 Vols. (London: Europa Publications Ltd., 1985)

18. The *New York Times* gave the following estimates of troop strengths: Israel, 250,000; U.A.R., 80,000; Jordan, 55,000; Syria, 70,000 (May 28, 1967, p. 1E). *Time* estimated 71,000 Israeli regulars and 230,000 mobilized reservists (June 9, 1967, p. 38). In the early 1980's, troop strengths for these countries were estimated as follows: Egypt: 460,000; Jordan: 76,000; Syria: 363,000. Also, each country has varying numbers of reservists, police and other combat units. As for Israel, "full mobilization to 500,000 can be quickly achieved." *The Europa Yearbook 1985: A World Survey*, Vol. II (London: Europa Publications Ltd., 1985), p. 1866.

19. *Life*, June 23, 1967, p. 32B.

20. Only then, apparently, did the Johnson Administration declare its "neutrality" in the Arab-Israeli conflict.

21. *New York Times*, June 18, 1967, p. 14E.

22. *Life*, June 23, 1967, pp. 70–74.

23. *Life*, June 23, 1967, p. 4.

24. *Ibid*. It should be remembered that, as late as 1967, the Palestinians were viewed and treated as if they were no more than "Arab refugees," i.e. not as a people. Thus, American press accounts referred to Palestinians only as "Arab refugees."

25. *Time*, June 9, 1967, p. 27.

26. *Life*, June 23, 1967, p. 3.

27. *Newsweek*, June 19, 1967, p. 82; *Life*, June 23, 1967, p. 3.

28. *Newsweek*, June 19, 1967, p. 82.

29. AIPC, *Domestic Communications*, p. 3; Oxtoby, "War of Words," p. 34.

30. AIPC, *Domestic Communications*, p. 2.

31. *Life*, June 16, 1967, p. 24B (italics added).

32. *Ibid.*, June 23, 1967, pp. 24B, 24C.

33. Charles W. Yost,"The Arab-Israeli War: How It Began," *Foreign Affairs*, XLVI (January, 1968), p. 313; Mr. Yost's article is one of the best studies written on the crisis and how it developed.

34. See in particular Nadav Safran and Stanley Hoffmann, "The Middle East Crisis: Guidelines for Policy," *The Nation*, June 26, 1967, pp. 806–8.

35. *Time*, June 23, 1967, pp. 24–25.

36. *New York Times*, Jun 11, 1967, p. 12E.

37. *Ibid.*, May 28, 1967, p. 1E.

38. *Life*, June 16, 1967, p. 38A.

39. Senator Gore also presented the issue in religious terms; see Howard, "Instant Potboilers," p. 50.

40. *New York Times*, June 18, 1967, p. 14E.

41. *Time*, June 16, 1967, pp. 16–17.

42. I.F. Stone, "Holy War," *New York Review of Books*, August 3, 1967.

43. Smith, "Reflections in a Mirror," p. 6.

44. Louis M. Lyons, in his introduction to Wilton Wynn's *Nasser of Egypt: The Search for Dignity* (Clinton, Massachusetts: The Colonial Press, 1959,), p. viii.

CHAPTER 4

Perceptions of the Middle East
in American Newsmagazines during the 1973 War

State policies are formulated by government officials who rely on the available information and a set of basic assumptions concerning their national interests, their country's political and military capabilities as well as the concerns, orientations, and capabilities of other parties to the conflict. This study demonstrates that the United States realized too late that its basic assumptions about the Middle East situation and the concerns and capabilities of the Arab states in particular were wrong. It is arguable that, had American policy-makers been better informed and not so willing to accept the Israeli view, the 1973 war—the war that shattered America's myths about the Middle East—could have been avoided.

Israeli and Western Assumptions About the Middle East

While all nationalist movements are in a sense attempts at redefining peoples' images of themselves, Zionism, the Jewish nationalist movement of the past century, can be defined almost solely in those terms. That is to say, the fundamental drive behind the Zionist movement has been a basic desire to change the image Gentiles have of Jews as well as the image Jews have of themselves. Viewed from this perspective, many Zionist and Israeli actions in war, foreign policy, and propaganda become more intelligible.

At first the emphasis was on changing the image of the Jew as a Shylock, a merchant and moneylender. Hence the push for a return to the land, seeking rejuvenation and a chance to prove to the Jews themselves as well as to the Gentiles that Jews are not "different." The image of the Jew as a coward or a nonfighter also had to be combated.

Here a great deal of emphasis on "fearlessness" was instilled in the young, sometimes at the expense of other emotions, including love and kindness.[1] Every precaution was taken to be almost completely certain of victory in any contemplated military engagement with the enemy. This involved the practice of outnumbering the enemy forces wherever possible.[2] Then, after the victory, the tactic was to use extensive propaganda to publicize what was termed a David-and-Goliath battle in which the "underdog" won. In this manner, and over a period of time, Israelis and many Jews outside the state began to gain confidence in the fighting ability and prowess of the Israelis.[3] But when this attitude generated overconfidence and arrogance, Israeli leaders began to underestimate the enemy, to ignore possible compromise options, to overestimate the ability of their own forces to respond quickly and effectively in a war situation, and to use flamboyant, exaggerative, and sometimes false statements in addressing their people as well as the enemy — exactly the behavior the Arab leaders manifested in 1948–49 and again in 1967.[4]

Turning specifically to the period immediately preceding the October war, the attitude of the Israelis and their Western, especially American, supporters was one of overconfidence. Especially after the 1967 war, the attitude of the Israelis toward the Arabs both within and outside Israel was one of superiority. To them, the Arab was not a good soldier. He was neither effective nor courageous. Furthermore, he was not likely to change for some time — if ever. As I.F. Stone has observed, it is ironic that a people who for centuries have suffered from humiliation, oppression, and persecution as a minority group should, once in the majority as in Israel, begin to develop an attitude of "contemptuous superiority."[5] Far more important than the irony involved is the threat to the peace this attitude has constituted and the price the Israelis themselves have had to pay for such miscalculation.

According to the then prevalent Israeli-Western view, not only was the Arab a poor soldier but the whole Arab fighting machine was an inefficient organization.[6] Allegedly this was due to some deficiency in the Arab psychological make-up whereby the Arabs' pride in and emphasis on "individualism" meant that cooperative work in large organizations was difficult, if not impossible, to sustain for long periods of time. In addition, this view cited the Arabs' senstivity to criticism, their unwillingness to convey bad news, and the prevalence of primordial (tribe, clan, family) rather than nationalist loyalties as additional "proof" of the inability of the Arabs to put together an efficient fighting force.[7] If such cooperation was difficult to attain within any one Arab state, one could hardly expect the Arab world to act collectively. In other words, it was not possible for the Arabs to be united in their fight against Israel and its supporters regardless of whether the weapon chosen was military or economic. Concerning the possibility of an Arab oil boycott, the United States in particular accepted the Israeli view that Arab oil-producing countries were "conservative" and would not be likely to join the "extremist" Arab states in an embargo against the West. One final element rounds out the old Israeli and Western view of the Arabs, namely, that the Arabs cannot keep a secret. Thus it was argued that even if the other assumptions about potential Arab actions were incorrect, any war preparation on the part of the Arabs would be leaked to the West and the Israelis.[8]

Another faulty assumption — one that perhaps overshadowed all the rest in importance and was even more firmly and unquestioningly held — was the belief that the Arab view of what constituted "rationality" in the Arab-Israeli conflict was the same as the Israeli and Western view. According to the latter, if it is known in advance that a war will result in a definite and major disaster for one side, then that side would be "mad" to start a fight.[9] Hence Israeli leaders were confident that Egypt and Syria would not launch a major offensive. This confidence was expressed in the form of warnings threatening the Arabs with new and untold disasters. The purpose was threefold: (1) to reassure the Israelis of the tremendous military might of the Israeli state — and hence of the security of the inhabitants and forthcoming immigrants; (2) to persuade the West, and especially the United States, that a major war in the area was not likely and therefore there was no reason to pressure Israel into any concession or compromise; and (3) to cow the Arabs into a situation of inaction and avoidance of fighting as a means of regaining some or all of their land.

The Arabs, needless to say, were and are quite sane. Some of their attitudes and their actions, however, differ from those of Westerners — and this has a bearing on the way they behave in a conflict situation. It is indeed a sad commentary on Western scholarship on the Arabs and the Middle East in general that so very many myths have been fostered and/or allowed to persist. It is indeed "logical" and "rational" for a weak person in the West not to pick a fight with a much stronger individual, even when the former feels right and justice are on his side. But this is neither "logical" nor "rational" behavior in the Arab world. Therefore, if a person feels that he has been cheated, mistreated, or generally maligned and humiliated, then honor, duty, and "logic" dictate that he should fight, regardless of the outcome. In other words, in such a situation it is "better" — more "logical" and "rational" — to fight and lose than not to fight at all.[10] If it were otherwise, the Palestinians would have long been suppressed because of the tremendous odds against them. This also explains the failure of the Israeli policy of force as the only language the Arabs understand. It might well be, however, that the so-called Israeli hawks, led by David Ben-Gurion, Moshe Dayan, and Golda Meir, have understood Arab psychology quite well, and that the strategy of "force as the only language" is intended not to end the dispute but to exacerbate it and provide Israel with a chance for further expansion or other advantages.

The Israeli-Western image of the Israeli, the negative mirror image of the Arab, was that of an excellent and heroic soldier. The Israeli military machine was one of the best, if not the very best, not only in the region but in the world. Soldiers and officers worked well together, and no sacrifice was too great for the defense of the homeland. Unlike the Arabs, whose main motivation was hatred of the Israelis, the latter found their source of strength in love of their countrymen and their land.[11] There were no divisions within Israel to weaken the people's resolve. The Israelis (and some outsiders) began to believe themselves invincible.

Apart from conveying the above images of themselves and their enemies to the West, the Israelis had to assure their Western supporters that the latter's interests were being protected and advanced in the area. This was done with the following arguments. First, the Arabs were too weak (and they knew they were too weak) to risk a major war that might bring about a superpower confrontation — which the West definitely wanted to avoid. Second, U.S. and Western interests were better served by maintaining the (pre-October) status quo: even a partial settlement would result in the opening of the Suez Canal, which would mainly strengthen the Soviet military presence in the area and around the world. Third, Israel (together with Iran) was willing to act in behalf of the United States in opposing or suppressing any "extremist," that is, "anti-Western," movements or regimes in the area. Since the Arabs could not keep a secret, or, put differently, since the Israeli and American intelligence network was virtually fail-safe, any contemplated violence from the Arab side would be nipped in the bud before the issue could be internationalized or constitute a threat to world peace.

Although, in general, European nations, especially because of their greater need for a functioning Suez Canal and their greater dependence on Arab oil, were prepared to pressure the Israelis into some sort of compromise, the Israeli-American view that prevailed saw "Western" interests as indivisible. Those interests definitely included oil. As stated before, the view was that the Arabs were unwilling and/or unable to use the oil weapon effectively; and even if it were used effectively, it would not really hurt the West, especially the United States. As Richard B. Mancke, a staff economist for the U.S. cabinet task force on oil in 1969–70 and professor of law and economics at the University of Michigan, wrote: "In sum it seems to me unlikely that distaste for our Middle East policy would lead to a general embargo of Arab oil sales: both because the U.S. would not be the principal victim and because non-Arab OPEC members would be the principal beneficiaries."[12]

Needless to say, almost as soon as the war started, it became obvious that the United States and its Western allies did not view their interests in the Middle East in quite the same light. Europe could not survive merely on American "assurances." And even the United States came to feel the pinch from the oil boycott.

Prior to the October war the Israelis had succeeded in keeping their Western supporters from making any attempt to break the deadlock and move the situation off dead center. In other words, the Israelis had managed to prevent any changes in the status quo except those that might advance Israeli interests. We have already outlined various parts of the formula the Israelis so successfully followed. Another and most important part of that formula was to persuade the Western powers to accept the Israeli view of the nature of the probem in the Middle East. According to this view, the basic question was one of "Arab refugees" and Israeli "security," and every other issue was ancillary or peripheral or artificial. Following this "logic," Golda Meir could announce in London: "There was no such thing as Palestinians. . . . It was not as though there was a Palestinian people in Palestine considering itself as a Palestinian people and we came and threw them out and took their country away from them. They did not exist."[13] If there are no Palestinian people, the Israelis and their supporters need not have a guilty conscience about the dispersion of another people to make room for the Jewish state. If the problem is one of Arab refugees, the solution is to have those refugees resettled among their brethren outside Palestine or Israel. And, since the Palestinians do not constitute a nation, they do not need or deserve a state of their own — a view that the Israeli leadership continues to espouse.[14]

Leaders in all states use "national security" as an excuse or justification for many acts. Among Israelis, however, even by their own admission, "security" has become something of an obsession. In such a situation, outside observers must determine whether or not in any particular instance the leadership is using "national security" as a cover for other, less acceptable objectives — namely, expansionism. It is not important here to determine whether or not Israel's Western friends recognized the presence of an ulterior motive behind the Israeli claim of "national security," for instance, in setting up numerous settlements in different parts of the occupied territories. The important point is that they did little if anything to prevent their establishment. As the moderate Arab states, namely, those that are pro-Western, failed to interest the West, especially the United States, in any reasonable scheme to attain Israeli withdrawal and an equitable settlement, the implications of the Western actions (or lack of them) became clear — that the United States in particular was not willing to effectively challenge the Israeli leaders' view that Israeli occupation of the territory captured from the Arabs in 1967 constituted the best security for Israel and served the best interests of the United States.

American Opinion and the October War

It is little wonder, therefore, that both Israel and its Western supporters, primarily the United States, were taken by surprise by the events of early October 1973. It was realized too late that most of the assumptions on which Israeli and U.S. policy were based were erroneous. This is the phenomenon that the American news media have referred to as the "shattering of myths" about the Middle East. It is interesting to note, however, that the American media, reflecting the then prevailing attitudes of the Israeli and American policymakers, presented the Middle East picture from the old perspective for one or two weeks after the war started. They changed only after it became obvious that Israeli casualties were quite high and that a decisive Israeli victory was unlikely. This change in attitude is reflected in the tables at the end of this chapter, which include data on coverage of the Middle East in ₋American newsmagazines. An important item not shown in the tables is the emphasis the American press placed on the Arabs starting the attack. Normally this would not and should not be viewed as unusual or biased. However, when this is compared with the 1967 situation, the pro-Israeli bias becomes obvious. During that conflict, the magazines under review either ignored or muddled the issue of who actually launched the attack.[15] The point is that if who strikes the first blow is important enough to report and emphasize, then this should have been done in both instances.

TABLE 1

NUMBER OF ITEMS ON THE MIDDLE EAST
IN CERTAIN AMERICAN MAGAZINES
JULY-DEC. 1956, MAY-JUNE 1967, OCT.-NOV. 1973

Magazine	'56	'67	'73
New York Times	187	26	45
U.S. News and World Report	100	43	31
Nation	31	5	7
New Republic	41	6	8
Newsweek	103	27	41
Time	95	10	47

In general, the tables illustrate the partisanship of the American press in its reporting of the Arab-Israeli conflict over the past two decades.[16] The evidence is clear that 1967 marked the lowest ebb of impartial reporting in these magazines, but that 1973 saw the beginning of a move toward balance.

Looking at each table individually, we find that the Western media have generally ceased to associate the Arabs with nomadic living, a low level of education, and a depressed standard of living (Table 2). Although during the 1973 war references to Arabs as dishonest or unreliable were numerous, and their disunity and rivalry were mentioned in *Time* and, to a lesser extent, *Newsweek*, the "good" qualities of the Arabs were also cited quite often.

In 1973 the actions and alleged intentions of the Arabs were reported with greater understanding, if not sympathy, as Table 3 shows. The most important change is to be found in the columns entitled "Arabs' achievements mentioned" and "Arabs' actions justified." With the exception of the *Nation* and the *New Republic*, the weekly magazines surveyed began to show a concern for, and a sensitivity to, the Arab point of view. Arab achievements on the battlefield were amply reported. More significantly, Arab actions or views were adequately justified, placed in context, or explained. This is, of course, what good reporting

TABLE 2

CHARACTERISTICS ATTRIBUTED TO ARABS IN CERTAIN AMERICAN MAGAZINES
JULY-DEC. 1956, MAY-JUNE 1967, OCT.-NOV. 1973

Magazine	Nomadic living			Low standard of living			Low standard of education			Undemocratic orientation			Dishonesty, unreliability			Disunity, rivalry			"Good" Qualities		
	'56	'67	'73	'56	'67	'73	'56	'67	'73	'56	'67	'73	'56	'67	'73	'56	'67	'73	'56	'67	'73
New York Times	12	15	—	17	1	—	5	1	—	2	3	—	—	18	1	12	24	1	—	—	—
U.S News & World Report	41	3	1	42	15	—	31	—	2	10	—	—	16	15	5	20	41	6	4	5	3
Nation	3	—	—	10	—	4	7	—	—	6	—	1	4	—	1	5	1	—	—	5	—
New Republic	—	—	—	9	—	—	4	—	—	5	—	—	8	2	1	2	3	—	8	—	—
Newsweek	24	2	2	16	2	5	1	—	—	2	3	2	—	11	11	2	9	2	—	10	10
Time	18	5	15	16	—	3	2	—	—	1	—	3	10	20	25	18	10	5	5	12	42
TOTAL	98	25	18	110	18	12	50	1	2	26	6	6	38	66	44	58	88	14	17	32	55

Notes: Figures indicate number of times mentioned.

TABLE 3

TREATMENT OF ARABS AND ARAB STATES IN CERTAIN AMERICAN MAGAZINES
JULY-DEC. 1956, MAY-JUNE 1967, OCT.-NOV. 1973

Magazine	Refugees Mentioned			Arabs' desire for peace and security mentioned			Arabs' achievement mentioned			Israeli "mistreatment" of Arabs mentioned			Arabs' actions justified		
	'56	'67	'73	'56	'67	'73	'56	'67	'73	'56	'67	'73	'56	'67	'73
New York Times	5	19	3	—	—	1	2	—	10	36	4	2	—	—	—
U.S. New & World Report	1	1	2	—	2	—	—	—	12	—	8	3	9	4	13
Nation	3	5	2	—	—	—	5	—	—	4	1	—	—	†	20
New Republic	2	3	1	—	—	—	—	—	2	3	7	1	2	†	—
Newsweek	2	13	5	—	1	2	—	—	24	6	31	6	—	†	2
Time	1	14	24	—	—	14	4	—	46	17	1	8	3	8	27
Total	14	55	37	0	3	17	11	0	94	66	52	20	14	12	62

Note: Figures indicate number of times mentioned.

† Not reported.

TABLE 4

CHARACTERISTICS ATTRIBUTED TO ISRAELIS IN CERTAIN AMERICAN MAGAZINES JULY-DEC. 1956, MAY-JUNE 1967, OCT.-NOV. 1973

Magazine	Modern, high standard of education			Heroism, self-reliance, capacity for hard-work, efficiency			Honesty, no envy			Democratic and Western-like orientation			"Bad" qualities		
	'56	'67	'73	'56	'67	'73	'56	'67	'73	'56	'67	'73	'56	'67	'73
New York Times	—	—	—	†	15	1	†	6	—	1	—	—	—	—	—
U.S. News & World Report	1	4	—	†	37	2	†	2	3	—	1	—	—	2	1
Nation	1	—	2	†	1	3	†	—	2	6	—	—	—	2	3
New Republic	4	—	—	†	7	—	†	—	—	3	—	—	—	—	—
Newsweek	—	5	—	†	4	5	†	5	3	—	3	—	—	—	3
Time	—	9	—	†	17	26	†	4	2	—	—	1	—	3	19
Total	5	18	2	—	81	37	—	17	10	10	4	1	—	7	26

Note: Figures indicate number of times mentioned.

† Not reported.

TABLE 5

ITEM PERCENTAGE OF ALL REPORTING ON THE MIDDLE EAST IN CERTAIN AMERICAN MAGAZINES
JULY-DEC. 1956, MAY-JUNE 1967, OCT.-NOV. 1973

Attitude	New York Times			U.S. News & World Report			Nation			New Republic			Newsweek			Time			Average %		
	'56	'67	'73	'56	'67	'73	'56	'67	'73	'56	'67	'73	'56	'67	'73	'56	'67	'73	'56	'67	'73
Pro-Arab leader	—	—	4	2	2	7	—	—	—	—	—	—	—	—	—	1	—	9	0.5	0.8	4.5
Pro-Arab	1	—	11	3	—	3	6	—	—	6	—	—	1	4	—	—	—	2	1.8	1.7	3.9
Pro-Israeli	8	31	16	16	40	16	22	—	57	15	33	13	8	37	15	1	50	17	9.5	35.9	17.3
Pro-Western	6	12	2	18	—	3	18	—	—	2	—	—	14	—	—	10	10	—	10.8	3.4	1.1
Anti-Arab leader	12	31	—	44	30	—	6	60	—	11	33	—	20	44	—	9	10	—	18.0	33.0	—
Anti-Arab	1	12	16	8	26	16	3	20	14	15	17	50	3	7	15	5	50	13	4.0	19.0	16.0
Anti-Israeli	—	—	—	3	2	—	—	—	—	—	—	—	—	15	2	1	—	—	0.7	4.0	0.6
Anti-West	—	4	4	6	2	—	33	—	—	4	33	—	2	4	—	5	10	—	4.5	5.0	1.0
Anti-U.S.S.R.	†	—	4	†	9	13	†	40	—	†	17	50	†	15	2	†	10	—	—	10.0	6.0
Balanced	57	23	29	17	2	23	19	—	29	26	—	13	31	—	42	46	—	23	39.0	6.0	28.5
Neutral	23	8	36	28	19	32	16	20	14	26	—	25	42	11	37	24	—	45	27.5	12.0	36.3

Note: All figures (except those under "Average %") indicate the percentage of number of items of press coverage. If added vertically, total exceeds 100 per cent because the same item can be and often is for one party and against another.

† Not reported.

is all about. However, in the past, as we can see from Table 3, this was a procedure reserved for reporting on Israel. In 1973 it was applied to both sides.

Turning to American press coverage of Israel, Table 4 shows *Time* as the only magazine studied that emphasized the heroic, self-reliant, hard-working, and efficient characteristics of the Israelis in 1973. However, there was also mention of "bad" Israeli qualities, such as lack of preparation, overconfidence, and underestimation of the enemy. If this is the beginning of a trend that will be followed by *Time* and other newsmagazines, then it is an important and healthy development — and one that accords with the basic objectives of Zionism, namely, to change the image of the Jew and have him or her be treated as a human being. In its zeal, Zionism has, at least in public statements, managed to change the image of the Jew from "subhuman" to "superhuman." This is a very serious error. The problem for Jews and non-Jews alike, in the Middle East and elsewhere, will continue to exist until Jews are treated as other human beings — until they are seen as people with good and bad qualities, capable of greatness but also capable of error, a mixture of strength and weakness, kindness and cruelty, courage and cowardice.

Table 5 reflects the extent of improvement in American reporting on the Middle East in 1973. Thus there was no condemnation of Arab leaders — a marked change from previous years. In the past, of course, President Nasser of Egypt was an easy target of blame for any and all "troubles" in the Middle East. His successor, Anwar Sadat, appears to have avoided antagonizing the Western media. In fact, he came in for some, though slight, praise from certain quarters. What is more significant, perhaps, is that he escaped criticism in the editorial columns of these magazines.[17]

The analysis shows that the American media did not by any means stop criticizing or condemning the Arab states. However, at least in the *New York Times*, the amount of pro-Arab reporting came close to the amount critical of the Arabs — a substantial improvement. Also, while it continues to be taboo to criticize Israel, it is clear from our Tables that, apart from the reporting in the *Nation*, a definite and significant drop in the pro-Israeli attitude of 1967 took place in 1973. Clearly, the erosion of pro-Israeli bias has not resulted in a pro-Arab gain. Instead, and quite properly, the media have shifted to a more neutral, balanced stance on Middle East issues. This is not to say that the situation is ideal, but that a beginning has been made in the attempt to present the Arabs as human beings—and not merely as the enemies of Israel or as trouble-makers for the United States and the West in general.

Remaining Myths

Much remains to be done before the press fulfills its duties properly. For instance, while the media generally acknowledged the "shattering of myths" about the Middle East, the following important questions were hardly raised, let alone discussed in depth: (1) Who fostered those myths and how? (2) What have been the policy consequences of such erroneous assumptions? (3) What other myths are there that need to be shattered before a major conflict exposes them? (4) Are there new myths developing and gaining popularity? (5) What can be done to stop mythologizing and begin accurate reporting on the Middle East? (6) Shouldn't the political opposition take the administration to task for failing so miserably in its assessment of a dangerous situation in a strategic area?

At least one question (the first) was not asked because the answer was known and quite embarrassing. The media themselves, as we have seen, have been, wittingly or not, a principal agent for propagating myths about the Middle East. Some of these were so shattered by the 1973 war that the media had to take notice of them. But what about the others? Surely the time has come for the American public to be informed of the true nature of the problem in the Middle East. Who are the Palestinians? How did most of them become "refugees"? What is to become of them? Is a solution to the problem in the Middle East that is unacceptable to them feasible or even desirable? These are questions that have yet to be adequately dealt with in the American press. Also, and despite evidence to the contrary, it is still the popular view in the United States that the "Arab refugees" left their homeland in Palestine of their own accord or through exhortation by Arab leaders in the neighboring countries. It is also still generally believed that the Arabs are out to destroy Israel *and* the Israelis. The explanation normally offered—an explanation that is even worse than the assertion itself—is that the Arabs hate the Israelis and are generally anti-Jewish. Since it is not stated that the Israelis hate the Arabs, the implication is that the hatred is one-sided and irrational. Occasionally, however, this alleged Arab hatred of the Israelis is explained in terms of jealousy generated by the lower standard of living of the Arabs and by the presumption (myth) that Palestine was basically desert or arid until the Israelis came along and made it bloom.

The theme that the Arabs do not have much of a case (if they have one at all) in their dispute with Israel is pervasive and one that is presented in various forms. For example, during and after the 1973 war numerous governments in the world expressed their disapproval of Israeli actions either through public statements of criticism or through the recall of diplomatic representatives from Tel Aviv. Almost invariably, the explanation provided in the American press echoed the Israeli claim that such change in policy was due to "blackmail" on the part of the Arab countries. The "reasoning" here is that if any government acts favorably toward the Israelis, it is doing so because it is the proper and right thing to do; but, since the Arabs do not have a case, or are assumed to be in the wrong, any favorable action toward them by third parties must be the result of "immoral," if not illegal, pressure. The legitimate rights of the Arabs and the national interests of third party governments are assumed to be nonexistent or unimportant.

Even as some myths were being shattered, the Israelis were actively spreading new ones intended to bolster their own self-image and to downgrade the enemy. For example, the early setbacks the Israeli forces suffered were supposed to be due to Arab treachery (the surprise attack), or American faulty intelligence, or an Israeli decision not to strike first. This argument, which implied that the Arabs' early successes were atypical and could not be duplicated, was clearly designed to revive or buttress the myth of Israeli invincibility.

On the question of oil, the embargo was presented as a form of blackmail — and the U.S. government, it was argued, should not succumb to it or in any way modify U.S. policy in the Middle East.[18] Furthermore, the boycott idea did not come from the Arabs but from the Soviet Union — and so the United States should intervene and deny the Soviets a victory in the area. Here again the Arabs are assumed to have had no reason to be angry with the United States, but to have merely been doing the Soviets' bidding. Stanley Karnow's remarks are illustrative of this view: "In short the Soviet aim has been to promote Arab unity directed against the U.S. in the expectation that American oil imports would be curtailed."[19]

The United States and the Middle East — A New Relationship?

Since we have detected a change in the reporting of Middle East news in American weeklies during the 1973 war, we need to ask what factors brought about the change and whether or not they are transitory or fundamental.[20] There is little doubt that the improved Arab performance in the October war forced the United States, the West in general, and, to some extent, the Israelis to carry out an "agonizing reappraisal" of the situation and of their basic assumptions (myths) concerning it. In other words, they were rudely awakened from their long sleep. This aspect we have already discussed. But apart from the war itself, the attitudes of the Arabs, Israelis, and Americans need to be examined for possible clues.

Following the 1967 war, certain Arab countries (Egypt and Jordan in particular), by agreeing to support U.N. Security Council resolution 242 of November 22, 1967, publicly accepted for the first time the possibility of peaceful coexistence with Israel. This was indeed a major shift in attitude and a significant concession to Israel. Most, though by no means all, Arab countries adopted a wait-and-see attitude to determine whether or not the Israelis would withdraw from territories occupied in 1967 in return for Arab recognition. Israeli "negativism" on this issue irritated many people, including the leaders of numerous countries. As the Israelis continued to consolidate their hold over the occupied territories — building new roads and new settlements and proposing to allow individual Israelis to purchase land there — the Israeli contention that "everything is negotiable" rang hollow. Hence an overwhelming number of countries voted to condemn Israel on March 22, 1972 (U.N. Commission on Human Rights), and in July 1973 (U.N. Security Council). U.N. Security Council resolution 242, the plan of U.S. Secretary of State William Rogers, and the Gunnar Jarring mission all failed, as the Israelis showed preference for land over withdrawal, recognition, and peace. When the war broke out and dragged on, many Western journalists pointed out Israel's previous intransigence as one cause. At this time many African countries broke off diplomatic relations with Israel.

Almost concurrent with the above developments, American public opinion, following the traumatic experience in Vietnam, was hardening against any new American military involvement abroad. Though generally sympathetic toward the Israelis, Americans were beginning to fear being dragged into "another land war" in Asia. Besides, there was hardly any doubt that Israel could more than adequately defend itself, and there was no fear of Israel being destroyed or Israelis being "thrown into the sea."

Two other factors seem to have helped in bringing about the change noted in the Tables. The first is détente — the policy of accommodation with the Soviet Union so that the two superpowers might cooperate in various economic, political, and even strategic weapons matters. This is the positive response to the fear of a nuclear confrontation between the two countries over a "problem" area such as the Middle East. Consequently, many Americans began to adopt the view that Arab-Israeli differences, squabbles, or even violent confrontations should not be allowed to escalate into a nuclear war, and began to support a peaceful compromise — a compromise that would include the Palestinians and one that would necessitate concessions Israel was reluctant if not unwilling to accept. Hence the irritation at, and criticism of, Israeli actions. The policy of détente also helps explain the fact that enthusiasm and support for Israel in 1973 came mainly (almost solely) from the American Jewish community — in marked contrast to the situation in 1967, when political, economic, emotional and symbolic support came from almost all sectors of American society[21] The second factor that has played a part, although an uncertain one, in changing public attitudes is oil. This factor has been more influential, however, in changing governmental policies both in the United States and the West generally.

Summary and Conclusions

I have argued in this chapter that Western countries, particularly the United States, by accepting the Zionist-Israeli view of the Arabs, the Israelis, and the nature of the problem in the Middle East, found themselves formulating policies based on erroneous assumptions (myths). Because of their misreading of the situation, they failed to enact policies that might well have prevented the fourth round of Arab-Israeli fighting. During the October war, many of the previously accepted assumptions were declared "shattered." Unfortunately, however, it is not certain that these "shattered myths" have been completely removed from the consciousness or, more appropriately, subconsciousness of Western policymakers and journalists. Furthermore, even though numerous assumptions were found to be erroneous, no over-all attempt was made to determine what other Western assumptions about the Middle East might be incorrect. Various factors combined to make American attitudes toward Middle Eastern peoples and American reporting about the Middle East less partisan (that is, less pro-Israeli).

Some of these factors will continue to influence policymakers to adopt a more "evenhanded" approach to Arab-Israeli differences. However, policymakers act within certain constraints, including public opinion, and public opinion on the Middle East continues to be shaped to a great extent by the propagation of pro-Israeli views. Therefore, the attempt to seek a more balanced presentation of facts on the Middle East should be applied to all the media of communication: the press, radio, television, the movies, textbooks, popular fiction, and so on.

NOTES

1. See Yael Dayan, *Envy the Frightened* (London: Weidenfeld & Nicolson, 1961).

2. For figures on the number of troops of each side in 1948 and 1967, see John Bagot Glubb, *A Soldier with the Arabs* (London: Hodder & Stoughton, 1957), pp. 94–95; Peter Young, *The Israeli Campaign, 1967* (London: William Kimber, 1967); and Edgar O'Ballance, *The Arab-Israeli War, 1948* (New York: Praeger, 1957), and *The Third Arab-Israeli War* (Hamden, Conn: Archon Books, 1972). For accounts by retired U.N. truce supervisors pertaining to so-called retaliation raids and general Arab-Israeli violence, see E.H. Hutchison, *Violent Truce* (New York: Devin-Adair 1956); Carl von Horn, *Soldiering for Peace* (New York: David McKay, 1966), pp. 71–139; and E.L.M. Burns, *Between Arab and Israeli* (London: George C. Harrap, 1962).

3. It is worth noting that while the Israelis are beginning to be seen by some Westerners as "good soldiers" or "militaristic," the same notion does *not* transfer to Jews in general. See Michael W. Suleiman, "The Middle East in American High Schools: A Kansas Case Study," *Middle East Studies Association Bulletin*, VIII, no. 2 (May 1974), 8–19.

4. The same observation was made in "The War That Broke the Myths," *Newsweek*, Oct. 22, 1973, p. 60.

5. *In a Time of Torment* (New York: Random House, 1967), p. 438.

6. See Terence Smith, "The October War Changed Everything: The First Israeli Revolution," *New York Times Magazine* (Compact edition), Dec. 30, 1973, pp. 120–121, 129–31. Earlier, the same author had written: "More and more [the Israelis] tended to dismiss the Arabs as bumbling soldiers who might gradually improve their equipment but could never mold themselves into an effective fighting force." See "Explosions on Two Fronts," *New York Times*, Oct. 14, 1973.

7. For an exposition of such views, see Sania Hamady, *Temperament and Character of the Arabs* (New York: Twayne, 1960); Y. Harkabi, "Basic Factors in the Arab Collapse during the Six-Day War," *Orbis*, XI, no. 3 (Fall 1967), pp. 677–91; and, to a lesser extent, Morroe Berger, *The Arab World Today* (New York: Anchor, 1964). For a critique of these views and others, as well as the "methodology," see Benjamin Beit-Hallahmi, "Some Psychological and Cultural Factors in the Arab-Israeli Conflict: A Review of the Literature," *Journal of Conflict Resolution*, XVI, no. 2 (June 1972), pp. 269–80.

8. "The War That Broke the Myths," p. 60.

9. This view was repeatedly echoed by Israeli and Western observers before and after the war broke out. For example, according to a dispatch in *U.S. News and World Report* (Oct. 22, 1973, p. 27), "Many military observers questioned the wisdom of Egypt's decision to break the March, 1970, cease-fire that had kept a tenuous peace in the Mideast. *Some called it a 'suicidal impulse'* " (emphasis added).

10. This concept appears to be quite "alien" and "illogical" to Westerners. A *Newsweek* reporter refused to accept it as "normal" or "rational," but speculated that "there may have been an element of desperation in the Arab move. Asked if the Arabs could win, Egyptian Foreign Minister Mohammed Hassan el-Zayyat said: "Frankly, no. But you don't struggle because you are assured of success. You struggle because you are right" (*Newsweek*, Oct. 15, 1973, p. 41).

11. Herbert Krosney, the *Nation*'s correspondent in Israel, writing in the November 26, 1973, issue of that magazine, quotes an Israeli soldier as saying of the Egyptian soldiers: "They're just poor slobs." Krosney then describes the Israeli soldier as intelligent and "willing to do that job, even at the sacrifice of life, including his own." The depth of the spirit of "devotion to country" surprised Krosney. Also, the Israeli soldier, according to this account, "detests war. . . . Perhaps his hatred of war is what pushes him to wage it so well." The last remark makes little sense, even as an apology for what may appear to be "love of war" by the Israelis.

12. "Blackmail by Oil," *New Republic*, Oct. 20, 1973, p. 9.

13. From Frank Giles's interview with Golda Meir, *Sunday Times* (London), June 15, 1969.

14. See Yitzhak Rabin's first speech to the Knesset as prime minister of Israel, on June 3, 1974, in *Middle East Monitor*, IV, no. 12 (June 15, 1974), 4–6.

15. See previous chapter.

16. The methodology followed is detailed in Chapter 2.

17. Of eleven editorials (five in the *New York Times*, three in the *Nation*, and three in the *New Republic*), only two (in the *New York Times*) were critical of the Arab states. Israel escaped criticism altogether.

CHAPTER 5

National Stereotypes as Weapons in the Arab-Israeli Conflict

Nations in conflict generally internalize a stereotype of their enemy that consists exclusively of evil or contemptible characteristics and a corresponding view of themselves and their allies as possessors of the best human qualities. In the battle to win the hearts and minds of world public opinion, each side attempts to transmit its own stereotypes of the other to third parties, and the result may well be to influence the policies of the latter. It is, for example, questionable whether the United States government, in the face of a massive threat to US economic and other interests in the Arab world, would have pursued its pro-Israeli policy of the past years, had its leaders not had to reckon with a powerful Zionist lobby, capable of bringing great public pressure to bear on the government to pursue this line of policy.

This chapter attempts to examine the images of the Middle East conflict communicated to the American public with a view to illuminating the stereotypes that have taken root during this battle for public opinion. Among the key areas of communication that will be touched upon are the more influential newspapers and magazines, and textbooks on the area in common use in high school. Through these sources it will be possible to understand both the components and the effects of the stereotypes used by the major parties in the Arab-Israeli conflict in order to advance their cause and/or to discredit and weaken that of the enemy. The evidence suggests that, by and large, the Israelis have had tremendous success in defining the problem in their own terms and having these accepted by Americans. When the background to the Arab-Israeli conflict is discussed, for instance, Jews in Israel are seen to be the victims of persecution, but the problem of the Palestinian Arabs is seen merely as one of victims of circumstance, lacking both the sharpness of suffering and identifiable source of oppression that are bestowed upon Jewish victims of Nazism.

The Background to Stereotypes of Arabs and Jews

Several background factors not directly related to the merits of the Arab-Israeli conflict make it easier for a favourable image of Israel and an unfavourable one of the Arabs to gain a foothold. The Western picture of the Arab has been built up, not through familiarity, but over a long period in which Arabs have appeared variously as non-Christian fanatics fighting the Crusaders; as the protagonists of fictitious romantic episodes such as those of *Arabian Nights* or the writings of Lawrence of Arabia; as the source of violent headlines in contemporary newspapers and, in the 1970's, as the cause of a sudden—and to the majority of Americans who pay little attention to the Middle East, arbitrary— embargo on oil to the U.S.

In contrast with the images gleaned by Americans of the Arabs from this random assortment of sources there has been a campaign led by Zionists, among other Jews, to change the malignant anti-Semitic stereotypes of Jews that prevailed until recently. Pressure has been exerted in particular on Jewish activists to become professional anti-anti-Semites. One aspect of this situation has been a Zionist attempt to intertwine the Palestine question with the identity and existence of the Jewish people as a whole; as David Riesman, a Jewish liberal irritated by the process, puts it, the result has been to go "a long way toward enforcing unanimity among Jews"[1] on the Palestine issue, by identifying an anti-Israeli with an anti-Jewish position. Traditionally anti-racist liberals in the West have also accepted this view, and not only refrain from attacking Zionism but campaign actively on its behalf.

Many of the myths circulated to expand support for Israel have thus given impetus to the effort to change the image of the Jew. Some of the current Western beliefs include:

1. As against the traditional anti-Semitic view of Jews as non-fighting people, the Israelis are the underdogs of the Middle East, capable of victory against enormous odds through their intelligence, courage and perseverance.[2]

2. It is contended that Jewish settlement in Palestine has not involved irreparable damage to the Palestinians; on the contrary the Palestinian Arabs were not evicted from their homes in 1948, but were invited by

the Jews to stay, and left only of their own free will and on the advice of their fellow Arabs.[3]

3. Jewish settlement has made the desert bloom while the Arabs through their indolence had left Palestine untended.[4]

4. Zionism is a basically liberal philosophy deserving the support of those who love freedom throughout the world.[5]

5. The Arabs are expressing the same anti-Semitic sentiments that have existed in the West, and the conflict stems from this hatred.[6] The Israelis on the other hand, possess basically good intentions towards the Arabs.[7]

The world has come, through the credibility accorded to these various themes, to see the Middle East problem as a conflict in which it is basically the Arabs who are the religiously bigoted aggressors, while the Israelis are just, peaceful, and productive (and also successful enough in their wars to complete the picture by appealing to the "Social Darwinist" tendencies of the West towards admiration for the winning side.)[8]

The Arabs have failed in communicating their own case for a variety of reasons. Some of the causes lie in their own lack of sophistication in the methods required, but underlying this there is a gap in Arab understanding of how the West operates. Western hostility to the Arabs, and inadequate reporting in the Arab press, combined with the Arabs' view of politics and the political process (particularly as influenced by Marxist theories) have provided educated Arabs with an incorrect picture of Western politics and the Western role in the Palestine-Israel and Arab-Israeli disputes. Many of the Arab intelligentsia, for instance, view authority as the sole possession of people in government, or, at least, of a small group, an elite, which run the country. The elite in many Western countries are then assumed to be automatically pro-Zionist, often as the inevitable and mechanical result of their "imperialistic" aspirations. The functioning of Western democracy, however, is far less comprehensible in terms of sweeping generalizations about imperialsim, capitalism, and the ruling class, than in terms of pluralism or polyarchy (where there is no over-arching ruling class but rather a multiplicity of elites vying for influence). So far as the Arab-Israeli conflict is concerned, the end result has been the overwhelming dominance of the Zionist-Israeli point of view as a result of pro-Israeli pressure groups. Nevertheless, within the context of Western pluralism, the Arabs would be better served if they sought effective groups to counteract or at least modify the numerous pro-Zionist lobbies in the West, instead of merely fatalistically condemning Western support of Israel as "imperialist."

Data On Western Attitudes

1. *The American Public*

The attitude of the American public to the conflict is illustrated in Table 1,[9] which demonstrates a dramatic rise in sympathy for Israel since the conflict became more violent in 1947. The emergence of Israel as a state, with its accompanying legends, and the tensions between the United States and revolutionary Arab regimes, doubtless account to no small extent for the development. Similar results are to be found in other Western countries. While Table 1 shows some decline in pro-Israeli sympathy since the 1967 war, the substantial amount that remains has been reflected in the greater willingness on the part of Americans to place the blame on the Arabs for hostilities in the Middle East region, as Table 2 demonstrates.[10]

The American public is clearly more willing to condemn the Arabs for fighting to regain territories seized by Israel with declared annexationist intentions, than it is to condemn Israeli territorial expansion. In part this situation reflects the ineptitude of the Arab information network, but it is very largely the result of the well-coordinated worldwide campaign of the Zionist movement to obtain support for Israel. These activities range from attempts to influence the public through constant publicity, to the employment of various means of pressure against individuals and the media who attempt to deviate from a line which is favorable to Zionism. The aim is not only to stamp out any false statements about Jews and Israel but, as several observers have noted, to impede the publication and/or distribution of material that is critical of Israel regardless of whether or not it has a factual basis.[11] What has taken place has been an extremely effective socialization process utilizing all the media of communication (the press, films, radio, television, newspapers, magazines, books, journals), schools and universities, peer groups, churches, and places of work to transmit Zionist images of the conflict.

2. *The American Press*

In my studies of American press coverage of Middle East news during the 1956 and 1967 wars, the pro-Israeli bias is also clearly indicated, as Table 3 shows.[12] However, it is also clear that in the press coverage

TABLE 1

SYMPATHY OF AMERICANS
TOWARD ARABS AND ISRAELIS,
1947–1973

Polling Agency	Date	Jews, Israel	Arabs	Both, Neither	No opinion
Gallup	Nov. 19, 1947	24%	12%	38%	26%
NORC	Feb. 1948	35	16	49*	—
SRC-C	Nov. 1964	25	7	28	40
Harris	June 10, 1967	41	1	40	18
Gallup	June War, 1967 (Informed opinion)	56	4	25	15
Gallup	Jan. 1969 (Informed opinion)	49	5	46*	—
Gallup	Oct. 6, 1973	47	6	22	25

* Both, neither and no opinion.

TABLE 2

ATTITUDES OF AMERICANS CONCERNING
THE PLACEMENT OF BLAME ON ARABS AND ISRAELIS,
1946–1973

Polling Agency	Date	Jews, Israel	Arabs	Both, Neither	No opinion
Gallup	Jan.1946	12%	10%	(British 33% Other 1%)	53%*
NORC	Nov. 1953	9	11	13	67
NORC	Nov. 1955	5	15	18	62
NORC	Nov. 1956	19	29	14	38
NORC	April, 1957	12	40	18	30
Harris	June 10, 1967	The Arabs have wanted to start a war with Israel for a long time: 63% Agree; 5% Disagree; 32% Not Sure. Israel has wanted to start a war with the Arabs for a long time: 16% Agree; 45% Disagree; 39% Not Sure			
Harris	Nov. 1973	"The Arab claim that they were 'justified in fighting this war to try to get back the territory Israel has occupied since 1967' is rejected by 49–24 per cent."			

* Some persons gave more than one answer.

TABLE 3

ATTRIBUTES CHARACTERIZING JEWS AND ISRAEL IN THE US PRESS*
JULY-DECEMBER, 1956; MAY-JUNE, 1967; AND OCTOBER-NOVEMBER, 1973

Magazine	Previous Ill-Treatment of Jews			Israel's Desire For Peace and Security			Israel's Achievements			Israel Strong but Small Underdog**			Arabs Intent on Israel's Destruction			Arabs "mistreat" Israel			Israel's Actions Justified		
	'56	'67	'73	'56	'67	'73	'56	'67	'73	'56	'67	'73	'56	'67	'73	'56	'67	'73	'56	'67	'73
New York Times	3	0	1	32	24	11	15	30	15	3	11	3	24	18	3	137	47	15	36	58	13
U.S. News & World Report	1	1	3	21	6	20	24	4	6	19	34	3	50	26	12	64	29	15	60	19	17
Nation	12	0	1	15	3	12	9	0	4	4	1	4	8	7	2	25	9	5	23	5	10
New Republic	0	0	0	13	0	4	1	1	1	4	1	1	24	2	3	49	4	4	18	3	5
Newsweek	15	4	4	3	8	7	1	2	27	0	0	3	2	5	3	11	22	20	4	7	39
Time	3	12	14	11	20	17	9	11	37	0	3	7	9	30	17	10	47	41	18	30	36
Total	34	17	23	95	61	71	59	48	90	30	50	21	117	88	40	295	158	100	159	122	120

* Numerals indicate the number of times an attribute is mentioned.

** This category was designated "Among hostile neighbors" in the 1956 study.

of the October war a slight turnaway from such stereotypes came about as the Arabs emerged as less bent on baiting Israel or seeking its destruction. Furthermore, the press displayed greater awareness of the Arab viewpoint by mentioning, relatively frequently, the Arabs' desire for peace and security and by generally justifying their actions. Their military successes also received adequate exposition and praise.

3. School Textbooks and the Conflict

In a study in which I am personally engaged of world history textbooks used in high schools in the United States,[13] the findings mirror the press reports. While, in general, an attempt is made to correct some widespread misconceptions about Islam, the presentation of the Arab relationship with Israel and the West in recent times leaves much to be desired. There is also considerable confusion concerning religion and ethnicity or nationality. Thus, Arabs are often referred to as writing the same language and having the same religion — Islam. Furthermore, Jews and Israelis are treated as if they were one and the same people, a notion that is reinforced by the frequent assertion that today's Jews are the "descendants" of the Jews of Biblical times, and that their "return" to Palestine and the establishment of the "Jewish state" there is "natural." Discussions of the Palestine and Arab-Israeli conflicts are predominantly pro-Israeli and anti-Arab. The following quotations are not untypical and illustrate our point:

> In spite of this Diaspora, or "scattering," the Jews clung to their religion and customs and dreamed of someday returning to the "promised land." This dream was not realized until the 20th century, when the Jews were permitted to re-establish a Jewish state in Palestine, which is now the nation of Israel.[14]

> Israel is an ancient nation working to become a modern nation.[15]

> [In 1967] Vowing to crush the 19–year old nation [Israel], Egypt, Jordan, Syria, Iraq, Kuwait, Sudan, Tunisia, Morocco, Lebanon, Saudi Arabia, Algeria, and Yemen joined the conflict against Israel. Arab radio stations spoke of a "Holy War," and Israel's 2.7 million people faced over 100 million hostile Arabs surrounding them.[16]

Finally, here is an explanation of Arab resentment against Israel that completely ignores the Palestine Arabs and the loss of their homeland:

> This hatred of the West helps explain the strong feelings of the Arabs against the state of Israel. . . . The social and economic achievements [of Israel] thus represented a constant challenge — and irritant — to the surrounding Arab world.[17]

4. *Stereotypes: A Sample of Teachers' Attitudes*

Pictures in peoples' minds about other peoples or countries are formed basically as a result of personal observation and experience and/or through written or audio-visual reports. Since the great majority of Westerners have never had the chance to visit the Middle East, their knowledge of events occurring in it has come primarily from press reports, radio, television, and the movies. What images have such people formed, then, of Middle Eastern peoples and countries? Table 4 records the answers of teachers of world history in high schools in Kansas, USA, to the question: "What characteristic do you associate with each of the following groups: Arabs, Jews, . . . ?"[18]

Several observations about the results are in order. To begin with, it is worth noting that 40 per cent of the respondents refused to answer the above question, some specifically stating that they are not bigots or that they do not like to deal in stereotypes. This attitude is indeed commendable and should be encouraged. Unfortunately, however, reluctance to express oneself in writing about stereotypes does not automatically mean that such stereotypes do not exist mentally as a basis for thought and action on a subject.

The second observation relates to Jews and Palestinians as people who have suffered. Though an equal number of respondents mentioned this "characteristic,"[19] almost without exception the reference to the Jews was in terms of "persecution" whereas that to the Palestinians was invariably phrased as "victims of circumstance." Needless to say, in an age of liberalism and tolerance, a persecuted people is more likely to invite sympathy and support than a people which is merely "a victim of circumstance." The persecution label is accusatory, implying guilt and involving some responsibility on the part of the observer for securing justice, whereas an "act of nature" as portrayed by the term "victim of circumstance" specifically relieves the observer of any serious responsibility or involvement.

TABLE 4

ATTITUDES OF KANSAS HIGH SCHOOL TEACHERS
TOWARD ARABS AND ISRAELIS

Group	People or Country	Religion	National Character	Mili-tarism	In-country Conditions	Govt-Int'l	Persecution/ Victims of Circumstance	
Arabs	29%	13%	27%	11%	19%	1%	— %	100
Egyptians	30	1	36	5	11	17	—	100
Palestinians	3	11	25	8	21	—	31	100
Muslims	8	58	21	4	8	—	—	100
Jews	10	20	46	1	—	—	23	100
Israelis	8	13	51	11	11	6	—	100

Finally, the references provide an insight about whether or not the respondents are sympathetic toward the people covered in this study. As has already been mentioned, Jews are often designated as persecuted. More important, perhaps, they are thought of as efficient, dedicated, industrious, educated, logical, and brave. Very few negative character-istics were mentioned. Thus, less than 7 per cent of the respondents used terms like "tight," "persecution complex" or "clannish." In fact, less than 4 per cent had anything negative to say about the Israelis. Also, while many thought of Jews as persecuted, none thought of the Israelis that way, with 11 per cent calling them militaristic, good fighters, war-riors, etc. On the other hand, respondents were far more critical of the Palestinians, the Egyptians, the Arabs, and Muslims generally. The stereotypes held, even by an educated sector of the American popula-tion, are generally similar to, and appear to be a reflection of, those stereotypes found in high school world history textbooks and the American press in general.

The Effects of Bias

Biased reporting on the Middle East is clearly harmful in the first place because it distorts the true picture of what the people and their countries are like. The circulation of mistaken views, unless corrected, inevitably spreads in such a way that even the most educated circles of a society entertain incorrect assumptions about the area. For example,

in a recent book, Robert Ardrey attempts to use the Middle East in
applying the theory that "man is a territorial animal" and, as such, will
defend his territory with the increased energy brought by property to
its proprietors. Ardrey quotes approvingly David Lack's statement that
"victory goes not to the strong but to the righteous — the righteous of
course being the owners of property," and extends this to human beings.[20] Even if one accepts Ardrey's argument, his conclusion that the
Israelis won in 1948 because they were defending "their" property is
patently false.[21] When the United Nations General Assembly suggested
the partition of Palestine in 1947, Jews owned less than 7 per cent of
the land. It was, in fact, the Palestinian Arab community that owned
most of the property and Mr. Ardrey should have done more research
about the resistance of the Palestinians against heavy odds (i.e., both
the British mandatory government and the Jewish community) before
coming to a snap conclusion. Indeed, if anything, the stubborn refusal
of the Palestinian Arabs to have their case liquidated should be the
evidence Mr. Ardrey seeks in order to document his case.

Most seriously, the partisan attitude of the Western media and intelligentsia to the conflict influences the approach of Western governments to the problem. There has been an unwillingness, for instance,
to seriously consider the implementation of United Nations resolutions
concerning the rights of the Palestinians to return, even though all
Western countries support these resolutions in principle. The freedom
of manoeuvre of Western governments in this respect is inhibited by
the prospect of taking far-reaching action of the kind that would be opposed by important sectors of public opinion.

In spite of this, it would be wrong to conclude that the situation is
irremediable. Part of the responsibility is due to the poor performance
of the Arabs when compared to the work of the Zionists and Israelis
in presenting their images of themselves and their adversary to peoples
and governments in the West. The latter, as indicated above, have effectively utilized all the resources available to them to transmit Zionist
images of the conflict. The improved reportage on the October war suggests that there is a distinct possibility of obtaining more balanced
coverage in the West, but this depends on the willingness of the Arabs
to similarly appreciate and undertake the methods open in a Western
pluralist society for different groups to present their case.

NOTES

1. David Riesman, *Individualism Reconsidered* (Glencoe, Ill: The Free Press, 1964), p. 139.

2. For an approximate estimate of the real forces in the 1948 war, see John Bagot Glubb, *A Soldier with the Arabs* (London: Hodder and Stoughton, 1957), pp. 94–95. In 1956, France and England fought on Israel's side. A full mobilization, even carried out alone, would have given Israel almost a 3:1 numerical advantage in manpower against the Egyptian army. See Kennett Love, *Suez, The Twice Fought War* (New York: McGraw-Hill, 1969), p. 491. In 1967, the number of fighting men on each side was about equal. See Peter Young, *The Israeli Campaign, 1967* (London: William Kimber, 1967), p. 56; see also the *New York Times*, May 28, 1967, p. 1E; and *Time*, June 9, 1967, p. 58. Young, writing of the 1967 war, states (p. 109) that "it seems likely that by concentrating their divisions the Israeli commanders succeeded in building up a local superiority in actual combat."

3. The myth that the Palestinian Arabs left of their own free will and at the urging of Arab leaders is no longer generally accepted. Erskine B. Childers provides an excellent analysis of what happened in 1948 in "The Wordless Wish: From Citizens to Refugees," in I. Abu-Lughod (ed.), *The Transformation of Palestine* (Evanston: Northwestern University Press, 1971), pp. 165–202. Some Israeli or pro-Zionist observers now admit to the expulsion of about half of those who became "Arab refugees." Nadav Safran, while providing an account of events till the end of May that supports the Israeli case, offers a first-hand report of how after June 1948, the Palestinian Arabs "were *expelled* from almost all new territories that came under Israeli control." See his *From War to War: The Arab-Israeli Confrontation, 1948–1967* (New York: Pegasus, 1969), p. 34 (emphasis in original).

4. This is one of the most widespread themes of Israeli publicity. In fact the Negev desert irrigation projects, which are the main focus of this publicity, have been found since 1955 to be an "absurd economic proposition," continued only "for military and political reasons." (Alex Rubner, *The Economy of Israel* (London: Frank Cass, 1960), pp 114–115.) An American expert quoted by Rubner observed that it was a serious economic mistake to draw water all the way from the Jordan to the Negev because this left "unirrigated equally large areas of just as good land nearer the source of water."

Another myth is that the Palestinian Arabs allowed the land to go to waste when they were the country's inhabitants. In fact, their exile from the land which they had so carefully tended until 1947–48 brought about a severe agricultural shortage because of the inadequacy of Jewish agriculture to meet the country's demands: as late as 1953, Ben-Gurion was citing the disappearance of Arab agricultural production as one reason for Israel's economic difficulties (*Keesing's Contemporary Archives*, 1953, p. 12666). Of course, the Palestinian Arabs lacked the massive advantage enjoyed by the Israelis of having huge amounts of capital sent into the country for development by Jews abroad.

5. This view completely overlooks the exile by Zionism of most Palestinian Arabs and its discrimination against those who remain (see Uri Davis, "Palestine into Israel," *Journal of Palestine Studies*, III, 1 (Autumn, 1973), pp. 97–105; Sabri Jiryis, *The Arabs in Israel* (Beirut: Institute for Palestine Studies, 1969), *passim*). Contrary to views of Israel as an oasis of freedom, censorship of news for "security" reasons has been a standing practice in Israel. In 1969, the Foreign Press Association in Israel complained that "on occasion details of pertinent news stories are withheld for what appear to be reasons of image or prestige." *International Herald Tribune* (Paris), Dec. 12, 1969, p. 4. The Israeli authorities have since 1967 resorted to the practice of blacklisting Israeli critics of their government's policies if the critics happen to be abroad, and refusing to renew their passports to force their return home. *The Times* (London), March 11, 1970, p. 10.

As far as the danger of a militaristic spirit in Israel is concerned, see, e.g., Jean Larteguy, *The Walls of Israel* (New York: Evans and Co., 1969) with a foreword by Moshe Dayan;

Yael Dayan, *Envy the Frightened* (London: Weidenfeld and Nicholson, 1961); Uri Avnery, *Israel Without Zionists* (New York: Macmillan, 1968); Paul Drake, "Victories Israel Cannot Afford," *The Telegram* (Toronto, Canada), March 22, 1969, p. 7.

6. This Western image prevails in spite of the fact that even some Israeli sources make it clear that the Palestine conflict cannot by any stretch of the imagination be seen as stemming from innate Arab hatred for the Jews. As Israeli publisher and politician Uri Avnery points out, "nothing like European anti-Semitism ever existed in the Arab world prior to the events [Zionism and the establishment of Israel] which created the vicious circle." (*op. cit.*, p. 212.) To say that today anti-Jewish feeling does not exist at all in the Arab world would be both untrue and unrealistic considering the seriousness, scale and emotionality of the conflict, but there is no evidence that it has spread very deep, and it certainly does not exist on the mass scale known in the West, even after so much suffering at the hands of the Israelis.

A 1968 survey of Arab students and professionals in the US conducted by this author as part of a larger study of Arab elites, asked the following question: "Do you believe that the Arabs should make a distinction between Jews and Zionists in considering who their enemies are or that they should not make such a distinction?" Only 9 per cent thought that no distinction should be made, whereas 75 per cent would have made such a differentiation and 15 per cent argued that their judgement would be based on the circumstances of each case.

Among the Arab intelligentsia — and the spheres of thought which they influence — it is clear that the predominant majority do not condemn either Jews or Judaism, although the actions of the Zionist movement and the state of Israel against the Arabs are condemned. Indeed, despite some anti-Jewish tracts that have appeared almost entirely since the 1967 war, Arab writings on Palestine and Arab-Israeli issues generally distinguish carefully between Jews and Zionists in defining the enemy.

7. For Israeli public attitudes, see the polls in *Time*, April 12, 1971. About "The Racist Challenge in Israel," I.F. Stone has written: "The usual Jewish attitude toward the Arabs is one of contemptuous superiority. Our driver northward (in Israel) was a Jew who had fled from the Nazi advance into Hungary but that did not save him from racist habits. When I suggested that we give a boy a lift, he refused, saying the boy was an Arab. When I asked what was the difference, he said Arabs smelled bad. I said that is what anti-Semites said of us Jews in the outside world but this made no impression. His attitude, it is painful to report, is typical. Israel is a country not only of full employment but of labour shortages. Thousands of Arabs do the menial tasks of Tel Aviv. They find it as hard to obtain decent lodgings as Negroes do in America and for the same reasons; many 'pass' as Jews to circumvent prejudice. In Haifa I visited the only secondary school attended by both Jews and Arabs but even there the classes turned out to be separate. The state of Israel has done much in a material way for the Arabs but the sense of humiliation outweighs any improvements. The spectacle fills one with despair. For if Jews, after all their experience of suffering, prove no better once in the majority than the rest of mankind, what hope is there for a world as torn apart as ours is by tribalism and hate?" I.F. Stone, *In a Time of Torment* (New York: Random House, 1967), p. 438.

8. This argument is advanced by A.B. Zahlan in his "Support for Israel: A Legacy," *Middle East Newsletter* (January-February, 1969), pp. 11–15.

9. Compiled from Hazel Erskine, "The Polls: Western Partisanship in the Middle East," *Public Opinion Quarterly*, XXXIII, 4 (Winter 1969–70), pp. 627–40; and *The Gallup Poll* (Chicago: Publishers-Hall Syndicate, October 16, 1973), p. 1.

10. Compiled from Hazel Erskine, "The Polls: Western Partisanship in the Middle East," *Public Opinion Quarterly*, XXXIII, 4 (Winter 1969–70), pp. 627–40; and *The Harris Survey* (mimeographed), Nov. 8, 1973, p. 2.

11. Alfred Lilienthal in *What Price Israel* (Beirut: Institute for Palestine Studies, 1969), pp. 121–147, gives an account of some of these pressures. See also *Israel and Palestine*, 26 (January 1974), p. 3.

12. The table is compiled from my studies of American press coverage of Middle East news during the 1956, 1967 and 1973 wars.

13. This is part of a study by a committee of the Middle East Studies Association (MESA) to look into possible bias in the treatment of Middle East countries.

14. T. Walter Wallbank and Arnold Schrier, *Living World History* (Chicago: Scott, Foresman, 1969), p. 54.

15. Ralph S. Yohe, et al., *Exploring Regions of the Eastern Hemisphere* (Chicago: Follet Educational Corporation, 1969), p. 406.

16. Daniel Roselle, *A World History: A Cultural Approach* (Boston, Ginn, 1969), p. 717.

17. Wallbank and Schrier, *op. cit.*, p. 704.

18. The questionnaire was sent to 425 schools in Kansas. Slightly over 40 per cent of those approached responded.

19. Though an equal number of respondents mentioned the two characteristics, the percentages are different because the total respondents for the two groups are not the same.

20. Robert Ardrey, *The Territorial Imperative* (London: Collins, 1969), p. 121.

21. *Ibid.*, pp. 329–44.

CHAPTER 6

American Images of Middle East Peoples:
Impact of the High School

In this study of the role of the high school in shaping the views of Americans on the Middle East and its peoples, we also attempt to compare and contrast the views of American educators and their students concerning the Arabs, specific Arab countries and peoples (such as Egypt, the Palestinians, etc.), Israel, Jews as well as Turks, Iranians, and Muslims generally. It should be remembered that Americans often confuse one Middle East group with another (e.g. Turks and Arabs). It is, therefore, useful to get information on how Americans view the different countries and peoples in the Middle East. But it should be remembered that views are not permanent and that they are strongly affected by governmental policy and media coverage as well as relations between these countries' peoples and the United States. In this regard, American views of the Shah of Iran at the time of this survey in 1974 were certainly different from American images of the Ayatollah Rouhollah Khomeini in the mid–1980's. Nevertheless, and despite extensive media coverage, much of which is inaccurate or inflammatory (as Edward Said pointed out in his *Covering Islam*), the American public's view of Middle East peoples, be they Arabs, Iranians, Palestinians, or Egyptians, remains mainly stereotypic, sketchy, and rather unflattering. This chapter provides detail and a comparative study.

This report about the state of Middle East studies in American high schools is also an attempt to determine which factors most importantly affect the amount and quality of teaching on the Middle East that takes place in American high schools. Furthermore, since teachers play a significant role in this educational process, their attitudes toward Middle Eastern peoples are also assessed and the determinants of these attitudes are delineated.

In the late 1960's, a cursory review of American high school textbooks by a few members of the Middle East Studies Association (MESA) left little doubt that the Middle East, its problems and its peoples, have often been inadequately covered and very poorly presented. Not infrequently, factual errors were detected, and definite bias against the region and/or some of its peoples was easy to spot. The MESA Committee on Middle East Images in Secondary School Texts was then formed to study more systematically the possibility of factual or attitudinal distortion of material on the Middle East in the various World History and Social Studies texts used in the U.S. and Canada. At the same time, though a member of that Committee, I undertook on my own a survey of Kansas High School teachers of World History to determine the state of M.E. studies at that level and to assess the attitudes of the teachers toward Middle Eastern peoples.[1] The Images Committee then decided that the same survey should be carried out in several states to get data more applicable to the U.S. as a whole. This chapter, then, summarizes the results of the study of high school teachers of World History in California, Colorado, Indiana, Kansas, New York, and Pennsylvania.

Methodology:

After securing copies of the directories of high schools in the above states, a decision had to be made as to whether or not to include all the schools in the sample, depending on the number in each state.[2] Because of their relatively small numbers, it was decided to survey all the schools in Indiana (449), New York (656), Colorado (247), and Kansas (420). For California (1,084) and Pennsylvania (848), a 50% sample was drawn by random selection.

In the pilot study, administered in Kansas in 1972, it was found that the name of the investigator had some effect on responses to certain questions.[3] In the Kansas survey, half the questionnaires were sent out under the name of the researcher, Michael Suleiman, and the other half under the name of a colleague, David W. Brady. Because the Arab-Israeli conflict forms an important part of what Americans, including high school teachers, read and discuss about the Middle East, three names were selected to use in the 1974 Survey, one Arab/Muslim-sounding (Mohammed A. Sulaiman), another Jewish-sounding (Leon C. Cohen), and a neutral-sounding name (Ken E. Brady). After the sample for each state was chosen, it was further divided into three equal groups, again selected at random, to determine which schools were to be sent questionnaires signed Brady, Cohen, or Sulaiman. Also, all "investigators" were given the title of "Professor" in order to avoid any bias affecting the rate of return based on rank. Apart from the signature, all questionnaires were exactly the same. For each state, however, the letter accompanying the questionnaire was printed on the departmental stationery of the participant from the MESA Images Committee regularly teaching in that state. It was believed that this procedure would net the highest rate of return, which was as follows: Pennsylvania, 33%; Indiana, 32%; Kansas, 29%; New York[4], 27%; Colorado, 25%; and California, 21%. In all, 772 filled questionnaires (out of 2788) were returned for an over-all return rate of 28%.[5] This was satisfactory, considering the recent public disaffection with surveys.[6]

The Sample:

World History teachers tend to be young, over half of them (55%) being under thirty-five years of age. The men outnumber the women three to one. One-third (33%) are Anglo-American and 19% are of German background.[7] However, fully one-fourth of the respondents specified an affiliation with more than one ethnic group. Generally approximating the national population, 57% of the sample expressed Protestant leanings and 28% were Catholic.[8] The majority (56%) live in communities of 10,000 population or smaller, while only 11% inhabit large cities of 150,000 or more. They are well-educated, with 95% of them having had course work beyond the Bachelor's degree. 61% have a Master's degree or higher. Their main areas of specialization are History (45%) and the Social Sciences (39%).[9]

The various World History textbooks used by these teachers devote some 8–10% of their coverage to the history, civilization and politics of the Middle East. Even though the area is of strategic importance and has been for the past several decades an arena of international conflict, yet the majority in the sample (51%) never had a single university course dealing with that region, as Figure 1 shows.[10] Only 12% had three or more courses on the Middle East. Figure 2 illustrates the content of the courses the teachers took which focused on the Middle East.

Despite the teachers' generally low level of formal education on the area, 62% of the sample stated that they were "adequately qualified or prepared to teach the section on the Middle East."

Figure 1

*Number of University Courses Taken
by Teachers on M.E.*

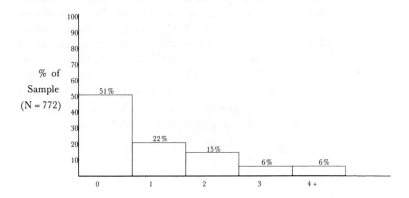

Number of Courses on M.E.

Figure 2

*Content of University Courses Taken
by Teachers on M.E.*

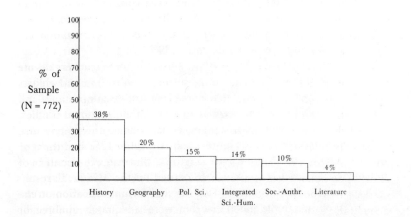

Content of Courses Taken on M.E.

World History teachers used a wide variety of textbooks. Some 55% of the respondents expressed satisfaction with their texts. For those who did not, the main complaints related to inadequate coverage of certain topics such as the Middle East (24%), or the view that the book is dated (16%), too difficult (15%), too simple (9%), or not suitable for the course (4%). Though only a tiny minority (1%) could point to a specific bias in their texts, some 38% stated that those same texts *reinforced* their students' "stereotypes" about the Middle East and its peoples.

When specifically questioned as to whether or not the text provides adequate coverage of the Middle East area, only 49% of the sample responded affirmatively. It should be remembered that the course in which the text is used is entitled World History, of which the Middle East section constitutes only one part. In fact, most of the material devoted to the Middle East deals with ancient civilizations. It is not surprising, therefore, to find that three-fourths of the respondents supplement their text with other material on the Middle East in the form of books, magazines, slides, speakers, etc. Two questions were related to textbook coverage and instructor emphasis given to particular periods of Middle East history, politics, or culture. Figure 3 shows that the textbooks appear to provide just the right amount of coverage on Islam so far as instructors are concerned. However, while textbook authors tend to emphasize the ancient history and civilization of the peoples of the Middle East, the instructors devote more class time to the recent period, especially the years since the end of World War II. Furthermore, as Table 1 shows, apart from Europe, the Middle East region is given greater attention by American High School teachers than any other world region.

Teachers display an uneven knowledge of the Middle East area and its peoples. The most familiar countries are Israel (44%) and Egypt (35%).[11] The countries mentioned as least familiar, i.e. ones that are somewhat familiar but which evoke an interest for greater knowledge, are Iraq (20%), Iran (15%), Syria (11%), and Saudi Arabia (10%).

Reflecting the inadequate knowledge of the region and its peoples, 85% of the respondents stated that they were "unaware of any misstatements of facts or opinion concerning the Middle East" in their textbooks.[12] About 4% thought their texts manifested a pro-Israeli bias, and 3% complained of over-generalization. Table 2 shows the results in answer to the question about how the teachers view textbook treatment of the various Middle Eastern peoples. These clearly reinforce the above results—except for opinions about the treatment of Jews and

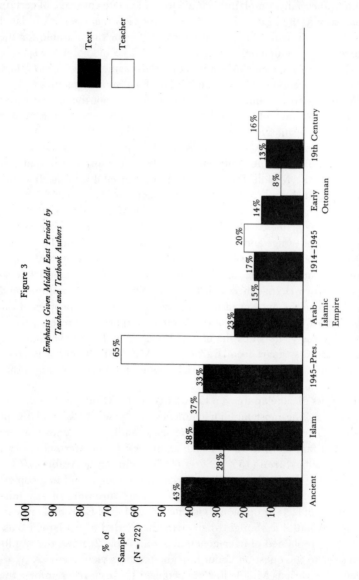

Figure 3

Emphasis Given Middle East Periods by
Teachers and Textbook Authors

Text ■
Teacher □

% of
Sample
(N = 722)

Ancient: 43%, 28%
Islam: 38%, 37%
1945–Pres.: 33%, 65%
Arab-Islamic Empire: 23%, 15%
1914–1945: 17%, 20%
Early Ottoman: 14%, 8%
19th Century: 13%, 16%

Middle East Period Emphasized

Israelis. Here, the teachers asserted that, though they were unaware of specific mis-statements, the over-all presentation was pro-Israeli and pro-Jewish about 20% of the time.

TABLE 1

NUMBER OF WEEKS AMERICAN HIGH SCHOOL TEACHERS DEVOTE TO DIFFERENT WORLD REGIONS*

Number of Weeks

Region	none or less than one	1	2	3	4	5	6	6 +
Middle East	12%	10%	17%	16%	12%	7%	9%	12%**
Europe	18	1	2	3	4	2	6	61
Southeast Asia	27	15	19	10	8	3	7	6
Subsahara Africa	28	15	15	8	6	5	6	13
Indian Subcontinent	28	15	17	10	8	4	6	8
Latin America	38	14	16	9	5	3	4	5

* Teachers were asked to state how many weeks they devoted to each listed world region.

** If added horizontally, totals do not add up to 100 per cent because the category "other" was dropped.

TABLE 2

TEXTBOOK TREATMENT OF MIDDLE EAST PEOPLES ACCORDING TO HIGH SCHOOL TEACHERS*

Group	Pro	Anti	Neutral/Balanced	Not Covered
Egyptians	9%	5%	77%	6%**
Muslims	6	5	83	4
Palestinians	4	4	56	33
Arabs	3	5	83	6
Israelis	20	1	66	10
Jews	19	1	71	6
Iranians	5	3	68	22
Turks	5	7	77	8

* Teachers were asked to state how their textbooks treated each of the above topics: "Pro, anti, neutral/balanced, or not covered."

** If added horizontally, totals do not add up to 100 per cent because the category "other" was dropped.

The teachers were asked to state (1) what do *most of your students* think of, and (2) what do *you* think of, when the various Middle Eastern peoples come to mind? 220 respondents or 29% of the sample refused to state an opinion on either question. Many claimed that they could not answer for the students and did not know their views. Others asserted that high school students view Middle Eastern peoples as "very often distant, maybe 'story book' people, almost non-existent." A few thought students "stereotype in their negative image if they have even heard of them at all." The failure of teachers to state their own views, however, can be attributed in the main to their reluctance to indulge in stereotyping. As one respondent put it: "Question calls for stereotyping; I'd look and feel stupid answering this." A variant of this theme is: "I think of them as human beings, each with his own culture, world view, problems and prejudices."

TABLE 3

STUDENTS' VIEWS OF MIDDLE EAST PEOPLES
AS REPORTED BY AMERICAN HIGH SCHOOL TEACHERS*

Group	People or Country	Reli-gion	National Character	Mili-tarism	In-Country Conditions	Gov't Int'l	Persecution/ Victims of Circumstance
Egyptians	70%	0%	5%	1%	2%	16%	— %**
Muslims	17	63	4	1	3	2	—
Palestinians	13	5	5	19	6	23	20
Arabs	44	7	6	3	15	18	—
Israelis	16	10	8	3	7	43	3
Jews	17	23	7	1	4	21	18
Iranians	75	1	2	1	7	5	—
Turks	64	3	7	9	5	4	—

*   Q. "What do you think *most of your students* think of when they think of the following groups? Turks, Arabs, etc."

** If added horizontally, totals do not add up to 100 per cent because the category "other" was dropped.

TABLE 4

CHARACTERISTICS OF MIDDLE EAST PEOPLES
AS DESCRIBED BY AMERICAN HIGH SCHOOL TEACHERS*

Group	People or Country	Religion	National Character	Militar-ism	In-Country Conditions	Gov't Int'l	Persecution/ Victims of Circumstance
Egyptians	50%	1%	9%	1%	13%	22%	— %**
Muslims	15	66	7	1	3	2	—
Palestinians	10	2	5	9	7	14	45
Arabs	34	7	11	1	17	22	—
Israelis	17	5	22	2	11	33	3
Jews	19	24	15	1	3	12	20
Iranians	61	1	3	0	18	10	—
Turks	58	1	9	4	11	11	—

*   Q. "What do *you* think of when you think of the following groups? Turks, Arabs, etc."

**   If added horizontally, totals do not add up to 100 per cent because the category "other" was dropped.

Tables 3 and 4 show the results for those who did express an opinion. Obviously, the teachers differ little, if at all, from their students on this point. Only with regard to three peoples do some noticeable differences appear. Thus, teachers tend to think of the Palestinians less in militaristic terms and more in terms of the suffering they have endured as "victims of circumstance." Another difference is the greater inclination on the part of teachers to think of Jews and Israelis in terms of "national character" traits.

One curious feature relates to both teachers and students, and is reflected in the following patterns: Egyptians, Iranians, Turks, and to some extent Arabs are identified with particular individuals, groups, their countries, physical properties, products, cultural artifacts, or history. A sizeable majority sees Muslims in terms of religion, whereas Jews are *not* pigeon-holed into one or even a few categories. Less than one-fourth of the respondents thought of them in terms of religion.

TABLE 5

STUDENTS' ATTITUDES TOWARD MIDDLE EAST PEOPLES AS REPORTED BY AMERICAN HIGH SCHOOL TEACHERS*

Group	Positive	Sympathetic	Neutral	Unsympathetic	Negative
Egyptians	2%	0%	85%	3%	8%**
Muslims	1	0	83	0	8
Palestinians	0	19	52	1	24
Arabs	0	0	79	3	15
Israelis	14	12	70	0	1
Jews	8	23	60	0	5
Iranians	2	1	87	1	5
Turks	2	0	80	1	13

* Q. "What do you think *most of your students* think of when they think of the following groups? Turks, Arabs, etc."

** If added horizontally, totals do not add up to 100 per cent because the category "other" was dropped.

TABLE 6

ATTITUDES OF AMERICAN HIGH SCHOOL TEACHERS TOWARD MIDDLE EAST PEOPLES*

Group	Positive	Sympathetic	Neutral	Unsympathetic	Negative
Egyptians	10%	2%	73%	0%	12%**
Muslims	7	1	82	0	6
Palestinians	0	42	41	1	11
Arabs	6	2	71	1	17
Israelis	25	8	57	0	6
Jews	16	22	54	0	4
Iranians	12	2	76	0	5
Turks	12	2	75	0	7

* Q. "What do *you* think of when you think of the following groups? Turks, Arabs, etc."

** If added horizontally, totals do not add up to 100 per cent because the category "other" was dropped.

When the above remarks are categorized in terms of whether they are positive, negative, or neutral, as in Tables 5 and 6, it is clear that the students' attitudes are surmised to be more neutral.[13] In other words, the teachers thought themselves to be more opinionated, i.e. more willing to take a position than their students. In general, however, the difference is slight.

Image of Middle East Peoples Among High School Teachers and Students

Unlike the reporting in Tables 3 and 4 above, we shall now attempt to present a composite picture with examples of each Middle Eastern group or people mentioned in the questionnaire, This will provide more detail and perhaps point up some additional differences between the students' and teachers' characterizations of, and attitudes toward, Middle Easterners. It is important to remember, however, that the survey was done in 1974, i.e. before the overthrow of the Shah of Iran and prior to Sadat's rapprochement with the United States.

Egyptians

The most well-known feature about Egypt and Egyptians is the ancient civilization of the Pharaohs. Over one-third of the respondents either referred to or expressed their great admiration for that civilization and for the outstanding monuments which continue to stand today. Some mentioned the "contribution to civilization" or the fact that Egyptians were "intelligent before their time." One teacher associated Egyptians with the "birth of Western civilization, immortality," while another wrote: "A great past, despite Elizabeth Taylor."

To students in particular, the Pyramids symbolize Egypt and Egyptians — almost as if present-day Egyptians are either non-existent or completely overshadowed by their past. In fact, some respondents claimed the Egyptians "have not done anything since the pyramids," or that they are "pale unworthy successors of great heritage." Others talked of the Egyptians' "search for past glories," or stated that they are "trying to prove today that they are as good as the pyramids."

Only among a relatively few respondents (about 10%) is the Arab-Israeli conflict the most important reference point concerning Egyptians. Somewhat related to this issue, however, is an anti-Egyptian sentiment based on Egypt's stand on the Arab-Israeli conflict and the relatively poorer Egyptian military performance in various encounters with the Israelis. Negative remarks included: Aggressive, disorganized, causing U.S. trouble, losing wars, leaderless and gullible, self-deluding, not able to back up their brag, poor soldiers, too stupid to drive a tank, etc.

About one-fourth of the respondents did associate the Egyptians with the more recent historical period. Thus, there were frequent references to Egypt, the Suez Canal, and the Aswan Dam. Also, presidents Gamal Abdel Nasser and Anwar el-Sadat were mentioned. Many respondents referred to Egyptians as the "leadership of Arab nationalism," perhaps having president Nasser in mind. Finally, there were some comments indicating backwardness, poverty, under-development, traditionalism, and overpopulation.

A fairly large minority of sample respondents (10–15%) expressed very favorable attitudes toward Egyptians. Thus, Egyptians were described as warm, hospitable, friendly, resourceful, hardworking, modern, "beautiful people," and "great people, great past."

To summarize, teachers viewed Egyptians mainly in terms of their ancient accomplishments, in which case the attitude was positive. The more recent period, however, produced either neutral or negative reactions. According to one teacher, his students viewed Egyptians as "proud, intelligent, warlike and poor."

Muslims

To teachers and students alike, Muslims were identified as people who adhere to the Islamic faith. This association was expressed through references to Islam, the prophet Mohammed, Mecca, mosques, minarets, and one or more of the five pillars of the faith. Prayers, the Koran, and Allah were also frequently mentioned. Even when a respondent wished to express a strong preference for or against Muslims, he/she referred to some aspect of the religion. Thus, anti-Muslim, uninformed, or negative remarks included: "Religious faith that stifles creativity," religious war, fanatical, fatalistic, slow in accepting change, holders of anachronistic beliefs, warlike people, "Islam has a retarding influence," very religious but misguided, devoted but exploited, and "false religion." Some claimed Muslims were a "religious group in war with Jews," or that they were out to "destroy Jewish faith." Especially among students, the element of "strangeness" is apparently a source of fear and hostility.

Thus, to some students Muslims are followers of a "strange religion, peculiar religion, weird," "people with a funny religion," "stupid religion," "infidels." Furthermore, Muslims "dress strangely and practice polygamy."

In general, teachers were much more favorably disposed toward Muslims than they believed their students to be. We now illustrate the number and variety of positive or favorable remarks. Frequent references were made to the devotion and sincerity of the followers of Islam. Also, Muslims were described as "proud, stubborn, determined," "organized, rich heritage, innovative," "good people, good religion," "dedicated, aesthetic, and sincere," "intelligent and reasonable," modern, "sincere in belief," "appeal to racial equality," tolerant and devout. Some teachers also mentioned that Muslims have "non-discriminatory" and "highly ethical" religious beliefs as well as "one of the world's greatest religions." Many respondents were impressed with the rich tradition and great civilization of the Muslim empire, specifically singling out Muslim contributions to science, the arts, and architecture in particular.

Students, relatively more than teachers, appeared to associate Muslims with the Crusades, and Christian-Muslim conflict of the Middle Ages, and referred to Muslims as Moors, Berbers, and the group that "once terrorized Eastern Europe." Furthermore, students tended to confuse Muslims with the Black Muslim and Black Power movements in the United States. ("How odd those Blacks to turn Moslem"), singling out Mohammed Ali (Cassius Clay) as their idea of what a Muslim is.

It is interesting to note that when reference was made to a particular Muslim individual from the Middle East with whom the respondents were familiar, it was the Shah of Iran who was mentioned almost in every instance, rather than the late King Faisal of Saudi Arabia, for example — this despite the fact that some respondents believe "Arabs" and "Muslims" to be and mean the same thing.

In summary, the Islamic religion or related matters were the most salient image for the survey respondents. Though most merely used neutral language to refer to the group or their beliefs, some expressed dislike for this "strange" religion, while others (the more knowledgeable) expressed great admiration for Islam and Muslims generally.

Palestinians

Teachers tended to see the Palestinians as refugees while students viewed them as guerrillas. In general, teachers appeared far more understanding of the plight of the Palestinians and tended to be more sympathetic to their cause than they perceived their students to be. While many, if not most, respondents referred to Palestinians merely as "refugees" or victims of circumstance, some pinpointed the blame for their homelessness and misery. The following examples are illustrative of responses not specifying who is to blame for the crime described: Vitims of Middle Eastern conflict, ripped off and oppressed scapegoats, homeless and outcasts, the poor relations, displaced, a group that has been cheated out of their own homeland, caught in the middle, evicted people, a forgotten people, etc. A few respondents not only avoided "naming the culprit" in the Palestinian tragedy but also seemed annoyed that Palestinians did not face facts, e.g. "unfortunate victims of history who refused to be realistic." However, quite a few others showed concern and specifically blamed a country or a group of people for the plight of the Palestinians, as the following examples illustrate: Victims of the Jewish state, victims of imperialism, victims of Arab-Israeli intransigence, victims of U.N., "victims of an imposed solution of a European problem."

As fighting or guerrilla units, the Palestinians were thought of in the following terms, among others: Violence, terrorists, hijackers, war, military, Al-Fatah, Black September, Palestine Liberation Army, revolutionary, and commandos. Others described them as "irrational terrorist groups," "Jewish homeland terrorist groups opposing Israelis," or they referred to "radical guerrilla atrocities involving the Olympics, hijacking, kidnapping." This picture of Palestinians as "refugees and terrorists" generates sympathy and understanding in some respondents, revulsion in others. The latter group, which is relatively smaller in number, shows its antagonism toward and hatred of Palestinians in such remarks as: sneaks, left-wing rebels and communist gangsters, extremists, troublemakers, causing U.S. trouble, very bad guys, fanatics, "unreasonable, violent, misguided," ruthless, foolish, crazy men, back-biters, "an artificial group maintained for propaganda purposes," or merely "a useless group of people." A larger percentage of respondents, however, especially among teachers expressing their own views (as opposed to student opinions) felt greater sympathy for the Palestinians and expressed the need for resolving their problem. For example, they referred to Palestinians as "unwanted, unloved, uncared for," most misunderstood, and "ignored by all." They pointed to "death, hopelessness, exploitation," no justice, tragedy, "some pity for their problems," and thought the Palestinians "want a simple life," and "deserve better treatment." Another respondent stated that Palestinians are "displaced persons; their anger is justified, their problem must be solved before there is peace in the Middle East."

Interestingly enough, relatively few respondents made references to the ancient history of Palestine, the Bible or the Holy Land. More importantly, however, very few respondents mentioned the heart of the problem, namely the Palestinian-Zionist-Israeli conflict in direct and specific terms. The most salient feature of Palestinians to these teachers and their students, then, is one of refugees or a homeless people using violent means in retaliation or to regain their homeland.

Arabs

Especially since this survey was conducted a few months after the October 1973 Arab-Israeli war, and at a time when Arab oil-producing countries enforced an embargo on oil sales to the U.S. and other countries considered supportive of Israel, the word "Arabs" was very much associated with oil in the mind of many (25%–30%) respondents. Most merely mentioned "oil" as their reaction. Others, however, specifically referred to "oil boycott," "embargo," "oil conflict," "blackmail," or "gas shortage." Some called the Arabs "oil price robbers," "oil hoarders," or "bad guys who cut off our oil."

Apparently oil and desert are closely associated in people's minds — at least so far as the Arabs are concerned. Thus, many respondents thought of the Arabs as desert people, camel-drivers, nomadic, bedouin, or, as one teacher put it, "homeless wandering groups in the desert." This image also includes pictures of camels, camel caravans, sheikhs, harems, and horses. To a few, it is a romantic life, and the Arabs are viewed as "bedouins whom I admire." To others, the Arabs are "nomadic who contributed little for 2000 years."

While the above image contains some negative attitudes, some respondents (10%–15%) specifically stated anti-Arab feelings and attributed "bad" qualities to Arabs. Thus, there were references to Arabs as terrorists, self-seeking, vindictive, semi-warlike, bad guys, inferior trouble-makers, pushy, self-deluding, clannish, fanatic, selfish, irrational, and back-biting people. Also, some respondents thought of Arabs in terms of "sexism and decadence," "conspicuous and abject poverty," or as "madmen with little logic." According to the teachers, students in particular harbored strong anti-Arab sentiments as expressed in the following responses: "Oil rich, power hungry war-mongers," "oil exploiters and primitive," cowards, inferiors, crooks, dirty, idiots, or uncivilized barbarians. To some students, the Arabs are "dumb nomads with tents," while others allegedly view them as "creeps who kill Jews and withhold oil."

In one surprising finding, only in a few instances (about 5–7%) did teachers mention the Arab-Israeli conflict in association with the Arabs, although it did color the feelings of the respondents in references to other issues (e.g. oil, anti-Arab sentiment, etc.). When such specific references were made, however, Arabs were mainly presented as adjuncts of the Israelis rather than in their own right. Examples of this follow: "Against the Jews," "threat to Israel," "hatred for Jews," "opponents of Jews," etc. One respondent called them "aggressors in the Middle East,"and another requested that Arabs "leave the Israelis be, stop fighting them." One teacher appeared to be "confused" and simply asked: "Was holy land promised by God to Jews or Arabs?"

The Arabs were also identified by some respondents as Egyptians, Saudis, Iraqis, "residents of the Arab countries," or people of the Middle East and North Africa. Furthermore, some teachers and students could make no distinction between Arabs and Muslims. Also, while some teachers pointed out the disunity among the Arabs, others referred to the uniting element of Arab nationalism.

While a large minority expressed anti-Arab sentiment, nevertheless a few (mainly teachers) stated strong positive or favorable attitudes toward Arabs and/or emphasized the Arabs' strengths rather than their weaknesses. Thus, they described Arabs as friendly and warm, "noble, proud, hospitable," progressive and intelligent, "shrewd, good businessmen," and "gentle hosts." These people who "have been pushed into the background and trampled too long" are "misunderstood" in the West and suffer from "stereotypes" spread through a "bad press." Other respondents mentioned Arab "contributions to civilization," especially in philosophy, literature, mathematics and the sciences. Furthermore, they are the "founders of one of the greatest religions in the world." The Arabs have given "so much in culture and enrichment to the West" and are a "proud religious people who feel they have been wronged." They are now actively modernizing and "emerging from sheikdoms to revolutionary governments." Finally, Arabs were viewed as an "emerging nation, struggling to regain identity."

In summary, then, Arabs were associated with oil and the desert and were more often viewed in negative terms, especially by the students. They were seen as primarily Muslim residents of the Middle East who are "enemies of Israel." Some teachers emphasized the Arabs' good qualities. Apart from the Arab-Israeli conflict, the following response adequately summarized the mixed reaction: "Bagdad, Mohammed, Islam, oil, bedouins, friendly."

Israelis

There is no question that, whenever the Israelis were mentioned, what stood out in the respondents' minds (especially the students') was the Arab-Israeli conflict or some aspect of it such as the 1948, 1956, 1967, or 1973 wars. In the graphic words of one teacher, the Israelis reminded him of a situation that was "the same as powder keg." The next most frequent association equated Israelis with Jews, Zionists, or the people of Israel.

The image of Israelis as hard-working and progressive was also widely-held. The richness of this picture is illustrated by the terms used to describe the Israelis: remarkable progress, well-organized, idealistic, dynamic, resourceful, and intelligent. Others merely stated their "pro" or favorable sentiments, without explicit reference, such as "respect, respect, respect." Another trait that respondents associated with Israelis was a determination to gain a homeland, fighting for survival, or "against great odds." One teacher put it this way: "People who have faced death so often that courage is a way of life." Another stated "being pushed into the sea by Nasser. Determined." The "fighting" itself was described mostly in favorable terms such as good soldiers, fierce fighters, strong army, brilliant military strategists, etc. Some, however, thought the Israelis were becoming militaristic, conquerors, or a military state. As the survey was conducted shortly after the October, 1973 war, some respondents merely mentioned the names of the Israeli leaders, mainly Golda Meir and Moshe Dayan.

Teachers in particular did express criticism of the Israelis in very specific terms. Some respondents described the Israelis as aggressors, irresponsible, arrogant, "too self-righteous," cocky, or "too racist and aggressive." Others called the Israelis "zionist expansionists," "intruders into the Arab world,' "nasty fellows with bombs," "aggressive twentieth century colonial power," "nation state occupying someone else's land," and "imperialistic, greedy for Arab land." One teacher described the

Israelis as "leeches of U.S." and another called them "the modern millstone around the neck of U.S. foreign policy."

In summary, there was little difference between the views of teachers and their students in their attitudes toward Israelis. The respondents mentioned the Arab-Israeli conflict, Jews and the excellent fighting as well as fighting spirit of the Israelis. However, some criticism centered on perceived Israeli arrogance and imperialist expansion. Perhaps a good summary is provided by one respondent's remark: "Modern, Western, proud, insufferable."

Jews

Students and teachers alike associated Jews with suffering, discrimination, persecution, and the Nazi and WWII experience. Further, they viewed Jews as underdogs in the Middle East. As Jews have been the "object of hatred" and "have been scapegoats for centuries," "struggling for survival," respondents expressed their sympathy for them, some stating that they "need understanding" or that they "should be left alone."

Respondents associated Jews with religion, monotheism, Moses, or the Ten Commandments almost as often as with persecution. Closely related to this were remarks expressly stating some respondents' affinity or strong identification with Jews on religious grounds. Examples of this are: "Admire strength of religion, basis for Christianity," "religious people of Christ's time," "fulfilling Old Testament prophecy," "God's chosen people," and "I am a Christian, so I am close to them in religious belief."

Many respondents (about 15%) tended to associate Jews with Israel, Zionism, or a related aspect. According to one teacher, Jews are people "interested in project 'Israel'." Others referred to Palestine, Jerusalem, the Balfour Declaration or the "creation of the Jewish state." Related to this, though to a lesser extent, were references to the Arab-Israeli conflict or some facet thereof.

Among both students and teachers, a substantial minority specifically mentioned some positive characteristics which they attributed to Jews. Some examples are: powerful, intellectual, love to learn, industrious, tenacious, builders, energetic, efficient, brave, etc.

The only difference detected between the attitudes of teachers and students pertained to one familiar stereotype of Jews. Thus, students were reported as thinking of Jews in terms of money and business. Such students viewed Jews as rich, exploiting, cheap, money-hungry, stingy, or greedy.

In summary, it can be said that the word "Jews" presented the respondents with a number of images which were largely sympathetic or positive. The variety of the respondents' images of Jews contrasts sharply with the overwhelming association found between "Muslims" and the Islamic religion. Jews were viewed as having suffered persecution, as belonging to a religion closely related to Christianity, and as a group oriented toward Israel or involved in the Arab-Israeli conflict. Specific positive attributes were also mentioned. The following remarks by two respondents seem to summarize most of the above: "Persecuted, industrious, self-centered, educated;" and "industrious, religious people that may have a chip on their shoulders."

Iranians (Persians)

Of all Middle Eastern peoples, the Iranians were the least known both by students and teachers. The remark that Iranians were "just another group of foreigners," though made by students, applies to teachers as well, to a lesser extent. For both students and teachers who were somewhat familiar with them. Iranians were thought of primarily in terms of ancient history and civilization. References were numerous to ancient Persia, Darius, Persian wars, Alexander the Great, Zoroastrianism, and "a great cultural heritage." Next in frequency of reference was oil and the wealth it has produced.

The Shah appeared to symbolize Iran in the U.S., especially for students. Though he was mentioned frequently by teachers also, the latter tended to mention Persian rugs, rug-weaving, and the crafts industry more often. Also, both groups, especially teachers, generally thought of Iran as a pro-Western country, friendly to the U.S. Others within each group merely stated that Iranians were the people who lived in Iran, a country in the Gulf area. A few merely expressed their favorable or friendly feelings toward Iranians.

There were, however, some differences between the views of teachers and what they believed their students thought of Iranians. Thus, hardly any teachers made any factual mistakes in their references to Iran. They claimed, however (and quite correctly), that students tended to confuse Iranians with Arabs and/or Iran with Iraq. Teachers showed greater sophistication also when they mentioned not only the backwardness of the country (much on the mind of students) but also the improvements and economic development being pushed by the regime. Perhaps more important and pertinent was the reference by many teachers to the "political stability of the country."

In summary, the main picture that emerged was that Iranians were not well-known. Teachers appeared to be more familiar with the ancient Persian heritage than with present-day Iran. Contemporary Iran was best-known for its oil and the Shah.

Turks

To American high school teachers and their students, the mention of Turks brought to mind the Ottoman Empire and its glory, cruelty, threat to Christian Europe, and some of the sultans that ruled the empire. Apparently, it is this period of Turkish history that also brings forth an image of the fighting, aggressive Turk. To students in particular, the Turks are a determined, tough people, fierce fighters, conquerors, pirates, savage horsemen, bloodthirsty, wild and barbaric. The teachers' descriptions are similar, though somewhat more positive, i.e. emphasizing the notion that Turks are good fighters or great warriors. Narcotics, drugs, and poppies are mentioned frequently by both groups. As one teacher put it, the Turks are "skilled politicians for getting the opium money from the U.S." It was surprising that a relatively large number of respondents (about 5%) referred to Turks merely as "people of Turkey," "live in the Middle East," "guys in the Middle East," or merely associated Turkey with Istanbul-Constantinople. Relatively few referred to the "backwardness" or poverty of the country or the fact that Turks are Muslim. A few teachers and students stated that the Turks are Europeanized Arabs, or, as one teacher put it, a "neutral Arab group."

Students, unlike their teachers, apparently often associate Turks with the Crusades, or think of them as "another people," "a place on the map," or as people who wear funny costumes, especially turbans and fezzes.

Teachers (but apparently not their students) recognize the Turks clearly as American allies in the Central Treaty Organization (CENTO) and the North Atlantic Treaty Organization (NATO). They are prized as friends of the West and enemies of the Soviet Union. Furthermore, there is a definite awareness of the strategic importance of Turkey for Western defense. Finally and in contrast to the students who allegedly see backwardness in Turkey, the teachers often referred to reform, modernization, and Westernization.

In summary, the sample respondents do not so much think in terms of present-day Turkey as of the Ottoman Empire, Muslim-Christian rivalry in the Middle Ages, the military prowess of the Turks, the drug (poppy-growing) issue and the country's economic backwardness. To teachers, Turkey represents a strategic location and membership in Western military alliances.

Conclusions and Recommendations

I. *Research on the Middle East: The Investigator-Respondent Interaction*

1. In survey research on the Middle East, even through mailed questionnaires, the name of the investigator, which identifies his/her religion, nationality or ethnic background, influences the answers provided by the respondents even when they are reporting "factual" material.

2. A mailed questionnaire on the Middle East signed by a person with an Arab/Muslim-sounding name or a Jewish/Israeli-sounding name is likely to produce one of the following reactions:

A. Net a low response rate (e.g. for Sulaiman in New York and Cohen in Colorado).

B. Motivate the respondents to answer in a manner that would convey to the investigator what they thought he/she wanted to hear (e.g. give a more positive response to Sulaiman concerning perceived student views on Arabs and Turks; claim that the teacher emphasizes Islam in the classroom; provide a more positive response to Cohen concerning Israelis and Jews, etc.)

C. Confuse the respondents and make them answer in a random manner.

D. Alert the respondents to the "foreignness" of the investigator and put them on their guard for the need to protect America's good name (e.g. significantly *fewer* Cohen or Sulaiman respondents than Brady respondents claimed their texts reinforced stereotypes about Middle Eastern peoples).

E. To most respondents, there is a greater concern with Cohen (Jews, Israelis) and a greater desire to respond in a manner acceptable and pleasing to him (them) than is the case with Sulaiman (Arabs-Turks-Muslims).

3. Women teachers are more likely than men teachers to avoid hurting the feelings of the investigators (e.g. women teachers, while assuring Cohen of the negative student image of Arabs, deemphasized the negative student image of Arabs when responding to Sulaiman).

4. Teachers of mixed ethnic background, unlike Anglo-American and German-American teachers, tended to show a lack of constancy, commitment or conviction in their views on some Middle Eastern issues and were, consequently, more influenced by the name of the investigator (e.g. Americans of mixed ethnic background responded in positive terms about the Palestinians only 35% to Brady, 48% to Cohen and 75% to Sulaiman).

5. Teachers belonging to the Catholic or Protestant churches were more likely than others to show constancy, commitment or conviction in their views on some Middle Eastern issues and were, therefore, less affected by the name of the investigator (e.g. Protestant and Catholic respondents gave somewhat similar responses about Palestinians to all investigators; not so the others who "tailored" their responses to please the investigator).

II. *Teachers, Textbooks, and Middle East Coverage*
in High School World History Courses

1. High school teachers, perhaps not unlike other educated Americans, have definite stereotypes and biases about Middle East peoples. However, they are mainly *unaware* that they are biased or of what these biases are.

2. Teachers and students display a generally neutral attitude toward peoples of the Middle East.

3. Apart from the "name of the investigator," the most important socio-economic factor in explaining the attitude of respondents toward Middle Eastern peoples is the number of university courses on the Middle East that the teachers have had.

4. World History textbooks usually devote 8–10% of their coverage to the history, civilization and politics of the Middle East. Often, most of the material deals with ancient civilizations. However, teacher interest and coverage in the classroom tend to center on the more recent, 20th century period.

5. Though World History textbook coverage of Middle Eastern peoples and countries is generally inadequate and biased, most high school teachers (85%) are *unaware* of the bias.

6. Young teachers (25 years or under) and/or those of Anglo-American background are more likely than older (26 years and over) teachers or those of German-American background to admit that their textbooks reinforce stereotypes about the Middle East.

7. A majority of high school teachers of World History (51%) never had any university courses dealing with the Middle East.

8. A majority (52%) of teachers who claim that they are adequately-prepared to teach the section on the Middle East in the World History class never had a single university-level course on the area.

9. Teachers who have had four or more university courses on the Middle East begin to have more positive attitudes toward Turks and to recognize student bias against Arabs.

10. The most familiar Middle Eastern countries to Americans are Israel and Egypt.

Recommendations

1. American professors and authors on the Middle East should alert their students and readers to the pre-existing biases concerning Middle Eastern peoples, especially the Arabs. As the students and readers are unaware of their own bias, if this is not pointed out to them, the material they read or hear will not have the intended impact.

2. Funds should be sought and provided for supporting the following activities which are designed to improve the competence of American high school teachers on the Middle East as a whole, including the Arab world. Since high schools treat the Middle East as a unit, material on Arabs and the Arab world has to be part of the Middle East course to facilitate and encourage its use by teachers.

A. Panel participation (clinics) at conferences of high school social science teachers for the purpose of presenting accurate information on the Middle East, especially the Arab World.

B. Setting up workshops or seminars on "the Middle East in high schools."

C. A comprehensive study of materials used in teaching social studies in American elementary and secondary schools should be undertaken to detect misinformation, bias and distortion concerning Middle Eastern peoples and cultures. The results should then be published and distributed among educators, textbook authors, and publishers.

D. Preparation and publication of a Teachers' Guide on the Middle East for elementary and secondary schools.

E. Preparation of well-constructed classroom slide-tape series on Arab/Islamic art, architecture, culture, etc. which high schools can rent for small fees.

F. Setting up summer institutes on the Middle East as a whole or on the Arab world for high school teachers.

G. Studies of the other media of communication (popular literature, magazines, newspapers, radio, television, and the movies) should be encouraged and supported.

NOTES

1. For the results, see Michael W. Suleiman, "The Middle East in American High School Curricula: A Kansas Case Study," *Middle East Studies Association (MESA) Bulletin*, Vol. 8, No. 2 (May, 1974), pp. 8–19.

2. Most directories included the elementary, junior high, continuing and vocational schools. The samples were drawn from the regular high or senior high schools only.

3. Suleiman, *MESA Bulletin, op.cit.*, pp. 12–13.

4. Within New York 50 questionnaires were sent out under the name of Marvin Fricklas, himself a high school teacher in Long Island and an observer on the MESA Images Committee. Since only seventeen responses were secured this way, it was decided to include them into the New York sample. Even if Long Islanders did constitute a distinct group, the sample was too small to adequately assess their characteristics. Other members of the MESA Committee on Middle East Images were Farhat Ziadeh, Chairman, Ayad Al-Qazzaz, William J. Griswold, John Joseph, Lorne Kenny, Don Peretz, and Glenn Perry.

5. The questionnaires were mailed out in March, 1974. About a month later, a reminder was sent out.

6. According to Irving Crespi, vice-president of the Gallup Poll, Inc., "There's no question that completion rates for surveys are lower than they were 10 or 15 years ago." In fact, they are 25% lower, according to the American Statistical Association. The quotation and information about why the completion rates have dropped appeared in Melvin Maddocks, "Does Gallup Speak Only to Roper?" *The Christian Science Monitor*, (April 15, 1974), p. F 1. While some researchers have noted differences between respondents and nonrespondents to mailed questionnaires, a recent study concluded that "there were no significant differences." See Edward C. McDonagh and A. Leon Rosenblum, "A Com-

NOTES

parison of Mailed Questionnaires and Subsequent Structured Interviews," *Public Opinion Quarterly*, Vol. 29, No. 1 (Spring, 1965), pp. 131–36.

7. Those constituting more than 1% of the sample were: Irish-Americans (9%), Italian-Americans (6%), Polish-Americans (4%), and Scandinavian-Americans (3%).

8. Of the others, about 8% expressed atheistic, non-religious or agnostic attitudes, and another 3% Jewish affiliation.

9. About 3% were Physical Education majors and another 3% had a combined Physical Education-Social Science concentration.

10. It is possible that some respondents understood the question to refer to courses that dealt with the Middle East even if only partially. If so, the number of teachers having taken courses specifically dealing with the area may be smaller than the survey showed. There may also have been a tendency for respondents not to admit the inadequacy of their preparation. Finally, in schools with more than one World History teacher, there may have been a tendency for the principal to refer the questionnaire to the better qualified one(s).

11. Next are Turkey (6%), Iran (4%), and Saudi Arabia (3%).

12. In contrast, the MESA Committee on Middle East Images reported as follows: "Of the forty-six books on world history, the history of the Middle East, or social studies generally reviewed by members of the Committee, twenty-nine were declared completely unacceptable because they are either biased, full of errors, one-sided, or generally inferior. The remaining seventeen range between being excellent, good, or tolerably acceptable even though there are minor errors or even slight distortions on the Arab-Israeli question." Farhat J. Ziadeh, "Report of the Middle East Image in Secondary Schools Committee," *Middle East Studies Association Bulletin*, Vol. 7, No. 1 (Feb., 1973), p. 52.

13. Examples of positive statements are: determined, a religious group with remarkable resilience, smart and tough, good guys, heroes, and modern. Sympathetic remarks include: struggling to find a solution, need help and education, centuries of being scapegoats, and "sympathy." Neutral statements are illustrated by "early inhabitants of Palestine," "history," European culture and "ancient." Examples of unsympathetic remarks are: "The modern millstone around the neck of U.S. foreign policy," and "feel prejudice." Negative statements include: troublemakers, very bad guys, unreasonable, and "stupid."

CHAPTER 7

American Public Support
of Middle Eastern Countries: 1939–1985

The purpose of this chapter is to present data concerning American attitudes, as reflected in public opinion polls, on various topics related to the Middle East and the peoples of that area. The time period stretches from the late 1930s to the mid–1980s. It is hoped that this will provide an adequate time frame (46 years) for proper analysis and sound conclusions.[1] This survey will also enable us to compare and contrast the various polling agencies in terms of both the wording and the content of the questions. It is not claimed here that public opinion determines or greatly influences government policy or foreign affairs. In fact, available evidence seems to indicate the opposite conclusion, namely that "opinion follows policy" and/or that the government in office often attempts to manipulate the public.[2] Nevertheless, attitudes are not easily or quickly changed. Furthermore, the existence of intense and widespread views on any issue, such as the Palestinian and Arab-Israeli conflicts, can set limits that policy-makers may violate only at the risk of popular and electoral displeasure.[3] The study of public opinion trends concerning the Middle East is, therefore, pertinent and worthwile.

American Attitudes Toward Arabs and Jews/Israelis

It is a sad commentary on the whole Middle East situation as well as on American attitudes toward the main combatants that some American racist or anti-Semitic feelings and attitudes continue to be fairly widespread — with one basic difference. While in the 1930s and 1940s existent anti-Semitism was directed against Jews, it is today directed mostly against the Arabs. This is the startling but clear con-

113

clusion that follows from the available public opinion data, which is detailed below.

In 1938, 58 per cent of the American public believed that the "persecution of the Jews in Europe" was entirely (10 per cent) or partly (48 per cent) their own fault.[4] The following results from a 1939 survey look strange and frightening today.[5]

Which of the following statements most nearly represents your general opinion on the Jewish question?

In the United States the Jews have the same standing as
    any other people and they should be treated in all
    ways exactly as other Americans..........................38.9%

Jews are in some ways distinct from other Americans,
    but they make respected and useful citizens so long
    as they don't try to mingle socially where they are
    not wanted...10.8

Jews have some different business methods and,
    therefore, some measures should be taken to prevent
    Jews from getting too much power in the business
    world...31.8

We should make it a policy to deport Jews from this
    country to some new homeland as fast as it can be
    done without inhumanity..................................10.1

Don't know...6.5

Refused to answer..3.0

                                               101.1%[*]

*Percentages add to more than 100 because some respondents gave more than one answer.

Numerous questions tapped attitudes concerning Jewish "power" in business and in government. In general about one-third of the respondents thought Jews had too much political power, whereas 50–60 per cent believed Jews had "too much influence in the business world."[6] Also, Jewish exiles from Nazi-occupied Europe were seeking a safe refuge, including the United States. Yet when Americans were asked in 1942: "Should we allow a larger number of Jewish exiles from Germany to come to the United States to live?", 77 per cent said no. In

1946, almost the same percentage (72 per cent) disapproved of President Truman's plan to ask Congress to allow more Jews and other European refugees into the United States than was allowed under prevailing law.[7]

Such sentiments are generally not present among Americans today. In fact, the American image of Jews and Israelis is today quite positive.[8] For instance, a study of social science high school teachers in southern California found that teachers generally thought Jews and Israelis to be good fighters, courageous, hard-working, and development-oriented.[9] Similar findings were obtained from a larger survey covering five states, including California.[10]

While American images of Jews and Israelis have changed for the better, the image of Arabs among Americans has suffered a change for the worse. The best illustration of current American images of both Arabs and Israelis, clearly showing the contrast, was obtained by a 1975 study in response to the question: "Does each word apply more to the Arabs or more to the Israelis?"[11]

	More to Israelis	More to Arabs	To Both equally	To neither	Don't know
Peaceful	41%	7%	9%	25%	19%
Honest	39	6	13	18	25
Intelligent	39	8	26	5	21
"Like Americans"	50	5	8	17	21
Friendly	46	6	15	11	23
Backward	6	47	7	15	25
Underdeveloped	9	47	10	10	25
Poor	21	34	9	15	22
Greedy	9	41	20	7	23
Arrogant	11	37	19	7	26
Moderate	31	8	10	21	30
Developing	33	20	21	3	24
Barbaric	4	38	8	23	28

It might be added that American Jews, in addition to their strong support of Israel and perhaps mostly as a consequence of it, are definitely the most hostile in their attitudes toward Arabs. Thus Jewish Americans, in their responses to the above list of words, were in every instance about twice as likely as other religious groups to attribute the good qualities to the Israelis and the bad qualities to the Arabs.

Also, a 1980 survey of American opinion showed that "a large percentage of the respondents feel that the Arabs can be described as 'barbaric, cruel' (44%), 'treacherous, cunning' (49%), 'mistreat women' (51%) and 'warlike, bloodthirsty' (50%). Furthermore, . . . a large percentage view 'most' or 'all' Arabs as 'anti-Christian' (40%) and 'Want to Destroy Israel and Drive the Israelis into the Sea' (44%)."[12] The same survey showed that Americans hold more negative views of "Arabs" as a general category than they do of specific Arab countries or peoples.[13]

As we noted earlier, there is some debate as to whether public images and attitudes "cause" or "determine" policy or whether policy determination comes first and that in turn colors a people's attitudes toward, and images of, another nation. The evidence does indicate, however, that if a government has friendly relations with another country, people's attitudes toward that country become friendly and their image of it is positive.[14]

Apparently, the American public is aware of the importance to US interests of cooperation with both Israel and the Arab countries. In the 1950s when a question about this was asked, comparable percentages (50–70 per cent) of the American people thought it was "very important" or fairly important" for the United States to cooperate closely with Israel and the Arab countries.[15] In 1985, almost equal numbers of Americans thought that it was "very important" or "somewhat important" for the United States to maintain friendly relations with the Arab countries (86%) and Israel (87%).[16]

Attitudes toward Israel and "the Arabs" have clearly been influenced by American perceptions of cooperativeness, friendliness, or hostility on their part toward the United States, and by whether or not each group has threatened US interests in the Middle East. Table 1 shows American attitudes toward Egypt and Israel since 1956. It shows a polarization in American attitudes occurring in the 1960s. Thus, the proportion of those indicating lack of knowledge or refusing to respond dropped by around 10 percentage points between the 1956 and 1966 surveys.

These data also indicate that the public has a generally favorable view of Israel. However, this favorable view is subject to some modification, upwards or downwards, in almost direct response to prevailing American-Israeli relations. American views are most favorable when cooperation is high, but some disaffection is clearly detected whenever Israel's actions are publicly criticized by the United States. A clear ex-

ample would be the drop of 20 points (from 75–55) in favorable opinion following the 1982 Israeli invasion of Lebanon and the reporting
of indiscriminate bombing and brutal killings carried out by the Israeli
forces.

TABLE 1

AMERICAN ATTITUDES TOWARD ISRAEL AND EGYPT*

		Favorable		Unfavorable		Don't Know/ No Answer	
	Year	I	E	I	E	I	E
	1956	51%	26%	24%	44%	26%	31%
	1966	63	46	20	36	17	18
	1967	74	39	19	53	7	9
	1973	—	37	—	51	—	13
	1974	66	48	25	43	9	9
	1975	60	44	29	45	11	11
	1976	66	49	25	40	10	11
	1977	62	51	25	36	13	13
	1978	60	45	28	41	13	14
Feb.	1979	68	63	24	28	8	9
Sept.	1979	68	67	22	22	10	11
Jan.	1980	74	71	21	23	5	6
Jan.	1981	75	71	19	23	6	6
Aug.	1982	55	55	37	36	8	9

*   The results are in response to the following interview question about Israel (I) and Egypt (E):
"You will notice that the boxes on ths card go from the highest position of plus five for a country
which you like very much to the lowest position of minus five for a country you dislike very much.
How far up the scale or how far down the scale would you rate the following countries?" In this
table the Favorable responses are combined into one rating and the Unfavorable responses are
combined as one rating. Totals are sometimes more than 100 per cent due to rounding.

Favorable American attitudes toward Egypt have also fluctuated —
but much *more* so than those toward Israel. While friendship and
cooperation with the United States are factors which affect American
views toward both countries, another factor is also important and might

explain the more consistently favorable American view of Israel. This is the cultural/religious factor, or what Americans often refer to as their Judaeo-Christian heritage. In other words, there is greater American understanding and a shared cultural background with Judaism (and by extension, Israel) than there is with Islam (and, by extension, any Arab country or people). This factor has also made it easier for Zionists to recruit supporters in the United States—so much so that it is estimated that about one quarter of the American public is firmly pro-Israeli and constitutes the only "veto group" in the American electorate.[17]

The increase in the level of favorable American orientations toward Egypt is evidently the result of perceived change in the Egyptian government's attitudes toward the United States and in Egypt's role in the Middle East. Although President Anwar Sadat came to power in 1970, it took him a few years to stabilize his power base internally and to persuade American policymakers of his interest in "solving" the Middle East problem along lines acceptable to the United States. After the 1973 war several factors combined to facilitate a change in American policy. Among these were Arab possession of a large percentage of available oil supplies and their ability to control the sale or non-sale of that oil to countries viewed as hostile to their cause; fear of instability in the Middle East area that might be combined with threats to conservative or moderate Arab regimes friendly to the United States; fear of a nuclear confrontation with the Soviet Union being triggered by a regional conflict; concern over disagreement and possible conflict with America's European allies over support for Israel; and concern over rising energy costs and oil imports and the concomitant trade imbalance with its deleterious effect on the value of the dollar. Sadat's "reasonableness" was warmly welcomed, therefore, and a push to resolve the Egyptian-Israeli conflict began. Realizing that it was not possible to reach a meaningful agreement that dealt only with this one issue, the United States sought a general "framework" for peace in the Middle East—one that would include some movement at least on the main issue, namely Palestine and the Palestinians. When the Israelis began to resist proposals along these lines, there were a number of American-Israeli "confrontations" or threatened confrontations. Israeli officials threatened to "unleash the Jewish lobby" on several occasions, and American officials generally backed off from these confrontations and tried other approaches more acceptable to the Israelis. With the election of Ronald Reagan as U.S. President, American-Israeli relations improved greatly and Israel was repeatedly presented as a "strategic asset" and, later, as a "strategic ally" for the United States. As a consequence, public attitudes became even more favorable toward Israel — and remained so until the 1982 Israeli invasion of Lebanon introduced some temporary irritations in American-Israeli relations. By 1986, however, the American-Israeli bond was so strong that "Israelis are beginning to wonder whether there is such a thing as drawing too close to the United States."[18]

Sympathy

Table 2 presents the results of surveys in which the American people were asked to indicate their sympathies toward the protagonists in the Middle East. The question is most often phrased as follows: "In the Middle East situation, are your sympathies more with Israel or more with the Arab nations?" Such a question limits the choices for the respondents and tends to inflate the figures showing "sympathy" when such feelings may not truly exist. Thus, when a third choice such as "or don't you have any strong feelings either way?" is explicitly made available, support for both parties declines, as is clear from the results reported in the Harris poll of October 1973.[19]

What do the results in Table 2 tell us? First, it is clear that sympathy for Jews and the state of Israel is generally fairly high throughout the 32–year period. At the same time, sympathy for the Arabs or Arab states is found among a very small portion of the American adult population. In fact, the largest sympathy "vote" (i.e. 16 per cent) was recorded during the struggle in Palestine just before the state of Israel was created.

A third observation based on the data is that a substantial proportion of Americans (approaching 50 per cent and often exceeding it) either do not know much about the situation, do not care about either party, or sympathize with both sides equally. In fact, until the 1967 war, at least 49 per cent, and more often a majority, of Americans did not display partisan sympathy. This withdrawal or withholding of sympathy for the two sides manifests itself when there is a deadlock in the negotiations between them and/or a breakdown of efforts to achieve a settlement with active US involvement.

Table 2 also shows that American sympathy for Israel is highest during periods of war, especially if the US government is viewed as openly or tacitly supportive of Israeli actions. This was the case for instance during the June 1967 war, the "war of attrition" in 1969 and the 1973

TABLE 2

SYMPATHY OF AMERICANS
TOWARD ARABS AND ISRAELIS

Polling Agency	Date	Jews, Israel	Arabs, Arab States Egypt	Both Neither	No Opinion
Gallup	Nov. 19,1947	24%	12%	38%	26%
NORC	Feb. 1948	35	16	49*	—
SRC-C	Nov. 1964	25	7	28	40
Harris	June 10, 1967	41	1	40	18
Gallup	June 12, 1967	55	4	25	16
Gallup	Ht.–'67 June War	56	4	25	15
Gallup	Jan. 1969	49	5	46*	—
Gallup	Jan. 1969 (whites)	50	5	28	17
Gallup	Feb. 6, 1969	50	5	28	17
Gallup	Feb. 27–Mar. 2, '70	44	3	32	21
Harris	Aug. 1970	47	6	25	22
Harris	Oct. 1970	47	6	26	21
Harris	June 1971	46	7	24	23
Harris	July 1971	44	7	22	27
Gallup	Oct. 6–8, 1973	47	6	22	25
Gallup	Oct. 19–22, 1973	48	6	21	25
Harris	Oct. 1973	39	4	16	41
Gallup	Dec. 7–10, 1973	50	7	25	18
Harris	Jan. 1975	52	7	31*	—
Harris	Jan. 1975 (leaders***)	56	5	29*	—
Gallup	Jan. 10–15, 1975	44	8	22	26
Gallup	April 4–7, 1975	37	8	24	31
Gallup	June 1977	44	8	28	20
Gallup	Oct. 1977	46	11	21	22
Gallup	Dec. 9–12, 1977	37	8	25	30
Gallup	Dec. 1977	44	10	27	19
Gallup	Dec. 1977	46	11	21	22
Gallup	Feb. 1978**	33	14	28	25
Gallup	March 3–6, 1978	38	11	33	18
Gallup	Apr. 28–May 1,'78	44	10	33	13
Gallup	Aug. 1978	44	10	33	13
Gallup	Early Sept. 1978	41	12	29	18
Gallup	Late Sept. 1978	42	12	29	17
Gallup	Nov. 10–13, 1978	39	13	30	18
Gallup	Jan. 5–8, 1979	40	14	31	15
Gallup	Mar. 16–18, 1979	34	11	31	14
Harris	July, 1980**	52	12	26	10
Gallup	July 31–Aug. 3, '81	44	11	34	11
Gallup	Jan. 1982	49	14	23	14
Gallup	April-May 1982	51	12	26	11
Gallup	June 1982	52	10	29	9
Gallup	July 23–26, 1982	41	12	31	16
Harris	Oct. 23–27, 1985**	64	14	13	9

Typical question: In the Middle East situation, are your sympathies more with Israel or more with the Arab Nations?

*   Both, neither, or no opinion

**   Telephone survey

***   See footnote 61

war. It was also the case during and after the Israeli invasion of southern Lebanon (Gallup, April-May 1978), and during the 1982 Israeli invasion of Lebanon. Finally, we note that after the establishment of the state of Israel (with decisive American support), sympathy for the Arabs declined and continued to hover around 6–7 per cent until the period following the 1973 war. Since 1977, Egyptian-American rapprochement has progressed rather steadily and with it has come a slight increase in the number of Americans sympathetic to the "Arab nations." There is little doubt that President Anwar Sadat's dramatic visit to Jerusalem in November 1977 and the following Egyptian-Israeli-American negotiations on the Middle East persuaded the public that Sadat and Egypt "want peace in the Middle East."[20] The "reasonableness" of Sadat (i.e. his willingness to accept American suggestions) and the "intransigence" of Israel (i.e. resistance to US suggestions), as displayed and reported on several occasions between 1975 and 1980, certainly contributed to a decline in American sympathy for Israel and a concomitant mild increase in sympathy for "the Arabs."

American sympathy for the two parties is obviously influenced by several factors. We have already mentioned war in the Middle East, the prospects of a peaceful settlement, and the attitude of the American government. Two other factors may be cited. One is the energy crisis, i.e. American dependence on oil from the Arab world, which will be discussed in more detail later. The other is the ability to manipulate the sympathies of the public through the use of the various media of communication. This is not the place to detail how the media have portrayed events and peoples in the Middle East.[21] While it is not normally easy to establish a link between what the American people read, listen to, or watch on television or in the movies and their sympathies toward Arabs and Israelis, a definite relationship was observed in at least two important cases. Thus, in a study of "public reaction to the Eichmann trial," it was found that over 30 per cent of the American public reported that as a result of exposure to the publicity attendant upon, and the proceedings of, the Eichmann trial, they became more sympathetic to Israel and Jews.[22] Also, in a survey conducted by the American Institute of Public Opinion (Gallup) during April 28–May 1, 1978, respondents were specifically asked if they had seen all or parts of the National Broadcasting Company's (NBC's) four-part series, "Holocaust," a show depicting the plight of Jews in Nazi-occupied Europe during World War II. According to the Gallup report:

"Among Americans aware of the situation in the Middle East who watched 'Holocaust', sympathies are significantly more pro-Israeli than among those who did not watch the show. Specifically, among those who saw at least part of the four-part special, 50 per cent side with Israel and nine per cent with the Arab nations. Among non-viewers, the comparable figures are 39 and 11 per cent, respectively."[23]

Blame

In discussing placement of blame, the situation is complicated by the fact that since 1957 the polling agencies have used varying question formats which are not easily comparable. Hence, we shall review the issue from different angles. Table 3 presents responses to a question that requests the placement of blame on one or the other of the two main parties involved in the Arab-Israeli conflict. Like the responses to the "sympathy" question, Table 3 shows that Americans tend to blame Arabs more often than they do Israel for causing continuing conflict. Unlike the case for the sympathy issue, however, the difference in the scores is not so great. Furthermore, most of the time, the majority could not clearly place the blame on either party.

TABLE 3

ATTITUDES OF AMERICANS CONCERNING
THE PLACEMENT OF BLAME ON ARABS AND ISRAELIS

Polling Agency	Date	Jews, Israel	Egypt, Arabs	Both, Neither	Don't know, No Opinion
Gallup*	Jan. 1946	12%	10%	(British 33% Other 1%)	53%
NORC	Nov. 25, 1953	15	20	24	41
NORC	Sept. 29, 1953	6	12	14	68
NORC	Nov. 23, 1955	5	15	18	62
NORC	Apr. 20, 1956	7	18	18	57
NORC	Nov. 15, 1956	19	29	14	38
NORC	Apr. 26, 1957	12	40	18	30

Typical question: Have you heard or read about the recent conflict between Israel and the Arab countries? If "yes," which side do you feel is more to blame in this dispute—Israel or the Arabs?

* Adds to more than 100 per cent because of multiple responses.

Another way to place blame is to ask whether a certain country was justified in acting in a particular manner. Responding to such queries, for instance, 53 per cent of Americans interviewed felt that Egypt was not justified in "taking over" the Suez Canal Company, whereas 40 per cent felt that Israel was not justified in "sending armed forces into Egyptian territory."[24] When asked as to whether they approved or disapproved of "Israel's action in Egypt," 47 per cent disapproved.[25]

When the question is phrased in terms of "who is right" or "who has more right on their side," then the results definitely favor the Israelis: 46 per cent in 1967 and 39 per cent in 1973, as opposed to 4 per cent and 6 per cent respectively on the Arab side.[26] Obviously, when the question is stated in moral terms, the respondents are less likely to judge the specific situation (1967 or 1973 war) on its own merits and are more inclined to choose up sides between "right" and "wrong," "good" and "evil." A similar situation obtains when respondents are asked to state their feelings concerning actions in which the warring parties might "want" to engage. Such was the case, for instance, on May 6, 1957 when Gallup asked: "If trouble does start there, which side — Israel or Egypt — do you think will be more likely to start it?" The response was Egypt 33 per cent, Israel 26 per cent, can't say 41 per cent.

Finally, it is interesting to note that when an open-ended question such as "who or what do you blame for this?" is asked, other parties receive much of the blame and only a small percentage of the public points the finger at either Israelis or Arabs.[27]

Energy Crisis

A detailed analysis of all aspects of the energy problem facing the United States will not be attempted here. Rather, our discussion will focus on the energy crisis as it affects attitudes toward the Middle East and its peoples. As early as April 1973, American officials as well as the public began to voice their recognition of an energy "shortage" or "crunch."[28] It was only after the Arab oil embargo of November 1973, however, that many Americans saw the "energy crisis/fuel shortage" as "the most important problem facing this country today." But whereas 46 per cent named the energy crisis as the most important problem in January 1974, only 3 per cent gave it that designation in October 1978.[29] Also, while about 40 per cent of the adult population continue to view the "energy situation in the US" as "very serious", a much smaller percentage appreciates how very serious it is and in what respects. Thus in May 1977, 33 per cent of the public believed that "we produce enough oil in this country to meet our present energy needs," and an additional 15 per cent did not know.[30] Furthermore, only 9 per cent of all adults had an accurate picture of the amount of oil (42 per cent) imported from abroad.[31]

In a survey of public attitudes carried out in December, 1973, almost immediately after the announcement of the Arab oil embargo, Americans tended to blame the energy crisis on the oil companies (25 per cent), the federal government (23 per cent), the Nixon Administration (19 per cent), or US consumers (16 per cent).[32] While 7 per cent blamed the "Arab nations," hardly anyone blamed the Israelis — the main focus of Arab concern and the motivating factor behind the embargo. Apparently, to most Americans energy was not their number one problem, and in any case the oil companies and "the government" were to blame. Somehow the message that the Arabs wanted to convey to Americans via the oil embargo was not delivered adequately, if at all — at least not to the general public.[33]

Palestine

The first and most striking finding that a researcher on this issue comes across is the centrality of the Jewish question and of Israel to the various agencies of public opinion assessment. Simultaneously, there appears to be almost total ignorance, or deliberate negligence, of the fate of the Palestinian Arabs. When one looks up "Palestine" or "Arabs in Palestine" in the index of the typical public opinion reports, for instance, one is referred to "Jews: Colonization" or to "Israel."[34] This is not merely because Palestine ceased to exist as a country in 1948. The following examples amply illustrate the total concern of Americans with Jews and Israel and their concomitant lack of concern for the Palestinian Arabs — an attitude that treats the Palestinians as a dehumanized non-people. In December 1944, NORC asked the following question: "Do you think the Jews should be given a special chance to settle in Palestine after the war, or do you think all people should have the same chance to settle there?"[35] It should be noted that "the Jews" were being discussed here in relation to others (presumably Europeans) who might be given a special chance to settle in Palestine — ignoring the fact that Palestine was already inhabited and ignoring those Palestinian Arab inhabitants. Even when some mention of the Palestinians is made, their needs and desires are not stated positively but only in relation to their adversaries, as in the following 1944 NORC question: "There are over a million Arabs and over half a million Jews in Palestine. Do you think the British, who control Palestine, should do what some Jews ask and set up a Jewish state there, or should they do what some Arabs ask and not set up a Jewish state?"[36]

The centrality of the Jewish problem is also evident in the 1948 NORC question about dropping the American ban on selling arms to Jews and Arabs. To those who thought the ban should be removed (10 per cent), a follow-up question was addressed: Should we sell to both sides or only to the Jews?"[37] Also, a few months earlier, in response to the question: "Can you tell me which groups of people have been having trouble in Palestine recently?" almost twice as many Americans named Jews (or Zionists) as Arabs (or Mohammedans).[38] Furthermore, in 1968 Gallup asked Americans the question: "What do you regard as the main cause of trouble between the Israelis and Arabs?" The responses were:[39]

Ancient enmity	22%
Territorial rights	16
Arabs claim	
Jews have taken their land	5
Communism	4
Economic causes	4
Political causes	3
Miscellaneous	10
No opinion	41
	105%*

* Some gave more than one answer

Thus, Palestinians continued to be a "non-entity" so far as Americans were concerned. Ignorance of Palestinian Arabs and their case is clearly illustrated in the results of a 1946 Gallup survey question that asked: "From what you have heard or read, why don't the British let more Jews into Palestine?"[40] — A question that also indicates the centrality of the Jewish problem.

British want to retain control	5%
Afraid to rouse Arabs	15
To appease Arabs and protect interests in India, Egypt, and Arabia	4
No room in Palestine	5
Prejudiced against Jews, afraid they will become leading power	10
Palestine	4
Afraid Arabs will get help from Russia	1
Miscellaneous	1
No answer	55
	100%

It is indeed remarkable that the Palestinian Arabs who inhabited the country for centuries, who constituted over 90 per cent of the population in 1917, who still constituted two-thirds of the population at the time of the survey, and who were seeking independence from Britain, should not register at all on the consciousness of Americans except as indicated in the responses of the 5 per cent who stated that there was "no room in Palestine." Apparently, what Americans "heard or read" almost totally discounted the significance of the Palestinian Arabs.

It is not surprising, therefore, that when Americans were asked about "permitting Jews to settle in Palestine," the over-whelming response (76 per cent) was positive.[41] This was the case whether the question was phrased in general terms, or whether it specified the entry of 100,000 Jews, as recommended in the Anglo-American report.[42]

Whereas support for the entry of Jews into Palestine and Jewish settlement there was strong among Americans, the idea of partitioning Palestine into two states, one Arab, one Jewish, did not meet with over-whelming approval. Thus in February 1948, only 38 per cent approved of partition, while 19 per cent disapproved and the rest were either unfamiliar with the subject (28 per cent) or undecided (15 per cent).[43] Also, among a "national cross-section of newspaper editors," 44 per cent favored a sectarian democracy for all, and 30 per cent opted for partition.[44] Furthermore, support for partition began to erode as the situation in Palestine turned violent. In any case, when respondents were presented with other options (such as "try other solutions"), as they were in June 1948, only 26 per cent favored partition.[45]

Once the state of Israel was established, there was a definite attempt on the part of Israel and its friends as well as of some Arab regimes to do away with the designations Palestine or Palestinians. Instead, terms such as the Gaza Strip, the West Bank, "Arab refugees", and Israel became the substitutes for various purposes. The Palestine question became the Arab-Israeli conflict, especially after "the Arabs" joined the war against Israel on May 15, 1948.

In 1964, and not before then to my knowledge, a question was asked about the treatment of "Arab refugees" in Israel. Surprisingly, less than 9 per cent thought they were treated very well (1.6 per cent) or pretty well (7.2 per cent). Approximately 15 per cent thought the "Arab refugees" were treated pretty badly (11.9 per cent) or very badly (3.0 per cent). The rest did not answer or had not read about the situation.[46]

After the 1967 war, however, the question of what should be done with the vast territories conquered by the Israelis was asked rather often by pollsters. At first, there was no mention of Palestinians or a Palestinian state. The question was usually phrased in such terms as: "What do you think should be done — should Israel be required to give back all this conquered land, keep it all, or keep some of it?" Even less than a month after the 1967 war, 24 per cent of Americans favored having Israel keep some of the territories and only 15 per cent said Israel should give back all conquered land.[47] Harris surveys in 1970 and 1974 showed reluctance on the part of the American public to see Israel return the territories conquered in 1967.[48] However, when different choices were presented, as in three Gallup surveys in 1977, 43–50 per cent favored return of all or part of the conquered land, with an additional 30–33 per cent expressing no opinion.[49]

Following Sadat's dramatic trip to Jerusalem in November 1977, there was increased speculation concerning a peaceful settlement and the fate of the Palestinians. Table 4 shows the results of three surveys, eliciting the American public's response to proposed plans for a Palestinian "solution." It is obvious that, by 1982, almost half (46%) of the respondents favored the establishment of an independent Palestinian state. Furthermore, a 1985 poll showed that 55% of the American public believed that "Peace in the Middle East will come only when the Palestinian people have a state of their own on the West Bank."[50]

TABLE 4

PLANS FOR A PALESTINIAN SOLUTION

Plan	1977	March 1979	July 1982
Establish a separate independent Palestinian state	36%	41%*	46%
Palestinians to continue to live as they do now	29	25	23
Don't Know, Other	35	28	31
Total	100%	100%	100%

* Based on those aware of situation in Middle East

Source: *Gallup Opinion Index*, May, 1979. p. 19;
               Gallup Report, August, 1982, p. 8.

Question Wording

As has already been indicated, the surveys discussed so far showed a definite bias against the Palestinian Arabs and in favor of Jews or of Israelis. We would like now to document this more fully. To begin with, we note that almost all polling agencies asked far more questions that are relevant to the Jews and Israel than to Palestinian Arabs. Thus, numerous questions addressed the problems of Jewish persecution, relocation, emigration to Palestine, entry into the United States, creation of a Jewish state, Israel's security needs, American assistance (how much and what kind), etc. By contrast, Palestinian Arabs and their problems were seldom explored or discussed.

Another form of bias involves question wording.[51] The pollster may work to lead the respondents in a certain direction by providing information favorable to one side. Thus in 1946 the public was asked: "As you remember, the (Anglo-American Committee) report recommends that 100,000 more Jewish refugees be admitted to Palestine in spite of protests by the Arabs there. President Truman has said he thinks this ought to be done. Now England says that the United States ought to help her keep order in Palestine if trouble breaks out between the Jews and the Arabs. Do you think we should help keep order there, or should we keep out of it?"[52] Another example comes from Harris and Associates: "(As you know) Israel has occupied all of Jerusalem, but has opened the city to all people who want to visit there, including all the religious shrines. Do you think Israel should be allowed to keep Jerusalem, or do you think the city should be an international city?"[53]

Another biasing tactic is to stack the cards against one of the parties, often eliciting sympathy for the favored party at the same time. A good example is provided by the following Harris survey statement with which respondents were asked if they tended to agree or disagree: "If it looked as though Israel were going to be taken over by the Russians and the Arabs, the US would have to do everything to save Israel, including going to war."[54] Still another Harris survey question of this nature asks: "The Russians want the UN to condemn Israel as the aggressor in the Middle East war and make Israel pay Arab nations for damage done in the war. Do you agree or disagree with such action by the United Nations?"[55]

Still another biasing technique is to use different wording for questions that are meant to be or are allegedly alike. In 1967, for instance, Harris and Associates *avoided* asking the public "who do you feel started the latest war in the Middle East — the Arabs or Israelis?" Yet this was the exact wording used in October 1973. In 1967, however, Harris asked the American people "whether they tended to agree or disagree that the Arabs wanted to start war; that Israel wanted to start war." Thus, instead of securing results that would show Israel starting the war, the data would reflect the American public's *attitude* toward the parties — already strongly anti-Arab and pro-Israeli.

The Harris Survey has continued to use tactics likely to influence the outcome in its public opinion polling on the Middle East. For instance, in July, 1982, at the height of the Israeli invasion, Harris asked: "As you know, Israel moved its troops into Lebanon to try to eliminate the PLO and Syrian military bases there which had been used to shell northern Israel. Let me read you some statements about Israel's move into Lebanon. For each, tell me if you tend to agree or disagree: The PLO leadership was wrong to deliberately put its strongest military force in the middle of the crowded city of Beirut, thereby making it inevitable that innocent people would be killed when Israel attacked PLO headquarters."[56] In this statement, as in others, it is clear that Harris sought to get the public to blame the PLO and exonerate Israel and justify its killing of innocent civilians. The tactic worked since 63% of the respondents agreed, while 24% disagreed and 13% were not sure.

Another procedure that might influence the respondents is question placement or the order in which questions appear. Thus, in a Harris survey conducted in October 1973, Americans were asked whether they tended to agree or disagree with several statements that showed sympathy for Israel or linked "the Arabs" with Russia, as well as the following: "If we yield to Arab restrictions over oil now, we will soon find the Arabs dictating much of US foreign policy, and that is wrong." After that, the respondents were presented with the statement: "We need Arab oil for our gasoline shortage here at home, so we had better find ways to get along with the Arabs, even if that means supporting Israel less."[57] It is at least plausible that the preceding statements might have reduced support for the last one.

Possible US Policy

In addition to American attitudes toward Middle East peoples and countries, some data are available concerning public reactions to possible policies and actions by the US government in the Middle East.

In the 1940s and 1950s, for example, American polling agencies asked whether respondents approved of the idea of sending UN and/or US troops to the Middle East to help keep the peace. In general, Americans first and foremost preferred to stay out of the conflict and not send any troops to the area. Thus, in a 1946 survey, only 7 per cent of those who had heard about the conflict in Palestine approved of sending US soldiers to maintain peace there, whereas 48 per cent disapproved.[58] Even when the question was rephrased and the respondents were told that the Anglo-American Committee on Palestine had recommended that 100,000 more Jewish refugees be admitted to Palestine and that President Truman had said that ought to be done, the reaction was overwhelmingly (61 per cent) in favor of "keeping out of it," with only 28 per cent supporting American involvement to "help keep order."[59] Only in the aftermath of the Suez invasion of 1956, when there was fear of Russian penetration into the Middle East, did Americans indicate relatively heavy support for direct involvement in a hypothetical situation. Thus, 50 per cent of the respondents in February 1957 indicated approval "if the United States were to promise to send our armed forces if Russian troops attacked these countries (in the Middle East)."[60] Otherwise, opposition to American military involvement in the Middle East has been strong and steady. Even the stationing of 200 American radar technicians or "monitors" in electronic watch posts in the Sinai in 1975 did not receive overwhelming approval. Only 43 per cent approved, while 41 per cent disapproved and 16 per cent had no opinion.[61]

For the most part, Americans have been reluctant to become militarily involved in the Middle East even "in the event a nation is attacked by communist-backed forces." Table 5 shows the generally negative responses to any form of military involvement, even in the defense of Israel, America's proverbial "ally" in the Middle East.

The discrepancy in the figures from the two polling agencies reflects differences in the wording of questions. Louis Harris and his associates generally linked "the Arabs" with "the Russians" in attempts to "take over Israel," then asked if the United States would send troops "to keep Israel from being taken over." Even under these circumstances, however, 39 per cent was the highest figure favoring such involvement in polls not limited to "leaders" (see footnote 61).

TABLE 5

SHOULD THE UNITED STATES SEND TROOPS
TO DEFEND ISRAEL IF ATTACKED?

Polling Agency	Date	Favor	Oppose	Not sure, No Opinion
Harris	June 10, 1967	24%	56%	20%
Harris	Oct. 9, 1967	22	29	19
Gallup	July 24, 1968	9	77	14
Harris	August, 1970	38	38	24
Harris	October, 1970	34	51	15
Harris	January, 1971	39	44	17
Harris	July, 1971	25	52	23
Gallup	Jan.-Apr. 1971	11	44	45
Harris	Feb. 1973	31	52	17
Harris	Dec. 1974	27	50	23
Harris	Dec. 1974 (leaders)	41	44	15
Gallup	Apr. 18–21, 1975	12	42	46

While questions concerning the possible defense of Israel were asked frequently, only rarely was a question posed concerning possible defense of "the Arabs" or a particular Arab country. Thus, a 1968 Gallup poll showed only 2 per cent favoring sending US troops "to help the Arabs . . . if a full-scale war were to start there." Also, in 1975, 7 per cent of the American public favored sending troops to Saudi Arabia "in the event [it] is attacked by communist-backed forces."[62] It should be remembered that the survey was done in the aftermath of the Arab oil boycott which began to awaken Americans to the realization that Saudi Arabia is of great importance to the United States in the area of energy.[63] This is so much the case that a 1979 poll asked the American public if they would "favor the use of nuclear weapons against the Russians . . . if Saudi Arabia were threatened with a Russian take-over." The majority (65%) opposed this option and a slightly smaller number (57%) did not believe the U.S. would use nuclear weapons in such an eventuality.[64]

During the 1948 war between Israel and the Arabs, the United States had a ban on arms sales to either side. In July of that year, Americans were asked if the ban should be lifted. Only 10 per cent favored changing the policy while 82 per cent wanted the ban to continue and 8 per cent were undecided.[65] In any case, in 1950, the United States joined Britain and France in formalizing what amounted to an arms embargo on the region. In their Tripartite Statement of Policy, they declared their opposition to the use of force between Middle Eastern states, and their resolve to supply Israel and the Arab states with only those arms needed for "legitimate self-defense."[66] When Egypt succeeded in concluding a major arms deal with the Soviet Union in September 1955, however, US polling agencies began to ask the public whether or not the United States should supply arms to Israel, and in 1968 a similar question concerning the Arabs was added.

Table 6 clearly shows that there is a stronger American sentiment for providing arms to Israel than to "the Arabs." It should be noted, however, that as Egypt began to move closer to the American view of Middle East issues, support for arms sales to "the Arabs" jumped to 16 per cent from a previous 2–3 per cent. As both presidents Jimmy Carter and Ronald Reagan found out, trying to persuade Congress to sell arms to "the Arabs," i.e. Arab countries friendly to the United States, namely Saudi Arabia, Egypt and Jordan, is an up-hill battle — and one they are not sure to win. In this struggle, the American president has to work hard to persuade the public to pressure Congress to vote for

TABLE 6

UNITED STATES ARMS SALES AND SUPPLIES TO ISRAEL AND THE ARABS

Polling Agency	Date	Israel			Arabs		
		Favor	Oppose	Don't know, No Answer	Favor	Oppose	Don't know, No Answer
NORC*	Nov. 23, 1955	25%	50%	26%	—	—	—
NORC	Apr. 20, 1956	19	63	18	—	—	—
Harris	June 1967	35	39	26	—	—	—
Gallup	July 1968	24	59	17	3	79	18
Harris	July 1971	36**	42	22	—	—	—
		39***	40	21	—	—	—
Harris	Oct. 1973	46	34	20	—	—	—
Gallup	Oct. 20–23, 1973	37	49	14	2	85	13
Gallup	March 3–6, 1978	28	54	18	15	68	17
Harris	Oct. 28-Nov. 3, 1981	—	—	—	42	48	10

*   Adds up to more than 100 per cent due to rounding.

**   Jet Fighters

***   Anti-aircraft missiles

the requested sale. By contrast, Israel's shopping list is hardly ever trimmed, let alone contested. Nevertheless, as Israel increased its attacks on various Arab countries, causing much destruction and thousands of deaths (mostly innocent civilians, as in the 1982 invasion of Lebanon), the American media and public began to question the Israeli use of American-supplied weapons. Thus, a Gallup survey conducted on July 23–26, 1982, found that 64 per cent of Americans agreed that "all weapons sent by the U.S. to Israel should be used only for defensive purposes."[67] A majority (52%) also thought "Israel was wrong to go to war and kill thousands of Lebanese civilians."[68]

The surveys discussed above specifically asked about supplying arms to Israel or the Arabs. When the question was phrased in such a way as to provide a choice between the dispatch of troops or supplying arms, the definite preference is for the supply of arms. Thus in 1975, 42 per cent selected that option (as opposed to 12 per cent favoring troop dispatch) for assisting Israel in case of attack by communist-backed forces. Also, the same survey showed that 27 per cent favored sending arms supplies to Saudi Arabia, whereas only 7 per cent favored sending troops.[69]

Perhaps a better measure of American attitudes is provided by surveys which ask open-ended questions like "what do you think the United States should do in this situation?" or "in the event of war?" Table 7 provides such data for the 1967–75 period. It is clear from this that the American public prefers to have the United States "stay out of conflict." It is also clear that while "support for Arab states" has remained almost nonexistent as a suggested option, the percentage of those who would support Israel, militarily or otherwise, declined fairly substantially in the 1970s. The main increase has been in approval of the United States playing the role of mediator and helping to negotiate a peace settlement.

While the definite preference of many Americans is to minimize US involvement in any Middle East conflict, it would be erroneous to conclude that this reflects an entirely isolationist sentiment. The dominant attitude favors staying out when that is a viable choice, i.e., when US interests could still be protected while doing so, and otherwise working with other countries or through the United Nations whenever possible. Only as a last resort would Americans agree to military involvement abroad. Thus, as early as 1946, Americans saw the UN as the agency which should "handle the problem of letting Jews settle in Palestine."[70] In 1946, 65 per cent preferred to see a UN volunteer army rather than US troops (3 per cent) keep the peace in Palestine if England pulled her troops out.[71] This support for action through the United Nations has held strong over the years — and in large majorities. In 1948, 62 per cent of the American public favored Big Power action to enforce UN recommendations;[72] in 1956, 70 per cent approved of a UN police force between Egypt and Israel;[73] and in 1967, 58 per cent thought that the UN Security Council was "the proper place where peace terms in the Middle East can be worked out."[74]

Following the Israeli invasion of Lebanon in the summer of 1982, a Harris Survey question inquired whether or not Americans favored stationing American troops as part of an international "peace-keeping" force in south Lebanon. The majority (54%) opposed the suggestion.[75] Even after U.S. troops were sent to Beirut as part of the multinational contingent, the American public opposed having the marines there (48% vs 47%), did not favor increasing the number of marines stationed there (55% vs 39%) and thought it was "both impossible and foolish" to keep them there (56% vs 38%).[76]

Cooperation with other major powers, friendly or otherwise, in attempts to solve outstanding issues is also much supported by the American public. Thus, as early as 1955, 49 per cent of Americans interviewed favored a suggestion to have the United States join other countries to prevent any attempt to change by force boundaries agreed to by Israel and the Arab countries.[77] Furthermore, Americans have fairly consistently and overwhelmingly favored Soviet-American cooperation to bring about a peaceful settlement in the Middle East. In fact, in the five surveys taken by Harris and Associates between 1969 and 1973, a minimum of 82 per cent favored the idea.[78] Also, in 1985, 66 per cent of the American public favored the idea of U.S. participation in an international conference including the Soviet Union, Israel, Syria, Jordan, Egypt and the PLO to "try to settle the Arab-Israeli conflict."[79]

It appears, therefore, that going from the most to the least acceptable response to Middle East "problems," the preferences of the American public are as follows: stay out of conflict; work through the United Nations and/or with other major powers to defuse the problem; provide economic support; provide military supplies; and, only as a last resort, send troops — hopefully and preferably as part of a United Nations force. This applies both to Arab countries and Israel, even though Israel received higher support from the public for military and troop assistance.

In the past decade or so, American authorities openly began to seek specific Middle East countries as friends or "strategic assets" or "allies."

TABLE 7

ALTERNATIVE UNITED STATES POLICIES TOWARD ARAB-ISRAELI CONFLICT

	1967	1968	1969	1970	Feb. 1975	April 1975
1. Stay out of conflict	41%	61%	52%	58%	55%	41%
2. Support Israel (military aid)	*	*	*	*	9	5
3. Support Israel (non-military aid)	16	10	13	13	7	*
4. Support Israel (send troops)	5	*	1	1	2	*
5. Negotiate/Act as mediator	14	8	11	10	7	24
6. Work through UN/Reconvene Geneva Conference	11	3	2	2	*	1
7. Support Arab States	*	*	1	1	*	*
8. Other responses, no opinion	13	20	20	15	29	31
	100%	102%**	100%	100%	109%**	102%**

* Less than ½ per cent

** Adds up to more than 100 per cent because of multiple responses.

Consequently, there have been repeated references in the American media to friendly countries, "strategic allies" as well as to unfriendly or "enemy" groups and countries. Polling agencies began to ask questions on these issues. In the mid–1980's for instance, Israel and Egypt were generally viewed as close allies (Israel 33%; Egypt 21%) or friendly (Israel 41%; Egypt 56%).[80] These were followed by Saudi Arabia and Jordan in that order. Arab countries and groups which the American public viewed as least friendly were the PLO, Libya, Syria and Lebanon.

Summary and Conclusions

The first and most important finding of this survey is the lack of sensitivity on the part of the American public (as well as the polling agencies) toward Arab, and especially Palestinian, concerns. Such insensitivity is an indication of bias and borders on racism. It may be that the pollsters, if not Americans in general, are biased but are unaware of their bias.[81] This might explain the slighting of the Palestinians in the way questions are asked by polling agencies. Thus, the Palestinians as a people are almost completely ignored in the questions addressed to the American public and the questions are at times constructed in a manner favorable to the Israelis. When the Palestinians are mentioned in the survey questions, their needs and desires receive little sympathy or support. This situation changed slightly after 1973, as "Palestine" and "the Palestinians" began to emerge as legitimate issues for consideration.

If Arabs, the Arab world, and the Palestinians are peripheral so far as American consciousness is concerned, the reverse is true of Jews and Israel. The perceived centrality of the question of Jews and Israel has not changed since the 1930s. At first, the issue was European Jews, their treatment, and whether or not they invited or deserved such treatment. Then the focus shifted to resettlement, a Jewish homeland, and a Jewish state in Palestine. After the state of Israel came into being the primary concern became the security of the state and its people — and how the United States could help. The different forms of assistance proposed included material and economic aid, military hardware, and a commitment to send troops in defense of the Jewish state. After 1967, the question of the occupied territories was often subsumed under or relegated to second place behind the concern for Israel's security. Only after 1973, as noted earlier, was there the beginning of discussion relating to a Palestinian entity of some form based on all or parts of the Gaza Strip and the West Bank — support for which was voiced by about one-half of the American public. However, questions concerning Israel's security continued to be dominant.

Despite the centrality of the Jewish question, however, American attitudes toward Jews and Israel have not always been favorable. In fact, especially in the 1930s and 1940s, the polls showed that a significant portion of the American public held what amounted to anti-Semitic (i.e. anti-Jewish) views. For these people, at least, support for Jewish settlement in Palestine and the establishment of a Jewish state there was motivated less by generosity than by ignorance (and ignoring) of Palestinian Arabs. It also manifested a desire not to have these Jewish refugees settle in the United States. American attitudes toward Jews and Israel improved after Israel began to be viewed as an American ally and an agent of US power in the Middle East. When there is disagreement between Israel and the United States, however, American attitudes show signs of becoming less favorable. It is possible, therefore, that if Israeli-American relations get strained or deteriorate, American attitudes toward Israel might become less positive.

While American attitudes toward Israel are affected by American-Israeli relations, Israel and its supporters, especially Zionists in the United States, have some ability to manipulate American opinion. For instance, it was found that both the Eichmann trial and the NBC showing of the presentation "Holocaust" generated added sympathy and support for Israel. It may be assumed that future reminders of Jewish persecution under Nazi Germany will result in increased sympathy for Israel and the Zionist cause.

While anti-Jewish sentiment was evident among some Americans in the 1930s and 1940s, anti-Arab feelings became quite evident in the 1970s and 1980s. Thus, in 1980, around 50 per cent of the American public thought of Arabs as backward, greedy, arrogant, treacherous, war-like, and even "barbaric."

In general, Americans sympathize more with the Israelis than the Arabs in the conflicts of the region and tend to place more of the blame for the troubles there on the Arabs. However, Sadat's "reasonableness" did at times earn him better ratings as a "man of peace" than Begin. Nevertheless, this did not translate easily or quickly into a positive attitude toward Egypt and the Egyptians — let alone "Arabs" and the "Arab nations." On the other hand, sympathy for Israel does not automatically translate into US commitment to actual involvement. In general,

Americans are very reluctant to see US troops sent to the Middle East. The definite preference is for staying out of the conflict unless vital American interests are at stake.

Our conclusion, therefore, is that public opinion on the Middle East changes slowly. It is influenced by US relations with the regimes in the area and by how the Administration in office views the situation.

NOTES

1. For other studies on American public opinion on the Middle East, see Hazel Erskine, "The Polls: Western Partisanship in the Middle East," Vol. XXXIII, No. 4, (Winter 1969–70), pp. 627–40; Seymour Martin Lipset and William Schneider, "Carter vs Israel: What the Polls Reveal," *Commentary*, Vol. 64, No. 5 (November 1977), pp. 21–29; Seymour Martin Lipset, "The Polls on the Middle East," *Middle East Review*, Vol. XI, No. 1 (Fall 1978), pp. 24–30; Andrew Kohut, "American Opinion on Shifting Sands," *Public Opinion*, Vol. 1, No. 2 (May-June 1978), pp. 15–18; Seymour Martin Lipset, "Further Commentary on American Attitudes," *ibid.*, pp. 16–17; also see Chapter 5.

2. For a discussion on the "after-the-fact-approval" model, see Robert Weissberg, *Public Opinion and Popular Government* (Englewood Cliffs, N.J.: Prentice Hall, 1976), pp. 24–25.

3. William B. Quandt, "Domestic Influences on United States Foreign Policy in the Middle East: The View from Washington," in Willard A. Beling, ed., *The Middle East: Quest for an American Policy* (Albany, N.Y.: State University of New York Press, 1973), pp. 263–285. See also Robert H. Trice, "Foreign Policy Interest Groups, Mass Public Opinion and the Arab-Israeli Dispute," *Political Science Quarterly*, Vol. 92 (Fall 1977), pp. 443–463.

4. Hadley Cantril, ed., *Public Opinion, 1935–1946* (Princeton, N.J.: Princeton University Press, 1951), p. 381. See also the questions about Hitler taking away the power of the Jews in Germany in *ibid.*, p. 383.

5. Cantril, *op. cit.*, p. 383.

6. *Ibid.*, *Public Opinion Quarterly*, Vol. II (Winter 1947–48), pp. 655–6.

7. Cantril, *op. cit.*, pp. 385, 387.

8. Harris, while showing that Americans are generally far more supportive of Israel and Jews than American Jews believe, states that "if we total all the unfavorable stereotypes, it can be estimated that 31 per cent of the non-Jewish public in the United States hold attitudes about Jews which can be described as anti-Semitic." See Louis Harris, "Oil or Israel?" *New York Times Magazine*, April 6, 1975, pp. 21–22, 34–35.

9. Yaqub Abdallah Abu-Helu, "Images of the Arabs and of their Conflict with Israel Held by American Public Secondary School Social Studies Teachers" (Ph.D. Dissertation, Stanford University, August 1978).

10. See previous chapter.

11. *The Cambridge Report*, Vol. 4 (Summer 1975), p. 180.

12. Shelley Slade, "The Image of the Arab in America: Analysis of a Poll on American Attitudes," *The Middle East Journal*, Vol. 35, No. 2 (Spring 1981), p. 147.

13. *Ibid.*, pp. 149–50.

14. As Buchanan and Cantril put it: "It appears that the individual, after deciding whether a nation threatens or reassures him, then fills in with a description of the people

of that nation, coloring them in predominantly attractive or predominantly unattractive characteristics to suit his purposes." See William Buchanan and Hadley Cantril, *How Nations See Each Other: A Study in Public Opinion* (Urbana, Ill: University of Illinois Press, 1953), p. 93.

15. See NORC surveys for 1952, 1953, 1955, and 1956. In December 1974, 68 per cent of the American public and 76 per cent of the leaders interviewed believed that it was "very important" to have good relations with the "Arab Countries." In this respect the Arab world ranked after Western Europe (75 per cent public, 97 per cent leaders); Soviet Union (71 per cent, 86 per cent respectively); Japan (70 per cent, 92 per cent respectively); and ahead of Asia (63 per cent, 60 per cent respectively); Latin America (62 per cent, 63 per cent respectively); Africa (56 per cent, 44 per cent respectively). See John Rielly, ed., *American Public Opinion and US Foreign Policy, 1975* (Chicago, Ill.: Chicago Council on Foreign Relations, 1975).

16. "Nation-Wide Survey of U.S. Attitudes on the Middle East," *Arab Studies Quarterly*, Vol. 8, No. 1 (Winter 1986), p. 64.

17. Seymour Martin Lipset and William Schneider, "Carter vs Israel: What the Polls Reveal," *Commentary*, Vol 64, No. 5 (Nov. 1977), pp. 21–29. Lipset later threw some doubt on the validity of the "veto group" argument. See Seymour Martin Lipset, "The Polls on the Middle East," *Middle East Review*, Vol. 11, No. 1 (Fall 1978), p. 30.

18. Mary Curtius, "Israelis to US: Push Hard for Peace, Too," *The Christian Science Monitor*, May 6, 1986, pp. 1, 48.

19. The question was worded as follows: "In the latest war between Israel and the Arab states, do you feel more sympathetic toward the Israelis, the Arabs, or don't you have any strong feeling either way?" See *The Harris Survey Yearbook of Public Opinion, 1973* (henceforth referred to as *Harris Yearbook, 1973* (New York: Louis Harris and Associates, 1976), p. 242.

20. On November 21, 1977 (two days after Sadat's visit to Jerusalem,), 76 per cent of the American public thought that Egypt "really wants a just peace" (58 per cent) or "reluctantly wants a just peace" (18 per cent) in the Middle East. Only 7 per cent said Egypt "really does not want peace" and 17 per cent were not sure. This was an increase of about 29 percentage points over October 1977 figures. See "Opinion Roundup,"*Public Opinion*, Vol. 1, No. 1 (March/April 1978), p. 31. Also, a Gallup poll conducted December 1–4, 1978 showed Anwar Sadat in fourth place after Jimmy Carter, Pope John Paul II, and Billy Graham and Menachem Begin in ninth place on the list of "most admired" men. See *World Opinion Update*, Vol. III, Issue 2 (March 1979), p. 52.

21. For a brief bibliography of studies on American communications media and the Middle East, see Suleiman, *American Images, op. cit.*, footnotes 1–3, p. 68. See also Janice Monti Belkaoui, "Images of Arabs and Israelis in the Prestige Press, 1966–74," *Journalism Quarterly*, Vol. 55, No. 4 (Winter 1978), pp. 732–38, 799. Ms. Belkaoui also demonstrates that there is some relationship between the content of the press on the Middle East and public opinion on the subject.

22. 61 per cent reported no change, whereas 7–8 per cent became more sympathetic toward Germany and the Germans. See Irving Crespi, "Public Reaction to the Eichmann Trial," *Public Opinion Quarterly*, Vol. 28, No. 1 (Spring 1964), pp. 91–103.

23. *The Gallup Opinion Index* (henceforth referred to as *G.O.I.*), September 1978, p. 1. It is possible, of course, that those who watched "Holocaust" were already more pro-Israeli than the general public.

24. 17 per cent felt that Egypt was justified while 30 per cent did not know. NORC poll of September 13, 1956, whereas 28 per cent felt that Israel was justified while 34 per cent did not know. NORC poll of November 15, 1956.

25. 10 per cent approved and 43 per cent did not know. Gallup poll of November 23, 1956.

26. Harris polls of June 10, 1967 and October, 1973. 42 per cent and 34 per cent respectively did not know, whereas 8 per cent and 21 per cent said "both"or "neither."

27. *G.O.I.*, May 1975 (Report No. 119), p. 9. See also *G.O.I.*, February 1974 (Report No. 104), p. 4 for similar diversified responses to the question "Who or what is responsible for the energy crisis?"

28. *Harris Yearbook, 1973*, p. 233.

29. See *G.O.I.*, March 1974 (Report No. 105), p. 10 and *ibid.*, November 1978, (Report No. 160), p. 18.

30. *Ibid.*, June 1977 (Report No. 143), p. 18.

31. *Ibid.*, p. 17.

32. *Ibid.*, February 1974 (Report No. 104), p. 5.

33. For an assessment and critique of the Arab public information effort in the United States, see Abdulrahman Abdulla Zamil, "The Effectiveness and Credibility of Arab Propaganda in the United States" (Ph.D. dissertation, University of Southern California, January 1973).

34. See Cantril, *op. cit.*, pp. xvi, xlii; George H. Gallup, *The Gallup Poll: Public Opinion, 1935*–1971, Vol. 3 (New York: Random House, 1972), p. 2365.

35. Cantril, *op. cit.*, p. 385.

36. *Ibid.*, p. 385.

37. "The Quarter's Polls," *Public Opinion Quarterly*, Vol. 12 (Fall 1948), p. 551.

38. NORC poll of October 1, 1947, *Public Opinion Quarterly*, Vol. 11 (Winter 1947–48), p. 654. Jews or Zionists were named by 75 per cent (under 21 years) and 82 per cent (21 and over); Arabs or Mohammedans were named by 40 per cent and 45 per cent respectively.

39. Gallup poll of June 26–July 1, 1968. See George H. Gallup, *op. cit.*, p. 2149.

40. Cantril, *op. cit.*, p. 387.

41. Gallup poll of December 5, 1945. *Ibid.*, p. 386.

42. Gallup poll of May 15, 1946. *Ibid.*, p. 386.

43. NORC poll of July 1, 1948. "The Quarter's Polls," *Public Opinion Quarterly*, Vol. 12 (Fall 1948), p. 550.

44. NORC poll of November 1947. "The Quarter's Polls," *Public Opinion Quarterly*, Vol. 12 (Spring 1948), p. 160.

45. Fortune poll of June 1948. "The Quarter's Polls," *Public Opinion Quarterly*, Vol. 12 (Fall 1948), p. 550. 31 per cent wanted to "try other solutions," 31 per cent "haven't thought about it," and 12 per cent had "no opinion."

46. SRC California, November 1964.

47. Gallup poll of July 9, 1967. 12 per cent said "don't know."

48. Respondents were merely asked if they tended to agree or disagree with the statement that "Israel should give back the territory it gained from the war of 1967" (1970), or that "the United States should not pressure Israel to give back all the Arab lands that were obtained in the 1967 Middle East war (1974)." 43 per cent disagreed with the first statement and 56 per cent agreed with the second. See also Harris, *op. cit.*

49. *G.O.I.*, April 1978 (Report No. 153), p. 12.

50. "Nation-Wide Survey of U.S. Attitudes on the Middle East," *Arab Studies Quarterly*, Vol 8, No. 1 (Winter, 1986), p. 64.

51. The problem of question wording and how responses on Middle East issues tend to vary according to question format has been briefly discussed in Seymour Martin Lipset and William Schneider, "Polls for the White House, and the Rest of Us," *Encounter*, Vol. XLIX, No. 5 (November 1977), pp. 24–34. See also George F. Bishop et al., "Effects of Question Wording and Format on Political Attitude Consistency," *Public Opinion Quarterly*, Vol 42, No. 1 (Spring 1978), pp. 81–92. Interviewer effect on the respondents, especially when sensitive questions are asked, has been well documented. For sources summarizing the results of studies showing interviewer bias, see Hadley Cantril, *Gauging Public Opinion* (Princeton, N.J.: Princeton University Press, 1944); Herbert H. Hyman et al., *Interviewing in Social Research* (Chicago, Ill.: University of Chicago Press, 1975): Seymour Sudman

and Norman M. Bradburn, *Response Effects in Surveys* (Chicago, Ill.: Aldine Publishing Company, 1974); and Eugene J. Webb, D.T. Campbell, R.D. Schwartz, and L. Sechrest, *Unobtrusive Measures*, (Chicago, Ill.: Rand McNally and Company, 1971). For studies demonstrating the effect of the race of the interviewer when racial questions are asked, see K.R. Athey, J.E. Coleman, A.P. Reitman, and J. Tang, "Two Experiments Showing the Effect of the Interviewer's Racial Background on Responses to Questionnaires Concerning Racial Issues," *Journal of Applied Psychology*, Vol. 44, No. 4 (August 1960), pp. 244–46; E.C. Bryant, I. Gardner, Jr., and M. Goldman, "Responses on Racial Attitudes as Affected by Interviewers of Different Ethnic Groups," *Journal of Social Psychology*, Vol. 70, 1st half, (October 1966), pp. 95–100; and Howard Schuman and Jean M. Converse, "The Effects of Black and White Interviewers on Black Responses in 1968," *Public Opinion Quarterly*, Vol. 25, No. 1 (Spring 1961), pp. 39–56. The social class of the interviewer was shown to be a contaminant in Daniel Katz, "Do Interviewers Bias Poll Results?" *Public Opinion Quarterly*, Vol. 6, No. 2 (Summer 1942), pp. 248–68; David Riesman, "Orbits of Tolerance, Interviewers, and Elites," *Public Opinion Quarterly*, Vol. 20, No. 1 (Spring 1956), pp. 49–73; and G.E. Lenski and J.C. Leggett, "Caste, Class, and Deference in the Research Interview," *American Journal of Sociology*, Vol. 65, No. 5 (March 1960), pp. 463–67. The effect of the interviewer's religion was demonstrated in Duane Robinson and Sylvia Rohde, "Two Experiments with an Anti-Semitism Poll," *Journal of Abnormal and Social Psychology*, Vol. 41, No. 2 (April 1946), pp. 136–44. The question of data contamination as a result of name identification when dealing with Middle East surveys has been discussed by Suleiman, *American Images, op. cit.*, pp. 32–42.

52. NORC poll of May 1946. Cantril, *op. cit.*, p. 386.

53. This question was asked in July 1967 and again in September. While 70 per cent of the American public opted for Jerusalem to be made an "international city" in July, only 33 per cent held that view in September. Those opting for Israeli control increased from 10 per cent to 45 per cent within two months. Those "not sure" constituted 20 per cent and 24 per cent of the respective samples.

54. *Harris Yearbook, 1970, op. cit.*, p. 100.

55. Harris poll of July 10, 1967.

56. *The Harris Survey*, No. 57, July 19, 1982, p. 3.

57. *Harris Yearbook, 1973, op. cit.*, p. 249. The statement was rejected by 50 per cent (vs 26 per cent in favor). In the summer of 1974, 61 per cent rejected the statement and 23 per cent agreed with it, whereas in January 1975, the percentages were 68 and 20. See Harris, *op. cit.*, p. 34.

58. Gallup poll of January 1, 1946. Cantril, *op. cit.*, p. 386.

59. NORC poll of May 1946. *Ibid.*, p. 386.

60. Gallup poll of February 4, 1957. 34 per cent disapproved and 16 per cent had no opinion.

61. Gallup poll of September 12–15, 1975. *G.O.I.*, October 1975 (Report No. 124), p. 5. It might be added that "leaders," i.e. "individuals, representing — as best could be determined — Americans in leadership positions with the greatest influence upon and knowledge about foreign relations," tend to be more pro-Israeli and more willing to see the United States send troops to defend Israel, if attacked, as Tables 2, and 5 indicate. See also Rielly, *op. cit.*

62. Gallup poll of April 18–21, 1975. *G.O.I.*, July 1975 (Report No. 121), p. 26. 27 per cent favored sending supplies, 54 per cent preferred to "refuse to get involved," and 12 per cent had no opinion.

63. It might be added that in December of 1974, 10 per cent of the public suggested military intervention "if the Arab nations impose another oil boycott on the United States." *G.O.I.*, February 1975 (Report No. 116), p. 5. In December 1974, it was found that 21 per cent favored (56 per cent opposed, 23 per cent not sure) US military involvement, including the use of US troops, "if the Arabs cut off the oil supply to Western Europe."

An oil embargo against Japan saw 14 per cent of Americans favoring US military involvement, with 63 per cent opposed and 23 per cent not sure. See Rielly, *op. cit.*, p. 18. The same survey found that only 6 per cent of the public (4 per cent of the leaders) favored a policy of "invade the oil-producing countries" if the United States, Western Europe, and Japan were faced with another Arab oil embargo. The overwhelming majority favored sharing oil with Western Europe and Japan or going it alone. *Ibid.*, p. 25. See also Harris, *op. cit.*, p. 34.

64. *ABC News — Harris Survey*, Vol. I, No. 51 (April 27, 1979), p. 3.

65. NORC poll of July 1, 1948. "The Quarter's Polls," *Public Opinion Quarterly*, Vol. 12 (Fall 1948), p. 551.

66. Fred J. Khouri, *The Arab-Israeli Dilemma*, 3rd edition (Syracuse, N.Y.: Syracuse University Press, 1985), pp. 295–6.

67. Twenty-six per cent stated that Israelis should be able to use the weapons in any way they feel is necessary; and 10 per cent had no opinion. *Gallup Report*, No. 203, (August 1982), p. 3.

68. *The Harris Survey*, No. 57 (July 19, 1982), p. 3.

69. *G.O.I.*, July 1975 (Report No. 121), pp. 17, 26.

70. 72 per cent thought it was a good idea, 19 per cent believed it was a poor idea, and 9 per cent had no opinion. Gallup poll of June 19, 1946. "The Quarter's Polls," *Public Opinion Quarterly*, Vol. 10 (Fall 1948), p. 418.

71. Gallup poll of November 19, 1947. "The Quarter's Polls," *Public Opinion Quarterly*, Vol. 12 (Spring 1948), p. 161.

72. 16 per cent disapproved and 22 per cent had no opinion. "The Quarter's Polls," *Public Opinion Quarterly*, Vol. 12, (Fall 1948), p. 550.

73. Gallup poll of November 26, 1956. 10 per cent disapproved and 20 per cent had no opinion.

74. Harris poll of July 10, 1967.

75. Forty-one per cent favored it and 5 per cent were not sure. *The Harris Survey*, No. 55 (July 12, 1982), p. 3.

76. *The Harris Survey*, No. 76 (September 22, 1983), pp. 2–3.

77. NORC poll of September 29, 1955. 36 per cent were opposed to such a suggestion and 15 per cent had no opinion.

78. There was, however, opposition (62 per cent) to having US and Russian troops occupy contested areas between Egypt and Israel in October 1973. See *Harris Yearbook, 1973*, p. 250.

79. "Nation-Wide Survey," *op. cit.*, p. 65.

80. The survey was carried out in May, 1983. See *The Harris Survey*, No. 76 (September 22, 1983), p. 3; and *ibid.*, No. 115 (December 27, 1984), pp. 2–3. It is worth noting here an additional method of manipulating the data to suit one's purposes. Thus, Harris neglected to report the data on Egypt in the September 22, 1983 report when attitudes toward Egypt were almost as favorable as those toward Israel. Also, in the December 27, 1984 report, the results presented were not for similar dates, but rather for May 1983 (Egypt) and November 1984 (Israel).

81. Louis Harris provides an example of writing by a national pollster displaying pro-Israeli sentiment mixed with anti-Arab and anti-Palestinian remarks. After reassuring the American Jewish community of the support of Americans (both public and leaders), Mr. Harris seeks to downplay American support for Arafat as a leader of the Palestinians (35 per cent) by downgrading and smearing Arafat as an "aggressor" — and displaying contempt for all Arab leaders as in the following remarks: "The reasons people think Arafat ought to have a seat at Geneva are interesting and reflect an underlying cynicism about world politics. It is a cynicism so widespread that it is becoming hard to find majorities of Americans who are ready to condemn aggressors. The head of the PLO is seen as being only a cut below many of the other figures who might be seated in Geneva. Moreover,

Americans have become used to seeing Secretary of State Kissinger holding cordial negotiating sessions with all kinds of previously hostile leaders: Brezhnev, Mao, the North Vietnamese, and every shade of Arab potentate. Why shouldn't Arafat sit in at Geneva, the reasoning goes, even if the PLO's acts of terrorism are despicable?" See Harris, *op. cit.*, pp. 22, 34.

CHAPTER 8

Stereotypes, Public Opinion and Foreign Policy:
The Impact on American-Arab Relations

In this chapter, an attempt is made to detail some of the harmful effects of the negative stereotypes which Americans have about Arabs and the Arab World. The impact of these negative views is not limited to politics, although this is the most crucial arena. Damage is also detected and discussed in terms of conflict between the United States and the Arab world as well as the suffering inflicted on the Arab community in the United States. Furthermore, the concept and practice of democracy are undermined when intelligent political discussion of a major foreign policy issue, namely Palestine, is prevented by pressure tactics, simplistic cliches, and the suppression of opposing views.

In the past twenty-five years, since I began my studies of American stereotypes of Middle East peoples, much work has been done on this subject.[1] This is gratifying in view of the fact that work in this area was often considered "peripheral" to other "important scholarship" on the Middle East.[2] In fact, Americans, including scholars and policy-makers dealing with the Middle East, resent the suggestion that they are biased or that they deal in stereotypes. My own research, however, has shown that while Americans (and Westerners) are often biased against Arabs, they are *unaware* that they are biased or that they use biased or stereotyped thinking on the subject.[3]

It may be worthwhile for us, therefore, to extract from the literature on Middle East stereotypes the basic notions which most Westerners, and Americans in particular, have internalized as a result of their exposure to the various forms of communications media, including school textbooks. Once this is done, we shall then discuss the implications of such stereotyping for American-Arab relations.

Without detailing at length the chronology of American images of

Arabs, it is nevertheless useful to present an overview of what stereotypes do exist. Americans today do, indeed, have numerous stereotypes of Arabs, some of which are positive or neutral, such as their admiration for Arab family life and the respect Arabs accord their elderly.[4] However, most American stereotypes of Arabs are negative and get repeatedly reinforced. It should be emphasized at the outset that it does *not* mean that when an American hears the word Arab or meets a person of Arab background that all the following stereotypes will flash in his or her mind. It *does* mean, however, that different individuals or groups of Americans hold a combination of such stereotypes which are easily conjured up if and when an "appropriate" situation presents itself. Hence the effectiveness of anti-Arab propaganda and the ease with which anti-Arab sentiment is sometimes whipped up.

II

The first and very significant finding is the absence of historical writings in America in which Arabs and/or their contributions and history are mentioned. It is as if Arabs either did not exist, had no impact on America, or were completely ignored by historians and social scientists. As Leuchtenburg put it:

> From the perspective of the American historian, the most striking aspect of the relationship between Arab and American cultures is that, to Americans, the Arabs are a people who have lived outside of history . . . . For one may read any standard account of this history of America, until the most recent times, and derive from it the impression either that the Arabs have had no history or that it was only of the most inconsequential sort.[5]

More recently, however, and especially in the twentieth century, as U.S. interests in the Middle East developed rapidly, American media began to cover the area extensively, and a definite "image" of Middle Easterners and Arabs in particular began to develop. It is this stereotype that will be detailed here. To many if not most Americans, the terms "Arabs" and "Muslims" are interchangeable. Ignorance about, and negative images of, Islam (and there are many)[6] are therefore readily transferable to Arabs. Furthermore, because there are many Muslim peoples, whenever there is a confrontation or a major conflict situation between a Muslim country and the West, particularly the United States, the end result is often for Americans to direct their hostility not only to that particular Muslim country (e.g. Turkey about WWI or Iran in the late 1970's) but to "Muslims" and "Arabs" *generally*. The same is true, and even more strongly, when the confrontation state is an Arab country.[7]

One often gets the impression that "Arabs" and the desert are almost synonymous — or at least they belong together. While at one time, early in this century, there developed a rather romantic image of the desert and its assumed inhabitants, i.e. the bedouins, the more recent view stresses the aridity and absence of development. Rarely, if ever, do Americans get exposed to the image of Arabs "making the deserts bloom." That picture appears to be the preserve of the Israelis. On the contrary, the usual emphasis is on Arabs doing little, if anything, to improve their conditions or the productivity of the land on which they live.[8]

In the desert, where Arabs are found, one also finds oil. Although oil is an indispensable energy source for the West (perhaps *because* it is such), Arabs are almost always associated only with the negative aspects of oil, i.e. oil boycotts, price increases (often referred to as "gougings," "robber," etc.) and the price-fixing "oil cartel." Furthermore, there is hardly any distinction, even by many national reporters for American media, between the Organization of Petroleum Exporting Countries (OPEC) and its Arab counter-part, the Organization of Arab Petroleum Exporting Countries (OAPEC). Very frequently, OPEC translates into "Arabs," who get blamed for its action. In fact, cartoonists' favorite depiction of OPEC is a barrel of oil looking like an Arab sheikh or having such a sheikh holding the gasoline nozzle as if it were a gun — and pointed at the American consumer. Only rarely is Saudi Arabia, for instance, given credit for its moderate views and its attempts to keep oil prices relatively low. Indeed, even this helpful action is sometimes debunked or explained away as not really done to help the U.S. and the West but in the self interest of Saudi Arabia. In other words, the Arabs find themselves in a no-win situation, being "damned if they do, damned if they don't." If they raise the price of oil, they are viewed as engaging in price gougings, if they try to keep the price down, some people's attitude is that "they are not doing us any favors!"

Based on American reporting about the Middle East, the general public gets the impression that Arabs are either fabulously rich or in dire poverty — with hardly a reference to the middle class. The fabulously rich Arabs squander their wealth, we are told, on consumer products and the leisure industry, gambling, wild parties, as well as "stupid" acts of generosity, like using a Rolls Royce in London for two days and giving it to the chauffeur as they reach the airport to leave the country.[9] As for the poverty-stricken Arabs, i.e. allegedly most of the population, these are believed to be denied the benefits of their countries' fabulous wealth by rulers who are despotic, corrupt, vicious, and/or uncaring. Among the possible exceptions are those viewed as pro-Western, at least as long as they are in total agreement with the United States on foreign policy issues, especially toward the Middle East.

The World War I romantic image of both the Arabs (bedouins) and the desert has been changed by Hollywood to one of mean-looking, dagger-wielding individuals lurking outside someone's tent (or door in a house) ready to stab him in the back at the first opportunity. In other words, this image of the Arab presents him as a liar and a cheat, one who cannot be trusted. He is, furthermore, dirty and immoral; that is, he does not subscribe to Western codes of morality. Arab women, on the other hand, are generally viewed as either completely and violently suppressed or they are willing and docile "slaves" or harem to their men-folk.[10]

At least until the 1973 war (and I think since then, though to a lesser extent), Arabs were viewed as united only in their opposition to Israel. Even in this case, however, they are believed to be unable to unite effectively. Furthermore, with some exceptions, Arab soldiers are seen as not good fighters and the Arab fighting machine as ineffective. To this should be added the view that Arab regimes are undemocratic and/or unstable and, therefore, they are undesirable and/or unreliable allies for the West and for the United States in particular.

In addition to the above, some stereotypes pertain to specific groups or countries in the Arab world. In particular, those concerning the Palestinians are worth listing because of their significance and the political motivations behind them. As I have written elsewhere: "There appears to be almost total ignorance, or deliberate negligence, of the fate of the Palestinian Arabs."[11] In fact, until recently, Americans did not think of Palestinians as a people; such individuals were referred to as "Arab refugees," i.e. neither a people nor Palestinian. In addition, Palestinians are often viewed as guerrillas and associated with violence and terrorism. The Palestinians (and Arabs generally) refuse to live at peace with Jews and Israel. In fact, they allegedly aim to destroy the state and its people. Palestinians, we are told, are either terrorists or destitute refugees. They are seldom presented as human beings with specific needs, desires, and aspirations.

III

Since it is obvious that Americans generally hold many negative stereotypes about Arabs, it is important to spell out clearly what the implications of this situation are. To begin with, it makes it difficult for reporters in any medium whether it be radio, television, the movies, or textbooks, to report objectively, honestly, and adequately. They first have to overcome their own prejudices—prejudices which are broadly shared by their colleagues, superiors, and the public in general. Thus, if they present views or even information different from the "accepted" ideas, they will have to fight, or have conflicts with, their bosses. Even if they win there, they will be reporting to readers who have strongly-held pre-conceived ideas. Consequently, their reports will often be viewed as shallow or prejudiced and, in either case, are likely to be easily forgotten or dismissed as the exception, rather than the rule. The alternative, which is the most comfortable option to choose, is for reporters to exercise a degree of prior restraint so that they refrain from reporting too favorably on Arabs or Muslims—even when the facts warrant such reports. Conversely, reporters often avoid reporting too negatively on Zionists/Israelis—again even if the facts warrant such reporting.[12]

Perhaps the best indication of how widespread and deep-rooted negative Arab stereotyping is in the United States would be the so-called Abscam operation. In this 1978 con game, an agency of the U.S. government charged with maintaining the law and deterring crime, itself resorts to the use of a reprehensible mechanism in which it both exploits *and* reinforces a popular image of Arab sheikhs as extremely wealthy individuals who are liars and cheats and who resort to bribery and corruption to get what they want illegally from American legislators.[13] I think it is important to discuss the facts of the case and their implications in some detail. As the reader might recall, Abscam was an operation in which the FBI invented an Arab sheikh, named him Kambir Abdul Rahman, and gave him a false business entitled "Abdul Enterprises Ltd." FBI agents then pretended to work for Kambir and proceeded to pay hundreds of thousands of dollars to American public officials in return for influence peddling in the areas of "investments, obtaining permission for Arab businessmen to reside in the U.S., and building hotels and gaining a casino license in Atlantic City, N.J."[14]

First let us look at the caricature or the stereotype of the Arab in the mind of both the FBI agents *and* the Congressmen involved. This fabricated Arab sheikh was not only rich and corrupt, he also had a non-Arab name, Kambir—albeit one which *sounds* Arab to Americans. Furthermore, "Abdul," as the name of the fake business enterprise, again reflects and reinforces popular ideas of the typical Arab name. Hardly anyone on either side of this sting operation appeared to know or stopped to reflect, it seems, that, in Arabic, "Abdul" is not only non-sensical but almost sacrilegious, since it leaves out the most important part, i.e. God's name. Even in English, one would think it rather silly to have as a name "The Servant of." Furthermore, the success of this operation demonstrates most clearly Hollywood's triumph in shaping the American image of Arabs. For how else can we explain this situation in which at least one United States Senator and seven U.S. Congressmen were completely taken in by this clumsy attempt at play acting, Hollywood style—a situation otherwise devoid of any reality or even real Arab characters?

In an era in which ethnic jokes are frowned upon and when the U.S. government is engaged in extensive programs to protect minorities against discrimination and prejudice, it is indeed most alarming that the FBI agents who carried out the Abscam operation did not even *consider* that they were maligning anyone or any group. In other words, this negative stereotype of the Arabs is so well-ingrained that it appeared to be the real thing! As has been asserted many times since then, no Jewscam or Blackscam, for instance, would have been contemplated, let alone tolerated or carried out.[15]

This lack of sensitivity to Arab concerns manifests itself even in public opinion surveys and, in the process, distorts the results of such polls. As has been reported elsewhere,[16] the question wording in public opinion polls on Middle East issues is such that it often leads the respondents in an opposite direction to the Arab view, either by providing information favorable to the other side or by stacking the cards against the Arab side. Whether this is done intentionally or unwittingly, it is definitely a consequence of bad or distorted reporting on the Arabs.

IV

The Arab-American community, now estimated at over two million, has suffered and continues to suffer in many ways because of negative stereotyping of Arabs. Thus, Arab-Americans are made to feel ashamed of their ancestors and their former homeland. As a result, some have avoided reference to their Arab heritage, for instance, often describing themselves in terms of the geographic region from which they came or the religious sect to which they belong. Also, in an attempt to "assimilate" completely in American society, some have changed their names to ones which sound more European, e.g. changing Haddad to Smith. Such a process, of course, adds to the fractionalization of the Arab-American community into groups based on religion or country of origin.

Arab-Americans are almost the only ethnic group that Americans feel they can attack or make fun of without fear of injury or punishment. This is done on occasion in all the media of communication. It is not much of an exaggeration to say that Arab-Americans find it difficult to enjoy watching television, going to night clubs or even going to the movies for fear of listening to adversary and derogatory remarks directed at their people.[17] Furthermore, there are numerous reports about job discrimination as a result of political stands Arab-Americans have taken on Middle East issues. Some of these cases are now being contested and adjudicated. Political harassment of specific individuals, groups or the Arab-American community as a whole have now been widely reported. Again, they reflect a hostile attitude (reflecting negative media stereotyping) on the part of some governmental agencies. Media campaigns have occasionally targeted specific groups as "terrorists." On November 27, 1978, for instance, the *Los Angeles Times* carried the following headline: "Ties to Arabs Carry Risk of Terrorist Acts in U.S." Other examples include the cases of Sami Ismail, Elias and Antoinette Ayoub, and Ziad Abu Eain.[18] The most serious infringement of the rights of Arab-Americans as a group, combined with illegal surveillance and political harassment, occurred in 1972 when the Nixon administration launched the so-called "Operation Boulder" campaign.[19] Only a strong reaction from the Arab-American community and other civil rights supporters succeeded in exposing and putting an end to that campaign.[20]

In the political realm, numerous grave implications follow from negative Arab stereotyping. Thus, both aspirants for political office as well as those already elected often end up not only supporting Israeli (thus anti-Arab) causes, but find it useful to say something nasty about Arabs or their viewpoint. As one former Congressperson confided to me: "I figured I would be hurt if I went against Israel or pro-Israeli interests and I would *not* be helped if I publicly sided with the Arab view. I had to play it safe." The lesson is learned early and is reinforced in every national election. A politician is thus hurt by "controversy" if he or she appears to be pro-Arab, even when such a stand is believed to be in the national interest. Furthermore, the politician hopes that moving in the opposing direction might well help. Aspirants for the presidency in particular have to be careful about what they say or write and how they vote practically throughout their entire political life. Appearing to be pro-Arab is viewed as a definite handicap — and possibly politically suicidal.

It is common knowledge that during election years, and more so during national presidential elections, United States policy on the Middle East is either at a stand-still or is very pro-Israeli and anti-Arab in tone, primarily to please Israel's supporters. Here again the feeling is that displeasing Arab supporters may be done with impunity. Even after the election is over, the president and his administration feel the strong pressure not to act in a manner which may be construed as pro-Arab. In the October 1981 debate (or rather drama) over the sale of AWACS planes and other military equipment to Saudi Arabia, for instance, President Ronald Reagan had to draw on almost *all* of his presidential "powers"[21] to be able to muster a bare majority in his favor in the U.S. Senate (52–48) after a resounding defeat in the House (111–301). Obviously there were other factors involved in the opposition to the sale, but the pro-Israel, anti-Arab element played a major part in the view of most observers, including that of President Reagan. Under such pressure, a weak president, or one whose popularity is low or slipping, is greatly tempted to go with the easy and "popular" decision. Jimmy Carter's presidency provides two recent examples. The first was in October, 1977 when a joint American-Soviet statement about how to proceed in the Middle East peace process was abandoned by the president shortly thereafter, under much Israeli and pro-Israeli pressure.[22] The second and even more glaring example of buckling under pressure and abandoning what was termed a pro-Arab stance by the Israelis was the "reversal" after the fact of the U.S. vote on a U.N. Security Council resolution which condemned Israeli settlements in territories occupied in 1967.[23]

Because of negative stereotypes, even Arab investments in the United States which bring in money and jobs and, therefore, help both our balance of payments and the unemployment problems, are viewed with suspicion and discouraged, if not severely restricted. Various headlines in the media illustrate this almost racial stereotyping which is meant to raise the spectre of "Arab" take-over of the U.S. Examples are: "Arabs buy up plush real estate in Hollywood;" and "Does Arab cash imperil U.S.?"

In the case of the Palestinians, negative stereotyping has practically made a non-people out of them. They have been dehumanized, and the consequence is to treat them and other Arabs generally as not having much, if any, demands on our conscience. Also, if Palestinians are a non-people, it is easy to wish them away, refuse to talk to them or their representatives, i.e. the PLO, and to persist in excluding them from any formula for a proposed solution to this nagging problem. Nevertheless, it is, to say the least, paradoxical that Palestinians are in the news almost every day, yet they are treated as if they do not exist. In fact, the official American attitude on the subject is best illustrated in the words of a comic poem which goes as follows:

> As I was going up the stair
> I met a man who wasn't there
> He wasn't there again today
> I wish to God he'd go away!

Furthermore, the language that is used to describe incidents involving the Palestinians is rather sanitized and almost non-committal. In 1980–81 encounters on the Lebanese-Israeli border provide good examples of this type of reporting. While we are provided much detail and many pictures and television coverage about the inconvenience, concern, fear, insecurity, suffering, injuries, deaths, funerals, sadness, and over-all rage of the Israelis after an attack by Palestinian forces, termed terrorists, we are then informed of the "retaliation" of the Israelis in which, "according to Palestinian" or "Lebanese" sources, tens or hundreds of individuals were killed or injured. The reports often merely repeat Israeli claims that "guerrilla" or "terrorist" bases were the target. Even Lebanese civilians are ignored or merely included among those counted as residents of "terrorist" camps.[24] The conclusion is inescapable: To the reporters or news directors, an Arab life is not equal to an Israeli life, and Arabs do not apparently suffer as much as Israelis or else their suffering is not as important or pertinent to Americans. While there was more of an uproar over the July 17, 1981 Israeli bombing of Beirut in which over 300 people were killed and about 800 injured, the true extent of the tragedy and the shattered lives of hundreds of civilians hardly received the attention it deserves in the U.S. Their frustration and anguish were reminders, if such were needed that, stereotypes to the contrary notwithstanding, Lebanese and Palestinians as well as Arabs generally are human too.

The way policy-makers view major issues greatly determines the policies followed in resolving those issues. Thus, American attitudes toward Arabs, including Palestinians, have at times caused them to make serious and very costly mistakes, leading to dangerous world situations. The 1973 war provides a good example of miscalculation on the part of American policy-makers, primarily as a result of stereotypic thinking about Arabs, Palestinians, and Israelis. It should be remembered that this situation was generally admitted and widely reported in the press — after the fact. When the war came, the U.S. was not only surprised but quite shocked to see so many of its ideas (now termed myths) about the area shattered.[25] One might add that those shattered myths or previously cherished assumptions by Americans also included a strong pre-disposition to accept as the "truth" the Israeli version of events in the Middle East, even when they should have had doubts, while simultaneously being skeptical of the Arabs' account of any particular situation. To the extent that such thinking lingers on, it hinders all attempts that seek to arrive at an acceptable and feasible settlement of the Palestine and Arab-Israeli disputes.

V

It is clear from the numerous studies on American attitudes toward Arabs that the American public has internalized many negative stereotypes of Arabs. But it should be reiterated that not all or even most Americans hold such negative stereotypes in their heads and recall them when they meet an Arab or hear the word Arab mentioned. However, such stereotypes can be, and often are, exploited by the mass media or acted on by public officials to generate anti-Arab sentiment or to propose policies clearly not in the best interests of Arabs or the Arab-American community.

Why do Americans have such negative stereotypes of Arabs and what would be the best way to change these stereotypes? The method one uses to combat bias and change stereotypes depends on one's view of what the main reasons are behind the spread of such stereotypes. If we believe that public opinion is autonomous, i.e. free of government influence or manipulation and subject only to private groups and competing interests, then attention is focused on such groups and the media. There is, however, some evidence to suggest that "opinion follows policy"[26] and that the primary change has to take place at the highest level of government in its attitudes to the Middle East and to Arabs in particular. While I share the latter view, I also believe that, in a democracy, the existence of intense and widespread views on any issue can set limits which policy-makers may violate only at the risk of popular and electoral displeasures. Nevertheless, the starting point has to be a change of heart and a basic change in policy at the highest level which then effects a general change in the attitudes of the public and the mass media.

But it must be added that even attitude changes at the highest level are certain to face formidable cross-pressures from the Zionists and their supporters in the U.S.[27] To counter-balance this powerful political lobby effectively, what is needed is a similarly powerful set of organizations representing the Arab side or general "American" interests. In addition, as the 1956 Suez Crisis demonstrated,[28] strong Presidential leadership is very crucial in any major American confrontation with Israel.

NOTES

1. Almost all conferences on the Middle East in recent years have included papers and panels dealing with American or Western images of the Middle East and its peoples. Many of the earlier studies, up to 1977, are included in Chapter 6.

2. The change in perspective on this issue is clearly illustrated in the fact that three articles on "Media and the Islamic World" appeared in the Autumn, 1981 issue of the *Middle East Journal*, Vol. 35, No. 4. They are John K. Cooley, "The News from the Mideast; A Working Approach" (pp. 465–480); Robert Hershman and Henry L. Griggs, Jr., "American Television News and the Middle East" (pp. 481–491); and Edward Mortimer, "Islam and the Western Journalist" (pp. 492–505).

3. See Chapter 6.

4. See Shelley Slade, "The Image of the Arab in America: Analysis of a Poll on American Attitudes," *The Middle East Journal*, Vol. 35, No. 2 (Spring, 1981), pp. 143–162.

5. William E. Leuchtenburg, "The American Perception of the Arab World," in George N. Atiyeh, ed., *Arab and American Cultures* (Washington, D.C.: American Enterprise Institute for Public Policy Research, 1977), pp. 15–25, 15.

6. For a detailed account of American media coverage of Islam during the Iranian crisis and the holding of American hostages, see Edward W. Said, *Covering Islam: How the Media and the Experts Determine How We See the Rest of the World* (New York: Pantheon Books, 1981). See also, by the same author, *Orientalism* (New York: Vintage Books, 1979).

7. See the different studies in William C. Adams, ed., *Television Coverage of the Middle*

East (Norwood, N.J.: Ablex, 1981). Afghanistan is included because the television networks began to treat it as if it were part of the Middle East. "Afghanistan became part of the Middle East-turmoil cluster, often accompanied by news of Iran." *Ibid.*, p. 24.

8. See William J. Griswold, *The Image of the Middle East in Secondary School Textbooks* (New York: Middle East Studies Association, 1975), p. 5. See also Glenn Perry, "The Treatment of the Middle East in American High School Textbooks," *Journal of Palestine Studies*, Vol. 4, No. 3 (Spring, 1975), pp. 46–58; Ayad Al-Qazzaz, Ruth Afifi and Audrey Shabbas, *The Arab World: A Handbook* (San Francisco, CA: Tasco, 1978), pp. 3–16; and the various studies on the media in Baha Abu-Laban and Faith T. Zeadey, eds., *Arabs in America: Myths and Realities* (Wilmette, Ill: The Medina University Press International, 1975), especially the piece by Ayad al-Qazzaz on "Images of the Arab in American Social Science Textbooks." *Ibid.*, pp. 113–132.

9. The point here is *not* that such acts have not happened but rather that isolated incidents of this sort are reported and emphasized and thus reinforce a negative image. Far less frequently, has there been reporting about the intelligent acts of generosity by the Arabs, namely Arab foreign aid. See, for instance, "Arab Aid," *ARAMCO World Magazine*, Vol. 30, No. 6 (Nov.-Dec., 1979), the whole issue.

10. Two papers have presented studies of American films with Middle East themes. These are: Karen Cedzo, "The Arab Stereotype and the Mass Media: An Emphasis on Film," paper delivered at the Association of Arab-American University Graduates Convention in Cleveland, Ohio, October 25–27, 1974; and Laurence O. Michalak, "Exoticism and Cruelty: The American Stereotype of Arabs," paper prepared for an Anthropology course at the University of California, Berkeley, June 1975.

11. See previous Chapter.

12. For discussions with reporters on Middle East coverage, its objectivity and problems associated with this enterprise, see Hudson and Wolfe, *op. cit.*, pp. 51–76; and Edmund Ghareeb, *Split Vision: Arab Portrayal in the American Media* (Washington, D.C.: Institute of Middle Eastern and African Affairs, 1977).

13. For a review of the facts concerning the incident and the individuals implicated, see *Facts on File*, Vol. 40, No. 2048, February 8, 1980, pp. 81–82.

14. *Ibid.*, p. 82.

15. Numerous such insults to Arabs and Arab-Americans are reported almost daily to the offices of Arab-American associations, especially the American-Arab Anti-Discrimination Committee, headquartered in Washington, D.C.

16. See previous Chapter.

17. See, in particular, Jack Shaheen's writings, especially the following: "The Image of the Arab on American Television," in Ghareeb, *op. cit.*, pp. 163–171; "American Television: Arabs in Dehumanizing Roles," in Hudson and Wolfe, *op. cit.*, pp. 39–44; "The Arab Stereotype on Television," *The Link*, Vol. 13, No. 2 (April/May, 1980), pp. 1–13; and "The Influence of the Arab Stereotype on American Children," *Arab Perspectives*, Vol. 1, No. 9 (Dec., 1980), pp. 15–20.

18. For these and other cases of attacks on and harassment of Arab-Americans, see the newsletters and reports of the American-Arab Anti-Discrimination Committee.

19. See M.C. Bassiouni, ed., *The Civil Rights of Arab-Americans: "The Special Measures"* (North Dartmouth, MA: Association of Arab-American University Graduates, 1974).

20. Elaine Hagopian, "Minority Rights in a Nation-State: The Nixon Administration's Campaign Against Arab-Americans," *Journal of Palestine Studies*, Vol. 5, Nos. 1–2 (Autumn, 1975/Winter, 1976), pp. 97–114.

21. On the question of presidential power, see Richard E. Neustadt, *Presidential Power: The Politics of Leadership from F.D.R. to Carter* (New York: Wiley, 1980).

22. The U.S.-Soviet joint statement was issued on October 1, 1977 and contained a set of guidelines for proposing Arab-Israeli negotiations and the reconvening of the Geneva peace conference, "with participation in its work of the representatives of all the parties

involved in the conflict including those of the Palestinian people." On October 5, 1977, successful pro-Israeli lobbying practically nullified the terms of the U.S.-Soviet joint statement, as the U.S. and Israel issued a joint statement of their own. See *Facts on File*, Vol. 37, No. 1926, Oct. 8, 1977, p. 759.

23. The March 1, 1980 U.N. Security Council resolution asked for the removal of Israeli settlements from occupied Arab territories, including Jerusalem. President Carter's "reversal" came on March 14 when he announced that the U.S. had not intended to vote for the resolution but did so as a result of a communication breakdown within the Administration. See *Facts on File*, Vol. 40, No. 3053, March 14, 1980, p. 179.

24. See, in particular, John Weisman, "Blind Spot in the Middle East: Why You Don't See More Palestinians on TV," *TV Guide*, October 24, 1981, pp. 6–8, 10, 12, 14.

25. See Chapter 4.

26. See Appendix.

27. The strength of the Zionist lobby in the U.S. has been discussed by many observers, most recently and fully by Alfred M. Lilienthal, *The Zionist Connection II* (New Brunswick, N.J.: North American, 1982); and Paul Findley, *They Dare to Speak Out: People and Institutions Confront Israel's Lobby* (Westport, Conn: Lawrence Hill, 1985).

28. Dwight D. Eisenhower, *Waging Peace, 1956–1961: White House Years* (New York: Doubleday, 1965).

CHAPTER 9

The Arab Information Effort
in North America: An Assessment

The main purpose of this chapter is to review and evaluate the Arab information effort in North America, particularly in the United States. The word "Arab" here refers to the pronouncements and activities of the League of Arab States, its agencies and bureaus, and any organizations or groups which openly work with the League in promoting its information activities. "Information effort" refers to any and all deliberations, suggestions, or campaigns by the League or specific Arab states to present the Arab viewpoint to Americans in a positive manner and/or to discredit attacks on Arabs generally or on specific members of the Arab League.

Most of the data for the study were collected from archival records and personal interviews conducted with members of the Arab League staff engaged in the information effort. Also, the few available studies on the subject, as well as the most important proposed "plans" for major reform, will be consulted and assessed.

When the Arab League was established on March 22, 1945, the Charter had no reference whatsoever to an information department or to potential activity in that area. In part, this was because the founding states themselves had no information ministries and knew little about the need for, or the importance of, information. Also, perhaps there was little thought given to the League representation to the outside world since it was established as an instrument to facilitate coordination, planning and cooperation among the Arab states themselves — and primarily, if not solely, in non-political, non-sensitive areas since each member state jealously guarded against any violation or impairment of its sovereignty.[1]

It was on April 4, 1946, a year after its founding, that member states charged the League with the formulation and dissemination of positive information or propaganda for the Arabs on the international scene. From the very beginning, Palestine was the main "information" issue with which the League had to grapple. Then, after the many political defeats suffered by the Arab side at the United Nations, the League recommended the establishment of, and later set up, a Department of Information and Publications in 1953.[2] In other words, only then did it occur to Arab leaders that information and the art of persuasion, far from being shameful or demeaning activities, were an essential component of the political process, at least on the international level.

But movement was at a snail's pace. Thus, it was not until 1959 that most of the structure presently in place was instituted. In addition to the Department of Information and Publications, this consists of the Permanent Committee on Information which is composed of the heads of the information bureaus in the member states. The Committee meets twice a year to formulate policy options to be discussed and decided upon by the Council of Arab Ministers of Information, which is supposed to be the highest policy-planning body.[3] Since the Permanent Committee meets only twice a year, its work throughout the year is carried out by the Permanent Bureau of Arab Propaganda composed of the Press Attaches at the embassies of the various member states found in the city where the Arab League is located. Funding for this information activity is secured through contributions from member states.[4]

Whereas the Arab League at the time of its founding in 1945 was completely oblivious to the role of information in international politics,[5] some members within it seem lately to have come full circle to the other extreme view that information is practically the be-all and end-all of any cultural development. In the words of one Arab Minister of Information,

The age in which we live is an age of information and communication. The information effort has become the cornerstone of every cultural act by which the progress of nations is measured. [This is so] because differences among nations, even when they [are reflected and have] consequences in the economy, society and culture, are basically informational in their essence and underlying causes.[6]

Arab Information Policy

Having set up the machinery to dispense information to the world, the Arab states had to decide what their message was. This is a continuous effort, of course, but the main themes and formulae have not changed much over the years, especially since the first meeting of the Council of Arab Ministers of Information in Cairo on 7–10 March, 1964. At that and subsequent meetings, the participants indicated that the Arab information effort should stress the fairness and justice of the Arab case, as well as Arab interest in international peace and human welfare. At the same time, the world should be informed about the Arab homeland and the many attempts at development and economic growth. Furthermore, opposing propaganda campaigns against the Arabs should be challenged, exposed and refuted. More specifically, the following are recurrent themes:

1. Arabs seek social and political progress and will fight bigotry, aggression and racism. Anti-Semitism, the historical root of Zionism, was a Western, not an Arab, phenomenon.[7]

2. Israel has deliberately distorted the truth about the Arabs and has presented them in a bad light so that the world, especially the West, has formed negative stereotypes of Arabs, their society, culture, art and even religion.[8]

3. Arabs have been greatly maligned and need to correct their bad image and change the negative stereotype. They also should inform the West about the great Arab and Islamic civilization.[9]

4. Israel claims to want peace but is hypocritical and its actions lead to war. Israel is an expansionist, exploitative country which acts as an agent of imperialism in the Middle East and other parts of the world.[10]

5. The Palestinian Arabs have been denied their rights within Israel. Also, Israel has caused them to become homeless.[11]

Arab heritage and rights in Palestine should be clearly spelled out. Armed Palestinian resistance is the natural consequence of the denial of Palestinian rights.[12]

Palestine is the Arab *cause celebre* and Arabs will offer all necessary moral and material sacrifices for the cause of Palestine.[13]

Arabs are committed to restore Palestinian national rights in accordance with the decisions of the Palestine Liberation Organization as the sole legitimate representative of the Palestinian people. This, coupled with Israeli withdrawal from the occupied territories, will make a peaceful solution possible.[14]

Arab Information Strategy

According to the League's members, then, the basic aim of the information effort was, and is, to defend the Arabs against malicious attacks especially from Zionists in the West, and to convey to the world the picture of an Arab world working for progress, welfare, and stability. If that is the message, who is supposed to develop it, how will it be delivered, to whom, and with what means? Who is to pay for it?

In the absence of a detailed plan of action or philosophical statement, concerning Arab information and its dissemination to the outside world, which has actually been followed by the League, we might arrive at this information indirectly by examining the annual reports on the activities of Arab League missions abroad. Such accounts can be brief or very detailed but usually organize League staff activities under the following categories: Speeches, conferences, publications, exhibits, and reports to the League headquarters in Tunis.[15] Quite often, the director of the main office in any particular country performs the major "visible" activities in communicating the Arab view to the host country. This is definitely the case in the U.S. Thus, the 1983 report summarizing the League information effort in the United States listed Dr. Clovis Maksoud's numerous public appearances as follows: fifty-five speeches and lectures, twenty-two press conferences, forty-three communiques, and participation in thirteen conferences and symposia. In addition, the Center printed and distributed various short booklets and a monthly magazine, *Arab Perspectives*. The regional centers were reported to have done "a lot" in providing information when requested to do so, and to have responded to false or defamatory propaganda.[16] Also, the League's center in Ottawa prepared a monthly report on the activities of hostile, mainly Zionist, groups. Among the various subjects covered under hostile propaganda are: Negative reports on the Arabs, favorable reports on Israel, and Canadian politics as it relates to the Middle East situation.[17]

Over the years, the Arab viewpoint has been presented primarily, if not almost exclusively, through the following media: speeches and lectures, press conferences, communiques and conferences, and in cooperation with "Friendship Societies."[18] However, the Council of Arab Ministers of Information has often recommended other forms of communication which have been rarely utilized, either because of lack of material resources, or because of the unavailability of trained personnel, or due to lack of enthusiasm for the specific projects suggested. Among the suggestions applicable to North America are the following: A travelling exhibit about Arab civilization and its contributions to humanity, including book exhibits; production of records and tapes for teaching Arabic to foreigners; a short course for foreign students on Arab civilization, to be offered at a university in the Arab world during the summer; strengthening and broadening the relationship between the Arab League and Arab communities abroad; setting up special exhibits on Palestine and celebrating Palestine week; production of long, feature films presenting the Arab view; strengthening and broadening contacts with influential personalities throughout the world in the fields of science and communication; preparation of a series of books, atlases, films, television shows, videotapes, etc. on specific Arab issues or on Arab cultural traditions or on various Arab countries for distribution abroad; paying attention to children's books and films and cartoons, especially in areas where the Arab image is distorted; contracting to do a comprehensive survey of Arab emigrants to determine how best to utilize their talent.[19]

It is clear from the above examples that the Arab Information Ministers have suggested almost every tactic imaginable in the hope that it might be the correct answer or the magic formula that would indeed turn the tide in favor of the Arabs and against Zionists/Israel in the struggle for the hearts and minds of Americans. It has also become clear to these ministers and their deputies in the past few years that they have issued the same recommendations over and over again — with no discernible change in the situation. The resultant frustration began to show in 1981 when the then president of the Permanent Committee openly decried the sad state of affairs in the Arab information campaign and bemoaned the woeful lack of resources and manpower necessary for success.[20] In 1982, the president of the Council of Arab Ministers of Information that year pointed out that, while Israel was practically free to do what it pleased, unchecked by the United Nations or world public opinion, the Arabs continued to meet — for at least fifteen consecutive years by then — without being able to arrive at a "strategy" for winning the information war.[21] Also, in 1984, the then president of the Council of Arab Information Ministers reminded the group that it was seventeen years earlier, in September 1967, when they first met to formulate a winning strategy for information abroad, but that no such plan had emerged.[22]

No over-all information strategy has as yet been formulated. Instead, there are many proposed tactics, presented in a rather haphazard, scattershot fashion, and intended to block specific Israeli or Zionist actions and/or to effect some changes in the Arab image among Americans. If there is an underlying assumption, it is the implicit notion that Westerners, and Americans in particular, are unaware of the true facts about the Arabs and the Middle East situation in general, and that Israel and Zionism have worked to keep them in the dark. The solution, therefore, is to devise some means to get the facts to the masses. Once the masses have been awakened from their sleep or coma, they will side with the Arabs and their just causes, especially in Palestine, and defiantly turn their backs on Zionism and Israel.

The above view has recently been articulated in more than one of the four major proposals or plans of action presented to the League with the purpose of advancing the Arab information effort in the United States. Since these are the most comprehensive proposals put before the League, and since they come in response to much frustration and disappointment at the poor results Arab information activities have yielded on the American scene, it is useful and necessary to review all four proposals briefly.[23]

Plan A is the most detailed and comprehensive in its approach and proposed plan of action. Its basic assumptions, however, are that while it is very difficult and expensive to effect a change in American foreign policy, an easier and cheaper way is to enlighten American public opinion concerning Arab issues. This will, in turn, lead American policy makers to take a more moderate and even-handed approach on Middle East issues. In order to correct the weaknesses of the Arab information effort, therefore, this plan suggests the development of a public relations campaign to be directed by three foundations, especially set up for this purpose. The first, to be financed from Arab and American sources, would employ the services of an American public relations firm to produce, package and disseminate accurate information about the Arabs to Americans, including those in remote, small villages. The second would be a political lobbying group, organized and financed entirely within the United States. The work of this group would focus on politicians and the political process and would work to counteract the activities of the Israeli lobby which presently has much control over the United States Congress. The third organization would be a tax-exempt group, devoting its efforts to long-term projects in research and publication to educate the public on Arabs and the Middle East generally.

Plan B calls for the establishment of an Arab Foundation for International Relations to act as an independent, social, cultural, and information agency whose primary aim is to cultivate better understanding and friendship between the Arabs and the rest of the world. This foundation, to be based in the United States, with branches in Europe, will act as a data bank storing and producing information about the Arab world, which will be disseminated widely. The foundation will also act to organize, direct and mobilize the various friendly and sympathetic groups around the world in an attempt to help them attain the common objective of greater understanding between Arabs and non-Arabs. The financing for this foundation will come from Arab governmental and private sources but it is proposed that its operation be separate from, and independent of, any Arab government or the Arab League, though its board will be appointed by Arab governments. Once the necessary capital has been raised, it will be invested and only the dividend used.

Plan C, like B above, also calls for the establishment of an independent foundation to be run by a governing board composed of well-known Arab-Americans. The initial financing should be substantial and might come from the Arab states. This foundation will undertake all kinds of projects of an educational nature about the Arab world, but also ones which deal with solar energy, American Indians, Hispanics, Blacks, etc. In other words, it will engage in whatever legal activity which its executive board deems effective and beneficial to advance the cause of friendship and understanding between Arabs and Americans.

Plan D suggests setting up an Arab- American foundation equivalent to the German Marshall Fund. The financing should come as a gift from the Arab governments and people. The foundation will then be set up as an independent entity to be run by an American board. Its activities will not be narrowly defined but will include any and all legal educational activities to release the Arab name and cause from "the ghetto" in which it has been placed.

These four plans were studied by the Arab League and deemed inadequate in one or more respects. Thus, it was pointed out, for instance, that educational foundations were being proposed to carry out activities which may be viewed as political — a situation that is likely to create legal and credibility problems. Other potential difficulties relate to the priorities of work suggested and the lack of unity among Arab-American communities. Finally, it was argued that on sensitive issues, it was possible to anticipate clear differences of opinion between a solely American board and the concerned Arab parties. Consequently, and at least for the present, the alternative is for the Arab League to carry out its own information functions but with greater efficiency and scope, provided added resources are made available.

Assessment and Critique

In part, the League's response to the four plans in the form of an alternative proposal, may be viewed as its answer to the implicit charge that it has not done enough to promote a good Arab information campaign. The League's answer, therefore, is that such a campaign requires more money, better and more personnel, and greater efficiency in administration. This is true as far as it goes, though it does not go far enough. However, it is necessary to discuss the main shortcomings of the Arab information effort before any changes or recommendations are offered.

1. The first and possibly most serious weakness of the Arab information effort is that Arab governments individually, as well as collectively through the League, have acted on the basis of a *mistaken* assumption concerning the proper meaning of "information." Thus, in practically all resolutions put out by the Council of Arab Ministers of Information and certainly in various tactics and plans of action advocated by the League, there is the underlying but clear assumption that 1) "information" is *merely* the dispensing of facts and/or that 2) information is propaganda i.e. a form of preaching designed to attract converts to one's cause or point of view.[24] These new converts must, in fact, accept *totally and fully* one's side of the argument. If that does not happen, then it is believed that the information effort has failed. There is very little understanding, or else definite negligence, of the fact that the main function of information in the twentieth century is to communicate effectively, on numerous levels and with different audiences, with the specific intention of accomplishing clearly-defined *political* objectives. It is, of course, useful and worth-while to try to convey factual information about Arabs and the Arab world as well as to seek converts to the Arab view. But if this is where the emphasis is placed, then it demands a certain strategy which often frustrates and defeats the other and more important objective — namely the need to persuade political decision-makers to accept and support Arab foreign policies and political objectives.

Another related weakness stems from the fact that "information" is often treated as an independent field, almost unrelated to the over-all political social, cultural, military, and political situation.[25] However, it is simply not practical to expect to make major strides in the information field if the other areas are weak, backward, or ineffective. In other words, it is not possible to regain by information what was lost in the battlefield or through bad political judgement. Neither will the most sophisticated public relations campaign get U.S. decision-makers to change their policies on the Palestine or Lebanese issues, for example, unless economic, political, and military factors are also brought to bear.

The review of Arab information materials as well as some resolutions of the Arab Information Ministers reveals a tendency to resort to general statements, platitudes, and moral exhortation, rather than an intelligent discussion of mutual or self-interest. However, as any textbook on international politics will tell us, nation-states, despite their profession of good-will, fair-play and justice for all, do not, in the end, act on the basis of moral laws but in accordance with their view of national interest. That does not mean that they will intentionally flout public morality. It *does* mean, however, that an appeal that is based merely on the presentation of facts and on showing the injustice suffered by the Palestinians or Arabs generally might perhaps win some sympathy, but is not likely by itself to move other countries to act on behalf of the Palestinians or Arabs. That action is far more likely to materialize when "information" is also used to communicate a concomitant economic, political, and/or military message.

2. Another area of confusion and weakness relates to the lack of clear policy and strategy with respect to Palestine and Israel. Thus, at times, Israel is viewed as an independent, expansionist state working for its own ends and using Zionism to extract concessions and support from the West, especially the United States. At other times, Israel is thought to be an agent of imperialism, especially American imperialism, in the Middle East.

On the question of Palestine, there was much vacillation and change until the rise of the Palestine Liberation Organization and then its recognition as the sole legitimate representative of the Palestinians in 1974. Since then, the PLO has formulated the policy on Palestine, which members of the League have generally accepted. If Arab governments once again claim the right to speak for the Palestinians or Palestinians are prevented from speaking with one voice, the information effort is bound to suffer.

3. A third area of major weakness stems from the fact that the Arab League is composed of twenty-one sovereign states and the Palestine Liberation Organization. Because it is an *official* organ of these states, it is impossible for it to present anything but the *official* version of events, facts and policies. In other words, the nature and make-up of the League oblige it to deal with information only as fact and/or propaganda. The consequence is to view information merely as a commodity to be handed out concerning specific topics on which Arabs present their point of

view.[26] Under such circumstances, debate (i.e. the presentation of opposing views) is possible, but a real constructive and fruitful dialogue is not. It also follows that a League-sponsored conference on any particular issue requires the participation of supporters, friends and allies. This is useful in that it encourages new scholarship to support the pertinent argument, keeps the issue alive and gains some publicity for it, and provides moral support for one's friends and oneself. However, it suffers from being very restrictive in the kind of audiences it can reach and often ends up being not much more than a forum where one is preaching to the converted. In other words, its usefulness is rather limited.

Also, if such conferences or other programs show the Arabs in the best light only, outsiders will tend to view them as crude propaganda attempts, even when the speeches and papers are objective and accurate. Under such circumstances, therefore, even excellent scholarship tends to become tainted and lose some of its credibility and effectiveness.

Within the League, policy is set by unanimous decisions, and any member state may exclude itself from approving specific resolutions. This situation leads to some negative results. One consequence is that major policies and objectives are difficult to agree upon and are, therefore, either ignored, or discussed and tabled. But even when such an agreement is reached,if one or more important members disapprove, they can frustrate its implementation by refusing to participate fully or effectively, especially in paying their dues or contributions.[27]

In order to avoid major disagreements and possible splits, the policies and decisions which receive approval are usually those of a general nature. An alternative that has often been used is to issue definite instructions to hold conferences on specific topics or carry out pointed media campaigns against the enemy. The weakness of this alternative is that, in the absence of broad policy objectives and guidelines, the message which the target audience receives is not clear and does not convey a total picture of who the Arabs are, or what their views and aspirations happen to be for their homeland, the Middle East region, world and regional peace, Arab-Western relations, or even Palestine. In the absence of such information which might normally constitute a "base" or a peg on which to hang other more specific news and information, any "new" information concerning Israeli annexation of Jerusalem or the Golan Heights, or repression of Palestinians and Lebanese, or the Israeli plan to dig a tunnel connecting the Mediterranean to the Dead Sea, and so on, would be interpreted by any target audience in the West as *discrete* events to be evaluated individually and separately — where Israel, in essence, is presumed to have equal rights and equally legitimate concerns. The end result is a definite loss for the Arab side.

Furthermore, divisions within the Arab world and the inability to formulate clear and definite objectives in foreign policy as well as information, means that events are not anticipated but followed. Israel is then given *carte blanche* to strike the first blow, formulate the major plans and seize the initiative. In other words, *Israel sets the agenda for the Arabs*. Thus, it is often *after* the enemy announces a plan of action that the League's Information Department is asked to formulate a media effort or an international conference to "expose" the action and condemn it — almost as if the information campaign is meant to be a *sufficient* response to the Israeli action.[28] Although it might make the Arabs feel good that right and justice are on their side, such an information effort is not likely to win many new friends nor reverse the Israeli action.

Not only is there no overall detailed Arab strategy of a positive nature as to what the message is, but there is also a lack of consensus on how to deliver that message and to whom, as well as who is supposed to deliver it and who should pay for the effort. Thus, there are many proposed projects to deliver what is assumed to be a well-known and agreed-upon formula or information packet which, it is further assumed, can *easily* be delivered if only some nasty individuals and groups (i.e. Zionists) out there did not oppose the Arabs. There is little or no discussion of Western audiences, their backgrounds, needs and aspirations, or their potential receptivity to Arab information messages. Western psychology and Western strategic plans and national interests also receive little attention.[29]

Sovereign Arab states and, by extension, the Arab League are always careful to deliver their messages in such a manner as to reflect exactly their views on all the main issues. Because they tolerate absolutely no deviation, unless it is a reinforcement or exaggeration of their case, they prefer to deliver their messages themselves or to entrust them to groups and individuals over whom they have control, i.e. the Arab League or a paid public relations firm, or through a paid advertisement.[30] Friendly groups or individuals might also be acceptable but only, or at least primarily, on specific issues where their views are already known. To rely on them for long-term support becomes problematic since it is feared that they might change their mind at some future date. Such a situation places great restrictions on the flexibility of the League and denies the information effort some of the best available talent in support of its overall media campaign. Thus, even when it is realized that emigrant Arab communities are generally sympathetic to Arab causes, their support as well as their extensive resources are, as yet, hardly tapped. In fact, no comprehensive studies of the Arab-American community have been carried out so far. It is true, of course, that there are many emigrant Arab organizations and that the level of cooperation among them is often rather low. While they are constantly urged to forget the divisions in their original homeland and work closely together, this is easier said than done — especially since the governments in the home countries insist on being the only conduit or connection for any activity concerning their former nationals.[31]

4. Another impediment to an effective information effort is the lack of agreement among the principal Arab parties, i.e. within as well as outside the League, as to who the target audience should be. Since the establishment of the state of Israel in 1948, different approaches have been discussed and advocated. One approach assumes that in a democracy, such as the United States, decision-makers formulate policies based on the needs and expressed desires of their electorate. The way to change American policy on the Middle East, therefore, is to win the hearts and minds of the American people who will, in turn, influence their leaders and policy-makers. In this process, the Zionist lobby is very powerful but should be overcome. Once that happens, the U.S. would become more pro-Arab in its policies. This approach advocates an information campaign that will reach the mass public. Another approach argues that in foreign policy matters, even in democratic states like the U.S., decisions are made by elites in the highest levels of government and supported by the influential media — which then communicate such views to the general public to assure its approval and support. It follows, therefore, that the preferred target audience for the Arab information effort should be the foreign policy elite. What is often not articulated, at least not openly and fully, is the debate as to whether the United States is basically a friend and ally of the Arabs, or a friend and ally of their enemies, especially Zionism and Israel. If it is the latter, as Fayez Sayegh concluded in 1970, then the Arab information effort in the U.S. is either useless and should be abandoned, or it should be directed at those individuals, groups, and forces within American society who are interested in changing American foreign policy.[32]

Here again, the divisions in the Arab world have made it difficult, if not impossible, to follow a consistent policy with full vigor. The two approaches are not necessarily mutually exclusive. The available evidence indicates that, under normal circumstances, opinion *follows* policy — that is, policy is first made by the foreign policy elite based on their conception of the American national interest, and then the media communicate this policy to the general public to get its support.[33] However, where there is an interested, committed and active minority or pressure group strongly supporting a specific foreign policy, the foreign policy elite has to take that view into consideration.[34] Thus, American policy-makers have not been able to ignore Zionist groups in the U.S.; they have had to deal with them in some way, either to support them, side with them completely or, occasionally, oppose them. It is when confrontation with the Zionist lobby has occurred that the overwhelming pressure from pro-Zionist forces became an irritant for American policy-makers.[35]

On the level of the general public, stereotypes and images (positive or negative) become important in facilitating or hindering the process of setting the right issues as agenda items for consideration by the attentive public, and ultimately by the policy-makers. Obviously it is much better to have a positive than a negative image among the population at large since that makes it easier to attain credibility and acceptance for one's media pronouncements — as the Israelis and their supporters do. This also makes it much easier for the Israelis to use "condensation symbols" to quickly convey a positive image of themselves or a negative image of the Arabs — as they do repeatedly and effectively. Thus, the American public often accepts, without much challenge, accusations of extremism or terrorism or anti-Semitism when they are hurled at Arabs or some of their supporters. On the other hand, hardly anyone challenges Israel's claim that it is "democratic," and Americans generally find it difficult to believe that the Palestinian Arabs have been *denied* their democratic rights by being removed from their homeland. Also, despite the heavy coverage of the Israeli invasion of Lebanon and the frequent display of Israeli violence, Americans do not generally think of Israelis as terrorists.[36]

However, public opinion does *not* make foreign policy, though it does set limits beyond which policy-makers venture at their own risk.[37] On the other hand, the foreign-policy elite discuss, propose, influence, and ultimately make policy. Without ignoring the general public, it should be made clear that, since there are scarce resources, the main task of the Arab information effort is to identify and influence the influential. But no information campaign is successful unless it is guided and supported by a clear strategy and well-defined objectives presented and pushed by political leaders willing to apply pressure on their counterparts in the West, whether these happen to be friends, allies, or adversaries.

5. The administrative and personnel structure within the Arab League has also been a factor in the Arabs' poor performance in the field of information. This is to be expected, since the administrative structure reflects the lack of unity among the member states. Thus, the various Arab states want to make sure that no information program takes place to which they object for any reason. The consequence has been for the members of the Permanent Committee (i.e. Deputy Ministers of Information) and the Council of Ministers of Information to spend much valuable time discussing and approving the holding of specific conferences. Thus, not only do these high level officials argue over the main topics to be discussed at such conferences, but also over the time and place of holding the conference and even, at times, the possible participants. Even more wasteful of time and effort are the follow-up discussions about such conferences, whether or not they were held, and further urgings to hold them on time and at the designated site.[38]

Since member states within the League have not been able to agree on a major information effort, that task has gone, by default, to the League's Department of Information, which has in the past few years been expected to formulate policies and information campaigns to present to the Permanent Committee and the Council of Information Ministers. However, the Department itself suffers from resources too inadequate (both in the number of qualified personnel and in support services and financing) to be able to propose grandiose plans, let alone carry them out. Despite such shortcomings, however, the Department has indeed worked with the Permanent Committee to put forth numerous projects which have also been approved by the Council of the Ministers of Information only to remain no more than paper resolutions because of lack of funding. Since the League's information effort is financed through contributions from member states, and since contributions have been generally few and small lately, the situation is rather critical. In fact, especially in the past few years, hardly any funds have been available to carry out anything but the very minimal information tasks. It should also be remembered that there has always been a definite structural weakness, namely the fact that an overwhelming percentage (75 –80%) of the information budget goes to cover wages and rents.[39] Thus, with the present financial crisis, the Arab information effort does little more than pay for wages and rents. Even under such circumstances, the various League information offices in North America could still deliver "the message" to American audiences, if indeed there was a clear and definite message, and if these League employees were relatively free to perform their duties as best they see fit. Unfortunately, however, that is not the case. For one thing, Arab ambassadors have a definite say and a veto power over what is said.[40] Furthermore, the personnel spend much of their time answering to their own, i.e. Arab League, constituency. Thus, the following reports are expected from all League officers: A weekly political report about news pertinent to the Arab world; a weekly information report; telegraphic reports on urgent or important events; a monthly report on office activities; a monthly report about hostile and opposing propaganda efforts; a 6-month report about office activities to be presented to the Permanent Committee; and a comprehensive annual report![41]

Basic Assumptions

The recommendations which follow are based on the preceding discussion and evaluation of the Arab information effort. They are also based on certain assumptions which should be made clear and explicit, as I shall now attempt to do.

1. The recommendations will be based on the present reality in the Arab world and North America. The emphasis will be on what is realistic and feasible, not on ideal or unattainable solutions.

2. Information is not an end in itself but a tool to advance certain policies. It can only be as strong as (certainly no stronger than) the proposed message, the messenger, or the original source about which it reports. Furthermore, information is only *one* possible tool or weapon employed by policy-makers. Arab policy-makers cannot and should not expect information campaigns to win military or economic battles for them.

3. Unless Arabs have clear and explicit objectives which are clearly pursued, even the best and most heavily subsidized information effort will not succeed.

4. Weakness of the Arab information effort outside the Arab world is very much related to the weakness of that effort *within* the Arab world itself.

5. For purposes of information dissemination, the Arab League is not an ideal tool or agency. The major drawback is the fact that the

League is a collectivity of sovereign states, each with its own definite view of "national interest." While there is, at times, a convergence in the views and perspectives of some of the member states, there is no *assurance* of the dominance of identity of interest. Furthermore, there is no enforcement mechanism to make member states follow the guidelines, let alone decisions, of the League as a whole — even when such member states have agreed to those guidelines or decisions. Consequently, whenever there is no consensus or even broad and general agreement on major foreign policy issues — which has been the case for most of the period since the establishment of the League — the information effort becomes crippled or, at best, ineffective.

6. The various Arab countries, like all sovereign states, can and should engage in propaganda to present their official positions. However, information is different from propaganda and is best disseminated by non-official agencies. Thus, the establishment of an Arab News Agency, as some have proposed,[42] is likely to create serious problems of credibility both within as well as outside the Arab world, especially in Europe and North America. Similar, though less serious, problems may be encountered by an agency set up strictly to convey "the Arab point of view" or to spread Arab propaganda.[43]

7. Despite disagreements and divisions within the Arab world, a joint strategy is possible, desirable and necessary. Such a strategy should focus on broad common objectives and aspirations, and should educate the world, including the West, about the cultural heritage, contributions and achievements of Arabs and Islam.

8. Arab information programs, in order to be effective, have to be prepared on a long-term basis, and with assured funding, in order to avoid discontinuity and chaos.

9. The Arab information effort has mainly focused on the Palestine question. With the establishment of the Palestine Liberation Organization and its recognition as the sole legitimate representative of the Palestinians, information on the Palestine issue should be the main responsibility of the PLO.

Conclusions and Recommendations

Based on the above assumptions, it is recommended that:

1. The Arab League information effort should focus mainly on Arab cultural, scientific, and educational achievements and on conveying the

news about such accomplishments to the outside world. In other areas, especially political issues, the League's offices would be expected to present the views which are agreed upon, and acceptable to, all member states. In pursuing this program, the League's efforts should include:

A. The establishment of Arab Cultural Centers similar to the British Council offices or the Goethe Institute. Such centers should be well-staffed by competent personnel who are chosen on the basis of a merit system and not nomination by member states. These centers should be furnished with adequate libraries stocked with books, journals, and periodicals dealing with the Arab world and focusing on the cultural-scientific-educational area. Also, they should be equipped with large selections of audio-visual materials, including slides, posters, films, videos, etc. The centers are to be used both as research libraries and lending institutions in order to broaden the impact and reach locations outside the main cities.

B. These Arab Cultural Centers should incorporate in their budgets plans to accommodate requests for speakers, films, exhibits, or conferences. They should also be in a position to initiate such activities on special pre-selected topics. For example, these might include the "dialogue-type" conferences which would bring together Arab and American literati specialized in a particular area, such as "Arab-Western Communication." Or they can focus on Gibran Kahlil Gibran as an Arab and an American, for example.

C. The Centers should arrange and facilitate exchange visits of prominent personalities in art, literature, the press, law, etc. *from* and *to* the Arab world. Such "visits" are not to be merely or mainly for recreational purposes. Rather, they are to provide better understanding of Arabs in North America.

D. In addition to brief exchange visits, scholarships, and fellowships can make it possible for some selectees to spend longer periods of time doing research and inter-acting with the host group.

2. Since almost all Arab states have extensive dealings with the major powers, especially the United States, Western Europe and the Soviet Union, it is imperative that several research and study centers focusing on those areas and countries be established. One such center might well be set up at the Arab League or as an agency of the Arab League but at a different location, especially if research and communication facilities mandate this. It is, indeed, difficult to see how Arab states can make rational long-term policy vis-a-vis these major powers without adequate research and information being available to their leaders and policy-

makers. Such centers would also carry out extensive research activities on American politics and society, with special emphasis on the presidency, congress, political elites, the media, public opinion, and the Arab-American community. They should also establish data banks which would make available easily-retrievable information for use of researchers as well as policy-makers.

3. There is a need for establishing an Arab Research Foundation, like the Ford Foundation, with the main focus of *all* its activities to be on studies and research on Arabs, the Arab world and Arab-Western relations.[44] It should be clear that this foundation would *not* be a propaganda tool nor would it be an agency for disseminating daily information about the Arab world. It would be set up in North America to foster, encourage and support scholarly research and publication by individuals, groups, institutions, and universities — the results of which would be better and more accurate information on the Arab world which would help dispel much of the negative stereotyping and misinformation currently found in the West, particularly in North America. Such a foundation would necessarily have to be set up as an independent body run by an American board of directors composed of prominent scholars, scientists and writers interested in the Arab world and committed to better and more objective writings on Arabs, their history, culture, and politics.

Such a foundation could also encourage better writings on the Arab world by offering prizes for excellent works and honoring major contributors to a better understanding between Arabs and Americans. It could also commission and/or support the production of films and the making of audio-visual materials on the Arab world.

Since the Foundation would also be concerned with Arab-American relations, it should encourage large and long-term studies dealing with public opinion and general American attitudes toward Arabs as reflected in textbooks, the movies, television, etc.

Both the centers for the study of major powers and the Arab Research Foundation would have to function away from overt or inordinate governmental pressures in order to do their job properly and produce good results. Arab governments and philanthropic individuals should contribute to their establishment as an investment in a better future.

4. Once it is understood that propaganda and information are not synonymous, it becomes clear that reports about the Arabs need not, indeed should not, all be positive, with no mention of any blemishes or problems. The emphasis should be on presenting the Arabs in their

totality. This is not to say that faults and weaknesses need to be pointed out all the time. It *is* to say, however, that generally positive reports which refer to some weaknesses or mistakes are not only to be tolerated but encouraged since, at the very least, they carry much greater credibility than efforts at white-washing all Arab activity.

Also, it is far more effective to present a positive view of one's accomplishments and aims than to dwell on a negative view of the enemy and its activities. In other words, *the focus should be on the Arabs*, not on their opponents. Also, audiences want to know what Arabs have to offer by way of *solutions*, and not merely what they say to refute what the Zionists/Israelis do or say. In this respect, recent tentative efforts by the Arab League to formulate positive aims are commendable and should be encouraged and made more elaborate and explicit. Such principles, examples of which follow, should form the basis for *all* information efforts.

A. Palestine is the crux of the Middle East problem and no Middle East peace is possible without finding a solution for it. There needs to be general acceptance of Palestinian rights to self-determination and a homeland and of the Palestine Liberation Organization as the sole legitimate representative of the Palestinians.

B. Arabs want peace but Israel is forcing the conflict and war to continue by refusing to withdraw from the occupied territories and by frustrating the hopes and desires of the Palestinians. The Arabs have confirmed their desire for peace, most recently through the Fez plan.

C. Arab efforts at social and economic development are part of the Arab peace initiative.

D. Arab civilization has made major contributions to world, that is human, civilization. This needs to become better known.

E. Peace is achieved through constructive dialogue and accurate information.[45]

These general principles should serve as the guidelines and the framework for whatever specific plans are forwarded or information campaigns carried out. They are also the main points that need to be conveyed to an audience, whatever the topic of discussion. Such discussion should focus on the essentials rather than on details which are easily forgotten, or on the opposing Israeli plans or actions, which are thereby unwittingly reinforced.

5. So far as the target audience is concerned, the evidence indicates

that, even in democracies such as the United States or Canada, the leaders decide foreign policy issues and these decisions are then followed by an after-the-fact approval by the public. Therefore, the focus should be on the politically influential. Within government, these are the President and his White House staff, the State and Defense Departments, and the Congress. Ouside the government, the major media agencies, i.e. the major television networks, especially CBS, NBC and ABC; the *Washington Post* and the *New York Times* and the press corps of the influential media generally — all these exercise much influence in public opinion formation.

As for the American public itself, the information effort is likely to be more productive if it concentrates on certain sectors of the population. Thus, non-Whites generally, and Blacks and Hispanics specifically, are likely to be more responsive. Furthermore, the established church groups have also shown greater concern for an equitable solution to the Palestine question and a fair hearing of the Arab case.[46] American labor unions as well as teachers' and lawyers' groups are influential and should be approached. Among voluntary groups, public affairs and service clubs as well as organizations such as the Chamber of Commerce, Rotary and Kiwanis, and the different Foreign Affairs groups, are important policy-molders.

In addition, one of the main targets should be the Arab-American community. Arab-Americans need to survey their members, coordinate the activities of their different groups, and mobilize the community to advance its own interests. In doing so, they can also form political alliances with like-minded groups, especially from among the Blacks and Hispanics. Obviously, regular and on-going public opinion surveys would be most helpful in identifying potential allies and possible problem areas — and how to overcome them.

Arab-Americans and their supporters can play a role in attempting to influence policy by political lobbying. However, in order to do this effectively, it is necessary to have a much higher level of organization, data gathering, and financial backing. In other words, lobbying needs to be done on a full-time basis by professionals who are indeed committed to the cause, i.e. Arab-Americans and friendly groups.

6. As Chedhli Klibi, the Secretary-General of the League, has pointed out, information is only *one* of the tasks used in advancing Arab interests. In addition to information, diplomatic activity involves political, economic and military pressures. Arabs are interested in a peaceful settlement and want to avoid the military option, if possible. Therefore,

they should make better use of economic and political pressures which are quite legitimate. In fact, their effective use can make the difference between success and failure in both the information *and* political spheres — and reduce the chances of a military confrontation.

In summary, the Arab information effort for the past forty years has been uninformed and ill-informed. It has been directed in a somewhat haphazard fashion because of a lack of understanding of what "information" is, or because of a lack of interest, or because of political divisions in the Arab world, or simply because of a lack of will, since blame can easily be directed at other people and at intervening events.

However, more recently, there has emerged a real awareness of the importance of information in attaining Arab political goals. While it is true that these goals are still not very clear, nor are they equally shared by all members of the Arab League, it is still possible to vastly improve the information effort, as has been detailed above. In order to do that, Arab leaders need to emphasize, and capitalize on, what is common and positive. They also need to make a major financial investment and to show trust in individuals and groups who, though they will not merely parrot the pronouncements of government officials, are strongly dedicated to a better future for the Arabs and their countries. These actions are necessary if long-term projects are to be successfully undertaken. The alternative is the continuation of a bad and worsening situation, namely denigration of Arabs abroad, negative stereotypes, and lack of access to power centers in North America. The resultant weak political position of *all* Arab states renders them incapable of bringing about a fair and honorable solution to their number one cause: The Palestine question.

NOTES

1. See Ghassan al-Atiyeh, "The Information Role of the Arab League," in *The League of Arab States: Reality and Aspiration* (Beirut: Center for Arab Unity Studies, 1983) (Arabic), pp. 411–436, 411–412.

2. *Ibid.*, pp. 413–414.

3. Abdulrahman Abdulla Zamil, "The Effectiveness and Credibility of Arab Propaganda in the United States." Unpublished Ph.D. dissertation, University of Southern California, January, 1973, p. 60.

4. Contributions may also be donated by the public, though these have never materialized. For this and general information about the League, see Muhammad Khalil, *The Arab States and the Arab League: A Documentary Record*, 2 volumes (Beirut: Khayats, 1962).

5. Munzer F. Anabtawi, *Reflections on Israeli Propaganda Policy* (Arabic) (Beirut: PLO Research Center, 1968), p. 179.

6. From a speech by Abdul-Razzak al-Kafi, in *Resolutions of the Arab Ministers of Information, 1984* (Tunis: Arab League, 1984), p. 41. From now on, references to resolutions of the Council of Arab Ministers of Information will merely state *Resolutions* and the year in which they were taken. It should be noted that these reports were published in Cairo until 1978 and in Tunis thereafter. Unless otherwise stated, all Arab League publications cited here are in Arabic.

The above view of information is the main theme offered in justifying the proposed establishment of an International Information Services Agency. See *The Permanent Committee on Arab Information, 11–13 October, 1984*, (Tunis: Arab League, 1984). (Hereafter, this will be cited as *Permanent Committee*). However, Chadhli Klibi, the League's Secretary General, has stated that information is only one of the tools which Arabs can utilize to change their image and defend their interests and very being. See *Resolutions . . 1984*, p. 55.

7. See *Resolutions . . . 1964*, pp. 2–3; *Resolutions . . . 1970*, pp. 2–3; and *Resolutions . . . 1979*, p. 11.

8. See *Resolutions . . . 1964*, p. 9; and *Resolutions . . . 1984*, p. 52. '

9. See *Resolutions . . . 1964*, p. 1; *1979*, p. 11; *1980*, p. 10; *1981*, p. 25; *1982*, p. 40; *1983*, p. 49.

10. *Resolutions . . . 1964*, pp. 3, 4, 28; *1970*, p. 2; *1979*, p. 1.

11. *Resolutions . . . 1964*, pp. 3, 27.

12. *Resolutions . . . 1970*, p. 3.

13. *Resolutions . . . 1979*, p. 11.

14. *Resolutions . . . 1979*, p. 12; *1980*, p. 8.

15. See, for instance, the *Report on Activities of Arab League Missions, January-September, 1984* (Tunis: Arab League, 1984).

16. "Annual Report of the Arab League Office in the United States, 1983." This is a brief 6–page report and a cover letter from the director.

17. See the various monthly reports on hostile propaganda for 1983 and 1984 forwarded to Tunis by the Ottawa Arab League office.

18. These were mentioned by the Acting Secretary General of the League, Ass'ad al-Ass'ad in a speech included in *Resolutions . . . 1983*, pp. 59–62.

19. These recommendations were made at annual meetings of the Council of Arab Ministers of Information. They are listed here in the order mentioned in the paper. *Resolutions . . . 1964*, p. 17 and *1977*, p. 14 and *1979*, p. 18 and *1981*, p. 34; *1964*, p. 18; *1964*, p. 18; *1970*, p. 5 and *1977*, pp. 18–19 and *1979*, p. 16; *1977*, pp. 14–15; *1977*, p. 15 and *1981*, p. 36; *1979*, p. 17 and *1981*, p. 15 and *1982*, p. 15; *1979*, p. 19; *1979*, p. 19; *1981*, p. 20 and *1982*, p. 13.

20. Issa Ben-Rashed al-Khalifa, Resolutions . . . 1981, pp. 63–64.

21. Michel Edde, *Resolutions . . . 1982*, pp. 44–50.

22. Mohammed el-Tazi, *Resolutions . . . 1984*, pp. 46–50.

23. These four proposed plans have been discussed by different committees. See *Studies and Programs Concerning Joint Arab Activity in America* (Tunis: Arab League, 1983). Hereafter, this will be cited as *Studies and Programs*.

24. For similar views, see Tahsin M. Bashir, *The Arab Propaganda in the United States* (Beirut: PLO Research Center, 1969), pp. 31–33. (Arabic).

25. In my interview with high level officials at the Arab League in Tunis (November, 1984), there appeared to be a clear understanding of the weakness of such an approach. However, League officials are unable to change the over-all Arab situation or even the views of policy-makers in the various Arab governments on this point.

26. This injunction is apparently strictly enforced. Thus, Arab League officers have to be extremely careful not to present, or allow themselves to appear to present, any views or comments which could be interpreted as a criticism of any aspect of policy or action

by any Arab government. If that happens, even if the over-all presentation was positive and effective, the consequences for the individual involved are likely to be severe and might well endanger his or her career.

27. The non-payment of dues or contributions has been a chronic and recurrent problem at the Arab League. As early as 1968, the Permanent Committee threatened to stop meeting until the financial problem was resolved. Al-Atiyeh, *op. cit.*, pp. 432–433. The issue has been raised almost every year since 1979. See, for example, *Resolutions . . . 1979*, p. 14; *1981*, p. 39; and *1984*, pp. 22, 29.

According to some Arab League officials (Interviews, 1984), one major cause of the financial problem faced by the League today is Egypt's blocking of about thirty million dollars of League funds (including about seven million earmarked for information) following Egypt's membership suspension and the transfer of the League headquarters to Tunis.

28. For example, after Israel's effective annexation of the Golan Heights, the action was condemned and an information campaign on the issue was proposed, which also included a proposed international conference in London under the title "The Golan and Israel's Expansionist Policy." *Resolutions . . . 1982*, pp. 26–27. Other examples about Jerusalem, the West Bank, etc. can also be cited.

29. This negligence is not the result of ignorance since at least some Arab League officials are familiar with writings about the American political system and how to improve communication efforts in the U.S. As one example, see Michael W. Suleiman, "Suggestions for Improving Arab Communication and Public Relations in the West," which was delivered at a meeting at the Arab League in Cairo, Spring, 1973.

30. Mohamed Hassanein Heikal estimates that Arab countries spend approximately five hundred million dollars a year on advertisements which are mistakenly believed to be "information." See the "Discussions" of the article by al-Atiyeh, *op. cit.*, pp. 450–451.

31. See *Resolutions . . . 1981*, p. 20 and *1982*, p. 13.

32. Fayez Sayegh, as cited in Zamil, *op. cit.*, pp. 121–123.

33. See Robert Weissberg, *Public Opinion and Popular Government* (Englewood Cliffs, N.J.: Prentice-Hall, 1976), pp. 24–25; M. Abravanel and B. Hughes, "The Relationship between Public Opinion and Government Foreign Policy: A Cross-National Study," in J.McGowan, ed., *Sage International Yearbook of Foreign Policy Studies*, vol. 4 (Beverly Hills, CA: Sage Publications, 1973); and Appendix

34. For a specific Middle East-related study, see Montague Kern, *Television and Middle East Diplomacy: President Carter's Fall 1977 Peace Initiative* (Washington, D.C.: Center for Contemporary Arab Studies, Georgetown University, 1983). See also Montague Kern, Patricia W. Levering and Ralph B. Levering, *The Kennedy Crises: The Press, the Presidency and Foreign Policy* (Chapel Hill, N.C.: University of North Carolina Press, 1983).

35. On the question of significant elites and how "systematic" and "government" agendas are defined, see Robert Cobb and Charles Elder, *Participation in American Politics: The Dynamics of Agenda Building*, 2nd ed. (Baltimore, MD: Johns Hopkins University Press, 1983). On this issue, as it relates to American policy-making on the Middle East, see William B. Quandt, "Domestic Influences on U.S. Foreign Policy in the Middle East: The View from Washington," in Willard A. Beling, ed., *The Middle East: Quest for an American Policy* (Albany, N.Y.: State University of New York Press, 1973), pp. 263–285; and *United States Policy in the Middle East: Constraints and Choices* (Santa Monica, CA: The Rand Corporation, 1970). See also Robert Holmes Trice, Jr., "Domestic Political Interests and American Policy in the Middle East: Pro-Israel, Pro-Arab and Corporate Non-Governmental Actors and the Making of American Foreign Policy, 1966–71." Unpublished Ph.D. dissertation, University of Wisconsin, 1974; and "Foreign Policy Interest Groups, Mass Public Opinion and the Arab-Israeli Dispute," *Western Political Quarterly*, Vol. 31, No. 2 (June, 1978), pp. 238–252.

36. For a discussion of symbols in politics, see Murray Edelman, *The Symbolic Uses of Politics* (Champaign, Ill.: University of Illinois Press, 1967). On American public opin-

ion concerning the Middle East and the ability of Israel to capitalize on its favorable image and the Arabs' unfavorable image, see Chapters 5 and 8.

37. There is much evidence to show that foreign policy formulation is not much constrained by preferences of the mass public. See, for example, Bernard C. Cohen, *The Public's Impact on Foreign Policy* (Boston: Little, Brown, 1973); James Rosenau, "Foreign Policy as an Issue Area," in James Rosenau, ed., *Domestic Sources of Foreign Policy* (New York: Free Press, 1967), pp. 31–47; Barry B. Hughes, *The Domestic Context of American Foreign Policy* (San Francisco: W.H. Freeman, 1978); Abravanel and Hughes, *op. cit.*; and Cobb and Elder, *op. cit.*

38. Examples of specific conferences proposed in the past few years are: Jerusalem and its future (*Resolutions . . . 1979*, p. 15; *1980*, p. 10; *1981*, p. 28; *1982*, p. 20; *1983*, pp. 22–23); the image of the Arabs in communications media (*1979*, p. 15; *1980*, p. 10); the conditions of Arabs in the occupied territories (*1979*, p. 15; *1980*, p. 8); Zionist designs on South Lebanon (*1979*, p. 15); the Camp David Accords and Palestinian rights (*1979*, p. 2; *1980*, p. 8; *1982*, p. 20); nuclear armament in the Middle East (*1982*, p. 19); the Golan Heights and Israeli expansionist policy (*1982*, p. 27); Israeli settlements (*1983*, p. 23), etc.

39. Al-Atiyeh, *op. cit.*, p. 434.

40. *Ibid.* pp. 426, 431.

41. The list is included in a memo detailing the duties of League missions abroad for 1984. The 1983 memo requested two additional 3–monthly reports!

42. See *Permanent Committee, op. cit.* Almost two-thirds of this document (i.e. 67 pages) are devoted to the presentation of this proposal.

43. Zamil recommends this and states that it was proposed by Libya in February, 1969. Zamil, *op. cit.*, p. 263. A similar proposal is contained in Plan A above. See *Studies and Programs, op. cit.*

44. A similar proposal was made about fifteen years ago. See Michael W. Suleiman, "The Repatriation of Arab Elites," *Middle East Forum*, Vol 47, Nos. 3 & 4 (Autumn & Winter, 1971), pp. 71–81.

45. *Permanent Committee . . 1984*, p. 3 of Part I.

46. See Basheer K. Nijim, ed., *American Church Politics and the Middle East* (Belmont, MA: Association of Arab-American University Graduates, 1982).

CHAPTER 10

Conclusion:
The Feasibility of Arab-American Dialogue

The evidence is clear, then, that American views of Arabs are quite negative and, furthermore, that the roots of prejudice are deep and well-entrenched. As we have seen, many factors are responsible for this regrettable state of affairs — and these factors tend generally to reinforce each other, with the consequence that the over-all picture is even worse than the sum of its various parts. In fact, apart from a temporary and slight but measurable improvement in the early 1980's (during the Israeli invasion of Lebanon),[1] and despite a more intensified effort by the Arab-American community, American views and orientations toward Arabs are as bad today as they have ever been. Under such circumstances, it is little wonder that hardly any protests have been voiced in the United States against the Reagan Administration for its attacks, both verbal and physical, on Arabs in general and the Libyan regime in particular.[2] Furthermore, the heightened tension and increased verbal violence against "Arab" terrorists has created an atmosphere that is, at the very least, tolerant of terrorism which is directed against Americans of Arab descent. Thus, while the killing of Leon Klinghoffer on the *Achille Lauro* was repeatedly and intensely condemned as a despicable crime, very little reporting and even less condemnation was evident following the killing of Alex Odeh in California.[3] Sadder still is the fact that, despite repeated and incontrovertible evidence of the negative stereotyping of Arabs in the United States, most Americans, including much of the educated elite, are unaware of the problem and often deny that such a problem exists[4] — which makes it very difficult, if not impossible, to find a solution.

A pertinent question presents itself: Is a solution possible? A solution, needless to say, will necessitate addressing the real causes. Many

183

of those active in combating the negative Arab image in America have concentrated their efforts on political lobbying, especially against the powerful Zionist/Israeli groups and propaganda apparatus. The media, therefore, become the primary target of a campaign whose central premise is that the American public is being systematically and deliberately kept uninformed or misinformed about Arabs, Muslims, Palestinians, etc., mainly, if not solely, because of inordinate Zionist influence in the press and on the air waves. The corollary to this is the further assumption that public officials, the press corps, and the public in general are being forced to put up with this undesirable and *undesired* situation, and once the truth is known and Americans are free to openly adhere to it, they will gladly do so.

There is no question that the Zionist lobby is powerful and very successful in conveying its point of view as well as in securing much support from the media and decision-makers alike. However, as our earlier discussion has shown, a good part of the success of Zionist/Israeli efforts in the information field is the fact that the public is already pre-disposed not to accept the Arab point of view and that many public officials, rightly or wrongly, see in the Zionist movement and the state of Israel an asset in the advancement of American interests in the area. Under such circumstances, therefore, the Arab counter-campaign is not likely to meet with great success if it *merely* targets the media and the Zionist lobby. Such an effort is definitely needed, but it has to be part of an over-all strategy which delineates what is and is not feasible and effective.

"Stereotypes should not be thought of as causative, but as symptomatic." This is the conclusion reached by William Buchanan and Hadley Cantril in their pioneering study on *How Nations See Each Other*. It follows, therefore, that if Americans view Arabs in negative terms, it is because they feel that "these people [e.g. Arabs] threaten us, they have fought against us . . . we cannot understand what they say, hence they *must* be cruel, conceited, domineering, etc."[5]

What is it, then, about Arabs, Muslims, or Arabism which makes them a threat to the United States? Is it possible to remove such threatening conditions and bring about an improvement in relations and perceptions? As was discussed earlier, Arabs (or at least most Arabs) are part of a larger group, namely Muslims. Also, Americans (or at least most Americans) are part of a larger group, namely Christians and Westerners. For over a thousand years, there have been contacts— sometimes friendly, sometimes unfriendly— between the two groups, that is Arabs/Muslims and Americans/Christians/Westerners. These old encounters impact on the two groups today on the basis of the kind of relationship, friendly or otherwise, they have. To quote Buchanan and Cantril again: "The raw material from which stereotypes are formed may be transmitted from generation to generation and may be absorbed by a child before he realizes what a 'nation' or a 'people' is. But the manner in which these materials are combined at any moment to produce a pleasant or an unpleasant image apparently will vary with the current state of relations between the governments of the two peoples."[6]

So stereotypes are flexible — or at least more flexible than is generally assumed. This, indeed, is also the case in terms of American views and orientations toward Arabs and Muslims. It is clear from the public opinion data as well as content analysis studies that, while American attitudes toward Arabs and Muslims are generally negative, they are also clearly more negative and definitely more hostile vis-a-vis certain Arabs and specific groups of Muslims.[7] This is also reflected in statements by American public officials who differentiate between moderate (i.e. good) Arabs and Muslims on the one hand and radical (i.e. bad) Arabs and Muslims on the other. During this century, and especially since World War II, Americans have generally viewed radical or revolutionary Arab regimes and movements as hostile and inimical to American interests. Similar negative orientations have been manifested toward integrative Arab nationalism, the Palestine national movement, and radical Muslim groupings or "resurgent Islam." On the other hand, local or country nationalism in specific Arab states, "establishment Islam", and Palestinians willing to accept a settlement short of a sovereign state are deemed non-threatening and, therefore, viewed positively.[8] Sometimes, however, the stereotypes are so strong that decision-makers fail to see a real change in the situation. Such was the case, for instance, when Anwar Sadat succeeded Gamal Abdel-Nasser as president of Egypt and began to signal the United States that he wanted to reorient Egypt and its people from Arab nationalism to Egyptian patriotism. It was not until *after* the 1973 war that the United States clearly recognized the message and began to view Sadat's Egypt as a potential ally and, therefore, to view it and its people favorably.

American-Arab relations, as we have seen, are multi-faceted and complicated by factors relating to perceived national interests, cultural/religious differences, and a historical legacy that was conflictual at times. It is even more seriously complicated by the fact that Arabs are not united in one state and that, as Muslims, (and most Americans think the two terms are synonymous), they suffer from bad publicity any time there is conflict between the U.S. and any Muslim country. On the other hand, the positive image of some Arab or Islamic countries does not automatically transfer to "the Arabs," either because it is not sufficiently positive or because the positive image is specific to a leader or a country friendly to America. Thus, the highly positive image of Anwar Sadat, especially after his Jerusalem visit, and the Egyptian-Israeli treaty and Camp David agreements, caused some (though not equivalent) change for the better in American views of Egypt and Egyptians. However, American views of Arabs remained basically the same, especially as most Arabs disagreed with and often condemned the very policies and activities which made Sadat so very popular in the United States and the West generally.[9]

What can be done to reverse the confrontation between the Arabs and the United States? Is Arab-American (or Arab-Western) dialogue possible and, if it is attempted, will it be fruitful? A meaningful and productive dialogue is possible only between two equals; the two parties to the dialogue should view each other as equals or at least not inordinately unequal. Furthermore, they should have mutual or shared interests. In other words, they need to have a symbiotic relationship in which they are interdependent on each other. A parasitic relationship in which one derives nourishment and sustenance from the other is not conducive to a proper dialogue.

The problem we face here is that, while it is possible to identify many mutual or shared interests between Arabs and the United States, the Arabs are not one unit and most certainly do not speak with one voice; neither do the various parts seek similar objectives, let alone the same objective. If they were fully integrated, or if they evidenced a moderate unity of purpose at least, then a dialogue with the United States would be possible. This was the situation, for instance, when president Gamal Abdel-Nasser was at the height of his popularity and power as the recognized leader of Arab nationalism in the 1950's. At that time, the United States began to look for ways to have a dialogue with the proponents of Arab nationalism—even though, in the end, the attempt failed or was frustrated.[10] Also, in the 1970's the Carter administration sought to have a dialogue with the Palestine Liberation Organization when the PLO was at the height of its popularity, power, and prestige.[11]

Dialogue is possible then, even between enemies. Any dialogue, however, is more likely to be successful if the two parties share a common heritage or similar value systems. If they do not, and if one side lacks respect for the other or looks down upon its people as inferior, then the discussions take place with much reluctance and the whole exercise is viewed as a necessary evil at best, to be abandoned if a better alternative presents itself. Such was the fate of the two attempts at dialogue with Nasser and with the PLO. In both cases, the weakening of the Arab side obviated the need for the United States to have a proper dialogue and establish a close relationship with them. Furthermore, President Lyndon Johnson's personal antipathy toward Nasser and his lack of understanding of, and sympathy for, the Arabs lessened the chances of a dialogue even more. The same is true, but even more strongly, in the case of President Ronald Reagan and his administration's attitude toward the PLO and Arabs generally. [12]

Individual countries in the Arab world are too weak in comparison to the United States and often too dependent on the latter to be able to carry on a proper dialogue, especially since they do not have much support from powerful groups within the U.S. to provide additional leverage. Consequently, even Arab countries friendly to the United States have great difficulty in securing the economic or military support they need. In fact, Arab-European dialogue has a better chance at success, exactly because West European countries, unlike the United States, are not superpowers; because they are more dependent on Arab economic and energy resources; because their images of the Arabs/Muslims are at times less negative than those in the U.S.; and because pro-Israeli sentiments and pressures are not as great. Here again, however, a more unified Arab approach has a better chance to succeed.

The bad press, the negative stereotypes, the Zionist and other lobbying and pressure groups — all contribute to the frustration of a good relationship between Arabs and Americans. However, in the end, these are contributing and secondary factors. The most important criterion is whether or not the two sides see each other in friendly or threatening terms. In the past, issues which have been quintessentially Arab — that is, of concern to the Arab world as a whole (such as Arab nationalism, anti-colonialism, Palestine and the Palestinian national movement) have been ones causing conflict between the Arabs and the U.S. While there is nothing inherently anti-American about *any* of these issues, the other factors cited above are likely to intervene to make sure that these or other issues become a major source of conflict between Arabs and Americans. Most importantly, as long as the Palestine and Arab-Israeli conflicts remain unresolved, Zionist forces will use any and all resources at their disposal (including negative media campaigns against Arabs, and political pressures on public officials) to get the United States to accept, adopt, and implement a view of the "national interest" which identifies as a serious threat any Arab party, group, government or movement which is perceived to be a threat to Israel. Thus far, they have been very successful indeed — never more so, in fact, than in the past several years since the Reagan administration came to power. While the predispositions, predilections, and psychological make-up of President Reagan and his two secretaries of state have had much to do with this development, these officials would certainly have had to consider other alternatives if the Arabs were more united and if they were able to present a strong and definite stand on the main issues.

Under such circumstances, what can be done to improve Arab-American relations as well as mutual perceptions? Obviously, for those, on both sides, who see an inevitable and irreconcilable clash between Arabs and Americans, and for those among the Zionists and Israelis who favor this clash for their own ends, nothing can or should be done to improve the situation. However, if both sides are desirous of a friendly and cooperative relationship, then accommodation through dialogue may be sought. In preparation for this, each side can discuss or review the situation to show that the attainment of its objective(s) does not necessarily mean the non-achievement of the other side's objective(s).[13] In other words, this is *not* a zero-sum game. In fact, it is certainly possible to argue that a non-solution is more dangerous and costly to all sides than a negotiated settlement.[14] Unfortunately, both sides have had major difficulty reaching this stage, in part because of the many factors discussed above. In any case, a dialogue requires two interested and, hopefully, committed partners. Arabs have found it difficult, at times extremely difficult, to get the United States to change its views on Middle East issues and peoples. In order for them to do so successfully, it is necessary to demonstrate to American officials in a persuasive manner that American interests would be better served if a different course of action was followed. The proposed approach should, at a minimum, push for even-handedness in American dealings with Arabs and Israelis, pointing out the dangers of total American identification with, and commitment to, Israel. It should also point out the need for America to have an amicable relationship with the Arab world, and to avoid resorting to confrontation and violence. Furthermore, it can and should be persuasively argued that an equitable solution of the Palestine question, including self-determination for the Palestinians, rather than posing a threat to American interests, safeguards and even advances those interests. In the United States, as elsewhere, what constitutes the national interest and how the country proceeds to advance its interest, are issues over which there are many difterences of opinion and much discussion. Within the U.S., therefore, what needs to be changed is the elites' views of the national interest concerning the Middle East and how to advance those interests.[15]

NOTES

1. Roger Morris, "Beirut — and the Press — under Siege," *Columbia Journalism Review* (Nov.-Dec., 1982), pp. 23–33.

2. One of the few exceptions is Claudia Wright, *The Politics of Liquidation: The Reagan Administration Policy Toward the Arabs* (Belmont, MA: Association of Arab-American University Graduates, 1986).

3. This situation has been the source of much bitterness among Arab-Americans, as reflected in the various publications of Arab-American associations.

4. This lack of awareness is in itself an indication of the extent of ignorance or blindness to the main issues, especially as they relate to Arabs and Muslims. Non-awareness of distortion and bias was one of the findings of the Middle East Studies Association Committee on Middle East Images, as reflected in its various reports.

5. William Buchanan and Hadley Cantril, *How Nations See Each Other* (Urbana, Ill.: University of Illinois Press, 1953), pp. 57–58.

6. *Ibid.*, p. 94.

7. See Richard H. Curtiss, *A Changing Image: American Perceptions of the Arab-Israeli Dispute* (Washington, D.C.: American Educational Trust, 1986), second edition; and Shelley Slade, "The Image of the Arab in America: Analysis of a Poll on American Attitudes," *The Middle East Journal*, Vol. 35, No. 2 (Spring, 1981), pp. 143–162.

8. See Wright, *op. cit.*, p. 1; and James A. Bill, "Resurgent Islam," *Foreign Affairs*, Vol. 63, No. 1 (Fall, 1984), pp. 108–127.

9. See Appendix; and Seymour Martin Lipset, "The Polls on the Middle East," *Middle East Review*, Vol. XI, No. 1 (Fall, 1978), pp. 24–30. See also, Doreen Kays, *Frogs and Scorpions: Egypt, Sadat and the Media* (London: Frederick Muller, 1984), although Kays tends to inflate the increase in Arab popularity as a result of Sadat's activities.

10. Henry William Brands, Jr., "What Eisenhower and Dulles Saw in Nasser: Personalities and Interests in U.S.-Egyptian Relations," *American-Arab Affairs*, No. 17 (Summer, 1986), pp. 44–54; and Malcolm Kerr, " 'Coming to Terms with Nasser': Attempts and Failures," *International Affairs*, Vol. 43, No. 1 (Jan., 1967), pp. 65–84.

11. Jimmy Carter, *Keeping Faith: Memoirs of a President* (New York: Bantam, 1983).

12. Donald Neff, "Libya and the United States," *American-Arab Affairs*, No. 17 (Summer, 1986), pp. 1–10.

13. On the Palestinian side, Walid Khalidi did this in his "Thinking the Unthinkable: A Sovereign Palestinian State," *Foreign Affairs*, Vol. 56, No.4 (July, 1978), pp. 695–713. Needless to say, unity among the Palestinians is essential for any successful dialogue with the United States.

14. Seth P. Tillman, *The United States in the Middle East: Interests and Obstacles* (Bloomington, IN: Indiana University Press, 1982).

15. This is the argument which is presented most persuasively by Cheryl A. Rubenberg, *Israel and the American National Interest: A Critical Examination* (Urbana, IL: University of Illinois Press, 1986).

APPENDIX

Trends in Public Support for Egypt and Israel, 1956–1978
(co-authored with Shanto Iyengar)

The importance of the Middle East in international politics has been
widely recognized (Fisher, 1971: 21-22; Glubb, 1971). United States'
interests in the area are immense and multifaceted. From the early work
of the missionaries and philanthropists in the nineteenth century to the
present concern about oil and geopolitics, United States involvements
in the Middle East have greatly expanded in number and complexity
(DeNovo, 1963; American Enterprise Institute, 1968; Congressional
Quarterly, 1977). Particularly since the end of World War II when the
United States emerged as a super power, the Middle East loomed as
an area of major American interest. Britain and France, greatly
weakened by the war, demonstrated their inability to protect Western
interests in the Middle East and were replaced by the United States
as the dominant force in an effort to "contain" the Soviet advance there.

While this is not the place to provide a detailed account of United
States involvement in the Middle East, it is helpful to present a brief
summary of American Middle Eastern policies in the past thirty years,
especially as these relate to the so-called Arab-Israeli conflict. The U.S.
role in the creation of Israel in 1948 was decisive (Truman, 1956:
143-169; Campbell, 1975), and alienated much of the Arab world, thus
ushering in a long period of difficult, often acrimonious, relations between the United States and the Arabs who had until then been favorably
disposed to America. Since then, U.S. actions in the area have been
motivated by the following major concerns:

First is preoccupation with the Soviet presence and influence in
the area. Second is the commitment to Israel's security and well-

being. Third is the fact that the Middle East contains nearly two
thirds of the known reserves of petroleum in the world [Quandt,
1977: 9].

Other major concerns include the avoidance of a nuclear confrontation
with the Soviet Union triggered by conflicts in the Middle East, as well
as the creation of stable conditions and the support of moderate regimes
friendly to the United States. The pursuit of these objectives has proved
difficult since progress in one area often undermines policies and actions in one or more of the other areas. For instance, the massive
American airlift of arms to Israel in October, 1973 and the large Israeli
aid bill of $2.2 billion proposed by President Nixon in 1973 prompted
the Arab response of an oil embargo against the United States.

Despite the massive American interests in the Middle East and the
significant involvement of the United States in the conflict between Israel
and the Arab states, the views of the American public concerning the
Middle East and United States policy toward the region have yet to
be investigated. Indicative of this scholarly neglect is the absence of any
question pertaining to the Middle East in the biennial opinion surveys
conducted by the Survey Research Center. The research reported here
attempts to correct this lack of interest by analyzing the level of congruence between American public images of the two principal combatants in the Middle East, namely Israel and Egypt, and American
policy toward the two nations over the past 22 years. Group variations
in American images of Israel and Egypt are also investigated.

The Relevance of Public Opinion to U.S. Middle Eastern Policy

While we argue that mass attitudes about the Middle East are worthy
of investigation, several caveats are in order. Foreign policy issues are
traditionally not a source of partisan conflict in the United States
(Pomper, 1975: 158–159). Moreover, it is well known that foreign policy
issues tend to be of low importance (Weissberg, 1976: 172–176; Miller
and Miller, 1977), and that public awareness of foreign affairs is minimal
(Gamson and Modigliani, 1966; Robinson, 1967; Smith, 1972; Glenn,
1972). Foreign policy preferences are thus relatively unstable (Converse,
1964: 240; Converse and Markus, 1979: 40) and tend to vary according to question format (Lipset and Schneider, 1977b). On the basis of
such evidence, most researchers have concluded that foreign policy

formulation is relatively unconstrained by mass policy preferences (see Almond, 1950; Miller and Stokes, 1963; Rosenberg, 1965; Rosenau, 1967; Cohen, 1973: 9–20; Hughes, 1978: 88–116; Abravanel and Hughes, 1973, 1975; Spanier and Uslaner, 1978: 98–102). As Converse, for example, has put it:

> Clearly, in foreign affairs, decision-makers are not convinced that the mass public has sufficient information to pass worthwhile judgement, and few of us who have had any contact with opinion surveys would dare say them nay [1963: 41].

Public approval or disapproval of foreign policies is nonetheless an important restraint on policy makers. As Weissberg and others have pointed out, opinion-policy linkage can take the form of an "after-the-fact-approval" model (Weissberg, 1976: 24–25; Nadel, 1972; Barton, 1974; Abravanel and Hughes, 1973). Policies that arouse large scale controversy and opposition (and which therefore endanger the reelection of elected officials), such as United States military involvement in Vietnam, are likely to be revised or terminated. After-the-fact-approval is realistic, for the direction of governmental policy can be influenced by mass policy preferences, yet the public is absolved "from making difficult, complex evaluations of policy impact" (Weissberg, 1976: 24).

Additional support may be derived from recent work in opinion consistency and issue voting. Nie et al., (1976), Pomper (1975) and others have demonstrated that since 1964, Americans have become increasingly sensitive to political issues and more ideological or consistent, in their issue opinions. Issue opinions also appear to be growing in importance as determinants of voting behavior (Repass, 1971; Pomper, 1972; Miller and Miller, 1975). While there is considerable doubt that the above findings represent a stable trend (Miller and Miller, 1977; Bishop et al., 1978), it may no longer be appropriate to dismiss foreign policy issues as nonsalient. This is especially so with regard to United States Middle Eastern policy given the importance of the Middle East as a major source of United States energy supplies and the growing role of the United States as an arbitrator in the Middle Eastern conflict. In addition, United States Middle Eastern policy is increasingly a source of partisan conflict as illustrated by the acrimonious debate over the recent arms sale package to Israel, Saudi Arabia, and Egypt.

Nothwithstanding the evidence concerning the growth of issue voting, it is still apparent that survey items which attempt to elicit specific policy preferences face the danger of being contaminated by "nonattitudes" and other sources of error. In this report, therefore, we steer clear of specific policy opinions and examine instead the level of public affection for the two major participants in the Middle Eastern conflict — Egypt and Israel. Specifically, we propose to investigate relative affect for the two nations — the extent to which one nation is favored over the other. Relative affect is then used as an indirect and approximate indicator of the public's policy preferences. For example, it is reasonable to infer, from a distribution of affect which clearly favors Israel over Egypt, that the public will approve of policies which align the United States with Israel in opposition to Egypt. Conversely, an alternative distribution of affect, under which the two nations are equally supported, suggests a preference for policies which are equally responsive to the demands of both nations, i.e., a policy of neutrality. In short, the congruence of opinion and policy is viewed indirectly, through the level of public support for Israel and Egypt.

Our specific objectives in this essay are as follows. First, we assess the level of public support for Israel and Egypt between 1956 and 1978. Second, the analysis compares trends in United States economic and military aid to the two nations with trends in public images of the two nations so as to assess congruence between changes in United States Middle Eastern policy and changes in public support for Israel and Egypt. Finally, the analysis investigates group differences in support for the two nations.

The Data

The data consist of cross-sectional surveys of the American electorate administered in 1956, 1966, 1967, 1973, 1974, 1975, 1976, 1977, and 1978. The 1974, 1975, and 1977 data are drawn from the National Opinion Research Center's Annual General Social Survey.[1] The remaining surveys were conducted by the Gallup Organization (AIPO Surveys 576, 738, 754, 868, 954, forthcoming).[2] The Gallup polls and N.O.R.C. surveys both use personal interviews and a probability sample of the voting age population. Sample size for all nine time points is approximately 1500.

All nine surveys contain the "Stapel Scalometer," an item designed to measure general evaluations of foreign nations. Egypt and Israel are among the nations included (Israel was excluded from the 1973 survey.)

The data set is complete in that it includes every survey containing the scalometer items administered in the United States between 1956 and 1978.

Scalometer ratings range from minus five to plus five. The exact wording of the question in the interview schedule is given below.

> You will notice that the boxes on this card go from the highest position of plus five for a country which you like very much to the lowest position of minus five for a country you dislike very much. How far up the scale or how far down the scale would you rate the following countries?

Since scalometers are single-item indicators, it is difficult to gauge their reliability. The wording of the item, however, strengthens the assumption that the responses reflect genuine evaluations of the nations. Since the scalometers use a general attitude object — the name of the country — responses do no require a substantial degree of political sophistication and awareness. The scalometer ratings are thus not likely to be contaminated by response error (for further discussion of this problem see Robinson, 1967). An additional advantage of the scalometers is that they focus on individual countries. Other items used to assess American public opinion toward the Middle Eastern conflict refer to the "Arabs" or "Arab states" — at best a highly ambiguous stimulus. The Gallup and Harris Polls, for example, have frequently asked this question: "As far as the Middle East situation is concerned, do you feel more sympathy with Israel or with the Arab countries?" In short, while the scalometers tap a general orientation, they do present the respondent with an unambiguous and recognizable stimulus.

Scalometer Ratings of Israel and Egypt, 1956–1978

The mean scalometer rating for the two countries at all nine time points is shown in Table 1.[3] The scores have been reflected so as to range from zero (minus 5) to nine (plus five). Also shown is the mean difference score (obtained by subtracting the rating of Egypt from the rating of Israel). The difference score can range from minus nine to plus nine, positive scores indicating higher affect for Israel, negative scores indicating higher affect for Egypt. Finally, Table 1 also shows the percent of the sample who rate the two nations positively, i.e., the sum of the plus one through plus five responses.

TABLE 1

MEAN SCALOMETER SCORES FOR EGYPT AND ISRAEL

	12/1956	12/1966	12/1967	4/1973	3/1974	3/1975	7/1976	3/1977	4/1978
Mean rating of Egypt	3.83 (.08)*	4.60 (.04)	3.92 (.07)	3.96 (.06)	4.36 (.07)	4.18 (.06)	4.48 (.05)	4.76 (.06)	4.41 (.07)
Mean rating of Israel	5.23 (.07)	5.54 (.03)	5.71 (.06)	—	5.60 (.07)	5.28 (.07)	5.50 (.06)	5.55 (.07)	5.27 (.07)
Mean Difference	1.40 (.09)	.94 (.04)	1.79 (.08)	—	1.24 (.08)	1.10 (.07)	1.02 (.05)	.79 (.07)	.86 (.06)
% positive toward Egypt	31	46	39	37	48	45	49	51	45
% positive toward Israel	51	64	74	—	68	62	66	64	59
N	1543	2851	1583	1528	1484	1490	1544	1530	1520

* The standard error of the difference score is given in parentheses.

It is apparent that Israel enjoys a positive image which has remained highly stable over time. The mean scalometer score for Israel in 1956 is almost exactly equal to the mean score for 1978. The mean rating of Israel is consistently over 5.0 (plus one on the original scale). More importantly, the distribution of the difference score indicates that Israel is viewed more positively than Egypt. The segment of the public rating Israel over Egypt ranges from 55 per cent (in 1956) to 40 per cent (in 1977) whereas those favoring Egypt constitute a smaller group, ranging in size from twelve to eighteen per cent.

Even though Israel's image has remained stable, the magnitude of the difference between the two ratings has clearly narrowed. This is the result of a steady upward trend (since 1967) in the rating of Egypt. In 1967 the percentage of the public rating Israel positively is almost double the percentage rating Egypt positively. By 1978, however, this disparity has been reduced to 14%. Between 1967 and 1978, the mean difference score has been more than halved.

Table 1 also shows that the public's image of Israel, though generally positive, was demonstrably less positive on three different occasions — 1956, 1975, and 1978. It is instructive that every one of these periods was marked by public and rather intense differences of opinion between the United States government and the State of Israel. Thus, in 1956, the Eisenhower Administration was instrumental in securing U.N. condemnation of the British-French-Israeli attack on Egypt and the passage of the resolution calling for the troops of these countries to withdraw from Egyptian territory. When Israel showed some resistance, President Eisenhower applied relentless pressure on the Jewish state to force compliance (Eisenhower, 1965). In any case, the American public was apparently aware of these differences. In 1975, after successfully negotiating two disengagement agreements by mid–1974 between Israel and Egypt and Israel and Syria, Secretary of State Henry Kissinger, anxious to keep up the peace momentum and show "moderate" Arab regimes such as Egypt and Saudi Arabia that their "moderation" and friendship with the United States could pay off, attempted to obtain a second Sinai disengagement agreement. However, it soon became clear that the Israelis were not as flexible or forthcoming as Kissinger and the Ford Administration hoped or thought they should be. The failure of Kissinger's attempt at shuttle diplomacy in March, 1975, resulted in the anouncement by President Ford that the United States was "reassessing" its policy toward the Middle East. It was clear to all, and was so reported in the press, that the reassessment was aimed at Israel. Thus, American-Israeli relations were clearly and publicly strained during this period (Sheehan, 1976: 165).

The 1978 poll came almost six months after President Anwar Sadat's "historic" trip to Israel. As a result of this dramatic gesture, Sadat has been generally viewed as sincerely desiring peace and, consequently, that Israel should reciprocate with a similarly major concession. When the Begin government did not live up to this expectation, disagreements between the Carter Administration and the Israeli government, particularly Premier Menachem Begin, became public knowledge, and charges and counter-charges were exchanged concerning what agreements, if any, were reached privately but were later broken. These differences were further exacerbated when President Carter announced his intentions of selling sophisticated war planes to Egypt, Saudi Arabia, and Israel as a package deal. When the Gallup survey was conducted in April, 1978, the debate had become a major controversy. Thus, it was reported that a high White House official claimed that Prime Minister Begin himself had to be replaced if peace in the Middle East was to have a chance; on the other side, Jewish and pro-Israeli groups were publicly accusing the Carter Administration of being anti-Semitic, or at the very least, of deliberately wanting to scuttle Israel's "special relationship" with the United States (Southerland, 1978).

Thus on all three occasions the decrease in support for Israel suggests after-the-fact-approval of United States Middle Eastern policy. The public seems to have been susceptible to the views of the administration in office as it aired its differences with the various Israeli governments. Further support for this contention may be gleaned from the fact that the public's support for Egypt was lowest in 1956, the period when the United States had its sharpest differences with the Nasser regime.

As noted above, the scalometer ratings of Egypt have changed considerably over the twenty-two year period.[4] Between 1956 and 1966, the mean rating of Egypt increases by .77, the largest increase between two contiguous time points for the entire period. Between 1966 and 1967, however, the rating drops precipitously. After 1967, the series for Egypt exhibits a steady increase. By 1977, the mean difference score is only .79, as compared to 1.79 in 1967. These are striking results and suggest that by 1977, Americans were only marginally favorable toward Israel. In terms of the 1977 difference score, the largest group of respondents (41%) rate both nations equally.

The major decrease in public hostility toward Egypt between 1956 and 1966 is also indicative of after-the-fact-approval of United States policy. Thus, after the tensions of 1956–1958, an atmosphere of accommodation and friendliness prevailed until about 1965 (Badeau, 1968; Nutting, 1972). This improvement in relations and attitudes was enhanced by the minimal number of violent conflicts between Egypt and Israel during this period (Khouri, 1968: 219). It may be recalled that United Nations troops (UNEF) were stationed along the border between the two countries following the withdrawal of the armies of Britain, France, and Israel from Egyptian soil until May, 1967, when Egypt requested their removal. Relations between Egypt and the United States were at their worst in this century just prior to and during the 1967 Middle Eastern war (Stookey, 1975; Bryson, 1977). In that war, Egypt accused the United States of collusion with the Israelis, and even of actual participation in the fighting on the side of Israel. This explains the marked decline in public sympathy for Egypt between 1966 and 1967. The period between 1967 and 1973 was characterized by an Egyptian determination to regain lost territory by political or military means. In the United States, first the Johnson and then the Nixon Administration supported Israel's hold on the vast territories it captured in the 1967 war until such a time that the Arabs (including Egypt) agreed to an overall peace settlement acceptable to the Israelis (Safran, 1978).

The noticeable improvement in Egypt's image (11%) between 1973 and 1974 can be traced to President Sadat's actions and pronouncements during and after the 1973 war which began to mark him as a "reasonable" Arab leader in the view of American policy makers. This, combined with his sharp public break with the Soviet leadership (his erstwhile friends and arms suppliers) provided the right opportunity for the United States to woo him. Pictures of Sadat and Kissinger in friendly embrace appeared frequently in the American media and the public began to get the message that the Nixon Administration viewed Sadat as quite friendly, if not yet fully a friend of the United States.

Since 1974 there is no question that American policy toward Egypt has become more positive. Richard Nixon in the latter years of his Presidency, Gerald Ford, and Jimmy Carter have treated Egypt's Anwar Sadat as a friendly, cooperative, moderate, and flexible leader who should be supported. As an indication of this approval, Nixon visited the Middle East, including Egypt in June, 1974 and was enthusiastically welcomed by the Egyptians. This was the first official visit by an American president to Egypt. Promises of American aid were announced including a nuclear reactor for peaceful energy uses. President Ford continued the policy of closer relations with Egypt and so has President Carter, especially since Sadat's "peace mission" to Jerusalem in November, 1977 and the Camp David Accords of November, 1978.

The 1977 poll was taken six months before Sadat's dramatic Jerusalem visit and the 1978 survey was carried out five months after that event. Yet it is clear that the American public image of Egypt became slightly more negative following Sadat's peace initiative. Why did this happen? Previous research on national images suggests an explanation for this apparent anomaly. Work by Abravanel and Hughes (1973, 1975) and by Deutsch and Merritt (1965) demonstrates that images of foreign nations depend on the long-term pattern of interaction between nations.[5] Since Egypt and the United States have experienced a largely conflictual pattern of interaction over an extended period (1952–1973), attitudes learned by the American public toward Egypt tend to be unfriendly. Conversely, American-Israeli relations from 1948 until at least 1974 have been consistently cooperative and friendly. As Deutsch and Merritt note (1965: 183), "almost nothing in the world seems to shift the images of forty percent of the population in most countries, even within one or two decades." A spectacular event, such as the Sadat trip to Jerusalem, might *temporarily* move some attitudes, but most attitudes "persist, or return at least part of the way toward their previous state, once the immediate external pressures slacken" (Deutsch and Merritt, 1965: 183). The Sadat trip, despite being a dramatic event which was extensively covered by the American media, thus did not noticeably raise the level of public support for Egypt. Five months after the Sadat visit, as the excitement of the event dissipated, the public image of Egypt returned to its previous state. In addition, the decline in the scalometer ratings of both nations in 1978 may have been influenced by the breakdown in the peace process following Sadat's visit to Israel. The American public may have been disappointed in the inability of Egyptian and Israeli leaders to arrive at a settlement—hence the lower rating for both nations.[6]

The preceding discussion suggests that public images of Israel and Egypt fluctuate in accordance with American Middle Eastern policy. As a more precise test of the after-the-fact-approval model, the mean scalometer scores are examined in relation to the amount of United States economic and military aid to the two nations. Table 2 shows the amount of U.S. assistance to the two nations between 1966 and 1977 (the only years for which annual-level data are available.)

The trends in Table 2, when considered in conjunction with the

TABLE 2

UNITED STATES ASSISTANCE (IN MILLIONS OF DOLLARS) TO ISRAEL AND EGYPT, 1966–1977

	1966*	1967	1968	1969	1970	1971	1972	1973	1974	1975	1976	1977
ISRAEL												
Economic Loans	35.9	5.5	51.3	36.1	40.7	55.5	53.8	59.4	0.0	8.6	268.0	252.0
Economic Grants	0.9	0.6	0.5	0.6	0.4	0.3	50.4	50.4	51.5	344.5	525.0	490.0
Military Credit Sales	90.0	7.0	25.0	85.0	30.0	545.0	300.0	307.5	982.7	200.0	850.0	500.0
Military Grants	0.0	0.0	0.0	0.0	0.0	0.0	0.0	0.0	1500.0	100.0	850.0	500.0
Other	0.0	9.6	23.7	38.6	10.0	31.0	21.1	21.1	47.3	62.4	117.3	0.9
Totals	126.8	22.7	100.5	160.3	81.1	631.8	425.3	438.4	2581.5	715.5	2610.3	1742.9
EGYPT												
Economic Loans	16.4	0.0	0.0	0.0	0.0	0.0	1.5	0.0	9.5	298.8	795.3	796.8
Economic Grants	11.2	12.6	0.0	0.0	0.0	0.0	0.0	0.8	11.8	71.3	221.5	110.9
Other	0.0	0.0	0.0	0.0	0.0	0.0	18.3	10.7	9.0	38.1	0.0	0.0
Totals	27.6	12.6	0.0	0.0	0.0	0.0	19.8	11.5	30.3	408.2	1016.8	907.7

SOURCE: Data for 1946–1974 from U.S. OVERSEAS LOANS AND GRANTS AND ASSISTANCE FROM INTERNATIONAL ORGANIZATIONS: OBLIGA-TIONS AND LOAN AUTHORIZATIONS, JULY 1, 1945–JUNE 30, 1974, pp. 12, 17; and data for 1975–1977 from the same publication for the years July 1, 1945-Sept. 30, 1977, pp. 14, 19 (Washington, D.C.: Agency for International Development).

*The data are for each fiscal year. Egypt received no military aid during the period. Pre-1966 figures are not shown as they are not aggregated annually.

scalometer ratings, suggest substantial convergence between mass ratings of Egypt and Israel and the level of United States aid to the two nations. Changes in the extent of United States assistance have been accompanied by changes in public attitudes. As Table 2 indicates, Israel received much more economic assistance than Egypt between 1966 and 1973. In addition, while the United States provided ample military supplies to Israel, Egypt received none between 1966 and 1977. More importantly, the economic assistance data reveal the distinct shift in United States policy beginning in 1974 in that aid to Egypt increases significantly between 1974 and 1977. During these four years Egypt received more economic assistance than Israel, a shift which is reflected in the gradual increase in the scalometer ratings of Egypt.

To assess the relation between the level of United States aid and the scalometer ratings in a more precise way, the difference in the amount of economic assistance received by Israel and Egypt was correlated with the mean difference in the scalometer ratings. The economic assistance figures are used, since military aid to Egypt is a constant (zero) during the entire period. This analysis is limited to the eight years for which aid and opinion data are both available.[7] The obtained correlation coefficient (r) of .54 (p 0.5) confirms the preceding discussion — when the United States provides Israel with more assistance than Egypt, the difference between the scalometer ratings increases in Israel's favor. As American policy shifts toward a more balanced approach vis-a-vis Egypt and Israel, the difference between the two ratings is reduced. Limiting the analysis to 1973–1978 raises the correlation coefficient to .92 (p .01), indicating a very strong relation between the difference in the amount of economic assistance provided by the United States and the difference in the scalometer ratings.

In sum, based on the trends shown in Tables 1 and 2 and the clear relation between the difference in the scalometer ratings, it is reasonable to infer that public evaluations of Israel and Egypt reflect considerable after-the-fact-approval of the overall thrust of United States Middle Eastern policy. When United States policy has clearly favored Israel, the public rates Israel over Egypt by a wide margin. Conversely, when United States policy has been more neutral, public ratings of Egypt improve and the image of the two nations converge.[8]

Group Differences in the Ratings of Israel and Egypt

Correlates of foreign policy opinions have been extensively investigated (Scott, 1965; McCloskey, 1967; Rosenberg, 1967; Willick,

1970; Bobrow and Cutler, 1968; Patchen, 1972; Hughes, 1978; Schneider, 1978). Most of this work was directed to general orientations such as isolationism and cold war attitudes. It is thus difficult to apply the results of these studies to public evaluations of Israel and Egypt. The analysis performed here, which is limited to the 1974, 1975, and 1977 data, explores group variations in the ratings of Israel and Egypt. The difference between the two scalometer ratings is examined in relation to basic demographic characteristics and general political orientations. (As noted previously, the difference score ranges from minus nine to plus nine, positive scores indicating a preference for Israel, negative scores a preference for Egypt.)

Table 3 shows the mean difference score broken down by seven demographic variables. Also shown is the analysis-of-variance-based measure of association—the eta coefficient.

Not surprisingly, religion is the strongest predictor of the difference score. Among Jewish Americans, there is an extremely wide gap between the ratings in favor of Israel. The mean scalometer score for Israel among Jews is consistently above 8.0 while the mean score for Egypt ranges from 1.3 in 1975 to 2.9 in 1977. Jewish respondents not only intensely support Israel, they are also highly critical of Egypt.

Males and females rate Israel over Egypt by the same margin. With respect to region, the difference score is lower in the Midwest and South. The larger difference scores for the Northeast and West may be the result of a more concerted and successful effort by Jewish and pro-Israeli groups (who are relatively more concentrated in these areas) to generate sympathy and support for Israel and opposition to Egypt. Trice (1977: 456–458), for instance, has found that "there is a moderate positive relationship ($r = .30$) between the relative size of a senator's Jewish constituency and his support [for Israel] score."

Age differences are visible in all three surveys. Preference for Israel is greatest among the older cohorts. Similar findings have been reported in other areas. Thus, in a study of Middle Eastern-related content of world history textbooks and courses in six states, it was found that the younger the teacher, the more likely he or she is to judge the content pro-Jewish or pro-Israeli as opposed to "neutral/balanced" (see Chapter 6). The effects of age may derive from a changed set of historical experiences. Younger Americans, not having lived through the dramatic events associated with the creation of Israel, such as the Second World War and the Nazi atrocities, are less prone to be emotionally committed to Israel. If this interpretation is valid, it may be anticipated that, with generational replacement, the difference between public evaluations of

TABLE 3

MEAN DIFFERENCE SCORE
BROKEN DOWN BY DEMOGRAPHIC VARIABLES

	1974		1975		1977	
RELIGION						
Protestant	1.17		1.10		.88	
Catholic	.67	(.36)*	.83	(.30)	.54	(.30)
Jewish	6.44		7.10		6.41	
EDUCATION						
Grade School	.67		1.10		.56	
High School	1.06	(.15)	.78	(.15)	.57	(.14)
College	1.76		1.62		1.29	
INCOME						
Under $5,000	.85		.77		.34	
5,000–9,999	1.38	(.15)	.94	(.15)	.77	(.12)
10,000–14,999	1.72		1.60		.95	
Above 15,000	2.02		1.47		1.09	
RACE						
White	1.39	(.14)	1.33	(.09)	.92	(.15)
Non-White	.07		.80		-.19	
SEX						
Male	1.46	(.04)	1.30	(.02)	.88	(.03)
Female	1.04		.94		.72	
REGION						
Northeast	1.64		1.52		.97	
Midwest	1.09	(.10)	.94	(.09)	.62	(.10)
South	1.03		.92		.63	
West	1.53		1.13		1.21	
AGE						
18–29	.92		.70		.30	
30–39	1.36		1.06		.80	
40–49	1.16	(.09)	1.29	(.10)	.94	(.15)
50–59	1.53		1.29		1.10	
60–69	1.29		1.28		1.07	
Over 70	1.55		1.30		.97	

* Eta coefficients shown in parentheses.

Israel and Egypt will be further narrowed.

Race, education, and income are all weakly associated with the difference score. Nonwhites, those with a grade school education and who earn less than $5000 annually, are more apt to rate the two nations evenly, while Israel tends to be favored among whites, the more affluent, and those with a higher level of education.

It is noteworthy that nonwhites are the only group to obtain a negative mean difference score (in 1977) indicating a slight preference for Egypt. In general, the images of the two nations converge among groups who are economically and socially deprived. It is possible that, as the under privileged, these groups are more prone to identify with Egypt — the weaker and less prosperous of the two nations. An alternative explanation is that these groups, lacking much interest, have little preference for one country over another.

It may be speculated that the smaller margin of preference for Israel among minorities, the poor, and less educated is a result of anti-Jewish sentiment. Selznick and Steinberg, for example, show that education and income are both inversely correlated with anti-Semitism (Selznick and Steinberg, 1969: 69–93, 135–143). These researchers also note (119–126) that blacks score higher than whites on an Economic Anti-Semitism Index (for contrary findings see Marx, 1967: 146–147). To test the anti-Semitism explanation, the scalometer ratings for Israel and Egypt are examined in conjunction with education, income, and race. The results are shown in Table 4.

These data do not substantiate the anti-Semitism hypothesis. The rating of Israel is consistently positive (above 5.0) among the groups presumed to be more anti-Semitic — nonwhites, those earning less than $5000 annually, and respondents with a grade school education. These groups obtain lower difference scores because they also rate Egypt positively. But while minorities, the poor, and those with less education tend to view both nations favorably, whites, the more affluent, and educated rate Israel positively and Egypt negatively. Note, for example, that those earning more than $15,000 have mean scalometer ratings of less than 4.0 for Egypt in 1974 and 1975. The mean rating of Egypt consistently fails to reach the positive half of the scalometer among the college-educated, whites and those with incomes over $15,000. Race, income, and education thus appear to reflect a greater dislike for Egypt, i.e., a form of anti-Egyptian and anti-Arab orientation, among whites, those with more education, and with higher incomes (for some evidence of anti-Arab racism among Americans, see Lipset and Schneider, 1977a: 22).

TABLE 4

ISRAEL AND EGYPT SCALOMETERS
BROKEN DOWN BY RACE, EDUCATION AND INCOME*

	1974		1975		1977	
	Israel	Egypt	Israel	Egypt	Israel	Egypt
INCOME						
$5000	5.36	4.50	5.20	4.40	5.54	5.20
$5–9,999	5.67	4.27	5.14	4.19	5.41	4.60
$10–15,000	5.84	4.14	5.47	3.88	5.61	4.67
Over $15,000	6.02	3.92	5.42	3.96	5.64	4.53
EDUCATION						
Grade School	5.17	4.54	5.34	4.14	5.26	4.67
High School	5.48	4.41	5.05	4.26	5.33	4.75
College	6.01	4.24	5.66	4.02	6.08	4.77
RACE						
White	5.68	4.23	5.30	4.09	5.60	4.66
Non-white	5.12	5.10	5.27	4.89	5.21	5.34

* Table entries are scalometer means.

The relations noted above have important political implications.
Citizens who tend to rate the two nations evenly rarely participate in
the political process. In contrast, Israel's "carriers of the creed" are
marked by a high level of political activity. In short, the potential for
politically relevant behavior is significantly higher among groups who
prefer Israel to Egypt.

Ratings of Egypt and Israel are generally unrelated to media exposure
and political attitudes (see Table 5). The correlation ratio between party
identification and the difference score is virtually zero in all three instances. Attitudes toward Israel and Egypt are not structured by partisanship (for similar evidence concerning attitudes toward foreign aid
see Pomper, 1975: 166–170). It may be noted, however, that the difference score for Democrats decreases over time to a greater extent than
the difference score for Republicans. Given the previously noted differences concerning education, income, and race, it is hardly surprising that nonvoters prefer Israel by a smaller margin than do voters.

A similar pattern of agreement is visible among liberals and conservatives. In 1974 both groups are more favorable toward Israel than moderates; but over time, the difference score for the liberals is reduced. Agreement between liberals and conservatives is likely to stem from differing concerns. As Schneider has pointed out with regard to mass attitudes toward United States support for Israel:

> Conservatives are likely to see American support for Israel as a Cold War issue; we must limit communist influence in the Middle East. Liberals probably see it as a moral and humanitarian issue; we must see to it that this small, courageous, democratic nation, surviving remnant of the European Holocaust, is not destroyed [Schneider, 1978: 45–46].

Thus, for conservatives and for Republicans in general, the communist threat continues to be a salient issue — hence the continuing support for Israel at a relatively higher rate. For liberals and for many Democrats, the threat to the existence of the state of Israel is no longer as great as it used to be believed — hence their greater freedom to recognize other salient issues, such as Egypt's importance to the United States.

Confidence in the executive branch of the federal government is curvilinearly associated with the difference score in 1975; those with a great deal of confidence and those with hardly any confidence at all are both more favorable toward Israel than respondents with some confidence. In 1977, the pattern is altered with the most trusting group showing preference for Israel by the smallest margin. This shift is probably a response to the policy changes adopted by the Carter Administration. With the Administration moving toward a more balanced position, supporters of the president alter their ratings of Israel and Egypt so as to rate the two nations more evenly.

To examine the combined effects of the variables included in Tables 3 and 5, a multivariate analysis was performed. Those variables which do correlate with the difference score (with an eta coefficient of at least .10) were dichotomized and used as predictors in a multiple regression analysis. The partial regression coefficients associated with each predictor are presented in Table 6.

Religion clearly overshadows all other predictors. However, it is not the only predictor to exert a significant impact on the difference score. The effects of race are significant in 1974 and 1977 while income-related

TABLE 5

MEAN DIFFERENCE SCORE
BROKEN DOWN BY POLITICAL ATTITUDES

	1974		1975		1977	
PARTY IDENTIFICATION						
Democrat	1.28		.98		.78	
Independent	1.27	(.00)*	1.10	(.04)	.70	(.04)
Republican	1.33		1.28		1.00	
POLITICAL IDEOLOGY						
Liberal	1.40		1.10		.75	
Moderate	1.12	(.06)	.97	(.06)	.79	(.04)
Conservative	1.51		1.30		1.10	
NEWSPAPER EXPOSURE						
High			1.21		.96	
Moderate	—	—	1.11	(.09)	.48	(.09)
Low			.62		.54	
POLITICAL PARTICIPATION						
Voted in last election	1.49	(.14)	1.34	(.13)	1.03	(.13)
Did not vote	.67		.60		.37	
CONFIDENCE IN EXECUTIVE BRANCH						
Great Deal	1.39		1.26		.54	
Some	.92	(.10)	1.10	(.02)	.94	(.07)
Hardly any	1.53		1.04		.84	

* Eta coefficients shown in parentheses.

differences are significant in 1974 and 1975. The regression coefficient for the voter-non-voter dichotomy also attains significance in 1975 and 1977 indicating that the smaller margin or preference for Israel among nonvoters is not spurious and cannot be attributed to demographic correlates of voting. The effects of education are significant in 1977. Finally, the impact of age on the difference score is also significant in 1977.

Summary and Conclusions

The data reported here show that American attitudes toward Israel and Egypt are affected by the views of the incumbent administration — if the administration is at odds with Egypt and supportive of Israel, then the public is both anti-Egyptian and strongly pro-Israeli. When the administration is in disagreement with Israel, then the public's support for Israel declines slightly. Finally, when the administration attempts to maintain harmonious relations with both nations, the public becomes less anti-Egyptian and the two nations are rated more evenly.

While public affect for Israel is generally high, these data do not support the general view tht American public opinion is overwhelmingly pro-Israeli (for similar conclusions see Trice, 1978b: 245; American Institute of Public Opinion, 1975). At the same time, it must be noted that even though public ratings of Egypt have improved since 1967, the mean scalometer score for Egypt in every year between 1967 and 1976 is in the negative range of the scalometer (4.5 being the dividing line between minus one and plus one). It is only in 1977 that Egypt's mean rating climbs into the positive half of the scalometer and both nations are viewed positively; but as previously noted, Egypt's mean rating returns to the negative half of the scalometer in 1978. In summary: Whereas American attitudes toward Israel and Egypt up to the early 1970s clearly favored Israel, the distribution of the two ratings has since moved closer to a point of neutrality. Israel is still favored over Egypt but the gap between the two nations is quite small.

TABLE 6

MULTIPLE REGRESSION OF THE DIFFERENCE SCORE

Predictor	1974	1975	1977
Religion	2.60**	2.79**	2.27**
Race	−.75*	—	−.76**
Income	.26*	.23*	—
Education	—·	—	.27**
Age	—	—	.42*
Voting	—	−.51*	−.37*

* $p < .05$;

** $p < .01$

Support for Israel is present among all groups. Jews, however, stand out as the most supportive of Israel and the most hostile toward Egypt, while nonwhites are the only group that tend to rate the two nations equally. The young, the less-educated, the less affluent, and the politically inactive are also more likely than their counterparts to have a balanced view of Israel and Egypt.

Based on these data what predictions can be made about public opinion and United States Middle Eastern policy in the future? It is clear that Egypt faces an uphill task. To begin with, the history of long-term conflictual relations between Egypt and the United States (1956–1974) and a parallel period of cooperative relations between Israel and the United States has produced a distribution of public attitudes favorable toward Israel and unfavorable toward Egypt. Apart from the direction of past United States Middle Eastern policy, Israel enjoys other advantages over Egypt. The number of Jewish Americans is much larger than the number of Arab Americans. Culturally, socially, and politically Israel resembles the United States to a greater extent than Egypt. Nations similar to the United States tend to be viewed more favorably by the American public (Nincic and Russett, 1979).

The Sadat Government has clearly sought better relations with the United States and a peace settlement with Israel (Dawisha, 1976). As previously noted, however, dramatic events, such as Sadat's Jerusalem visit and the Camp David Accords, cannot produce lasting attitude changes by themselves. Such changes might come about if the spectacular event is combined with or reinforced by government policies in the same direction. Whether or not this occurs depends on a multitude of factors. These include the ability of American leaders to promote initiatives for a settlement of the major Middle Eastern problems and their willingness to pursue such initiatives forcefully. Also to be considered is the extent to which the United States continues to depend on Arab oil. Experimental evidence suggests that a moderate degree of threat is associated with greater receptivity to a source's message (Berelson and Steiner, 1964). If the American public comes to perceive the importance of Arab oil to the United States economy, it may be easier for future administrations to mobilize public support for pro-Arab or neutral policies. The most critical factor will be the public stance of the incumbent administration. If the present trend of American support for Egypt is continued, we are likely to witness a gradual shift in public attitudes (increasing affect) toward Egypt. It must be cautioned, however, that such attitude changes are likely to be conditioned by various cross-pressures, most notably, pro-Zionist lobbying. The power of the Zionist lobby to limit an incumbent administration's Middle Eastern policy is well known (Quandt, 1973: 274–275; Trice, 1978a: 238–239).[9] Unless an equally powerful set of organizations representing the Arab cause are established to counter the influence of the Zionist lobby,[10] the development of pro-Arab sentiments is likely to be impeded even if future administrations maintain policies of neutrality or friendship toward the Arab states.

NOTES

1. The N.O.R.C data were made available by the Inter-University Consortium for Political and Social Research. The Gallup data were provided by the Roper Center. Neither the Consortium nor the Roper Center bear any responsibility for the analyses or interpretations provided here.

2. The authors are indebted to Mr. George Gallup Jr. of the Gallup Organization for providing the results of the 1978 survey.

3. Mean scores were computed after excluding "don't know" and "no opinion" responses.

4. The change in the public image of Egypt is notable from a comparative perspective in that the increase in Egypt's scalometer rating between 1956 and 1976 is exceeded only by the scalometer rating for Britain. The ratings for five other nations (for which 1956–1976 data are available) reflect greater stability (Nincic and Russett, 1979: 76) suggesting that public evaluations of Egypt have improved at a relatively rapid rate.

5. This is in marked contrast to the "mood theory" formulated by Almond (1950) which specifies that foreign policy opinions are volatile and susceptible to short-term changes. Empirical tests of the mood theory, however, have yielded negative results (see Caspary, 1970).

6. While the Sadat trip to Israel did not significantly increase the level of public support for Egypt, it must be allowed that dramatic events concerning the two Middle Eastern nations can artificially strengthen the link between United States policy and public images of the two nations. The Camp David Summit, for example, could have affected the attitudes of United States policy makers and thereby the content of United States policy, as well as public attitudes toward Israel and Egypt.

7. The eight scalometer ratings used in the computation of the correlation were 1966, 1967, 1973, 1974, 1975, 1976, 1977, 1978. The scalometer for Israel in 1973 was estimated using the mean for the entire period. The aid figures used are for 1966 and 1967 and 1972–1977. The 1966 and 1967 scalometers were obtained at the end of the year and hence can be correlated with the 1966 and 1967 aid data (since we are assuming, that policy affects opinions). The 1973–1978 scalometers, however, were obtained during the early months and were therefore correlated with the aid figures from the previous year, i.e., the 1978 scalometer difference is correlated with the 1977 aid difference.

8. Correspondence between public opinion and official policy may also reflect governmental manipulation of mass opinions: Citizens may become more positive toward Egypt merely to agree with official policy. Mueller (1970: 20–21), for example, has detected a "rally around the flag effect" on presidential popularity, in that major international developments boost the President's standing with the public. Other researchers have noted

that public approval of policies tends to increase immediately following presidential endorsement of these policies (Weissberg, 1976: 234–237; Barton, 1964; Abravanel and Hughes, 1975: 52). Unfortunately, it is not possible to empirically differentiate between the after-the-fact-approval and governmental manipulation models of opinion-policy linkage.

9. For the argument that pro-Israeli organizations constitute a "veto group" on Middle Eastern issues, see Lipset and Schneider, 1977a; Lipset, 1978. For a more recent analysis which questions this argument, see Lipset, 1978.

10. Several recent journalistic reports have indicated the beginnings of an Arab-American lobby. These reports demonstrate that at present the Arab lobby has little if any political clout. There are presently five members of Congress who are of Arab-American background, but they do not vote as a bloc on Middle Eastern issues.

REFERENCES

ABRAVANEL, M. and B. HUGHES (1973) "The relationship between public opinion and governmental foreign policy: a cross-national study," pp. 107–133, in J. McGowan (ed.) Sage International Yearbook of Foreign Policy Studies, vol. 4. Beverly Hills, CA: Sage Publications.

— — —(1975) "Public attitudes and foreign policy: behavior in western democracies," pp. 46–73, in W.O. Chittick (ed.) The Analysis of Foreign Policy Outputs. Columbus, OH: Charles E. Merrill.

ALMOND, G. (1950) The American People and Foreign Policy. New York: Harcourt, Brace.

American Enterprise Institute (1968) United States Interests in the Middle East. Washington, DC: AEI.

American Institute of Public Opinion (1975) Gallup Opinion Index, Report 119. Princeton, NJ.

BADEAU, J.S. (1968) The American Approach to the Arab World. New York: Harper & Row.

BARTON, A.H. (1974) "Conflict and consensus among American leaders." Public Opinion Q. 38: 507–530.

BERELSON, B.R. and G.A. STEINER (1964) Human Behavior: An Inventory of Scientific Findings. New York: Harcourt, Brace.

BISHOP, A.W., A.J. TUCHFARBER, and W. OLDENDICK (1978) "Change in the structure of American political attitudes: the nagging question of question wording." Amer. J. of Pol. Sci. 22: 250–269.

BOBROW, D. and E. CUTLER (1968) "Time oriented explanations of national security beliefs: cohort, life-state and situation." Peace Research Society Papers 11: 217–222.

BRYSON, A (1977) American Diplomatic Relations with the Middle East, 1784–1975: A Survey. Metuchen, NJ: Scarecrow Press.

CAMPBELL, C. (1975) "American efforts for peace," pp. 249–310 in M. H. Kerr (ed.) The Elusive Peace in the Middle East. Albany, NY: SUNY Press.

CASPARY, W. (1970) "The 'mood theory': a study of public opinion and foreign policy." Amer. Pol. Sci. Rev. 66: 536–547.

COHEN, C. (1973) The Public's Impact on Foreign Policy. Boston: Little, Brown.

Congressional Quarterly (1977) The Middle East: U.S. Policy, Israel, Oil and the Arabs. Third Edition. Washington, DC: Congressional Quarterly.

CONVERSE, E. (1964) "The nature of belief systems in mass publics," pp. 206–261 in D. Apter (ed.) Ideology and Discontent. New York: Free Press.

— — —(1963) "Comments on the three studies." Council for Correspondence Newsletter 24: 37–42.

CONVERSE, P. and G. MARCUS (1979) "The new CPS election study panel." Amer. Pol. Sci. Rev. 73: 32–49.

DAWISHA, A.E. (1976) Egypt in the Arab World: The Elements of Foreign Policy. New York: John Wiley.

DENOVO, J.A. (1963) American Interests and Policies in the Middle East, 1900–1939. Minneapolis, MN: Univ. of Minnesota Press.

DEUTSCH, K.W. and R.L. MERRITT (1965) "Effects of events on national and international images," pp. 132–187 in H.C. Kelman (ed.) International Behavior. New York: Holt, Rinehart & Winston.

EISENHOWER, D.D. (1965) Waging Peace, 1956–1961: White House Years. New York: Doubleday.

FISHER, W.B. (1971) The Middle East: a Physical, Social and Regional Geography. London: Methuen.

GAMSON, W.A. and A. MODIGLIANI (1966) "Knowledge and foreign policy opinions: some models for consideration." Public Opinion Q. 30: 187–199.

GLENN, D. (1972) "The distribution of political knowledge in the United States," pp. 273–284 in D. Nimmo and C. Bonjean (eds.) Political Attitudes and Public Opinion. New York: David McKay.

GLUBB, J.B. (1971) Peace in the Holy Land. London: Hodder & Stoughton.

HUGHES, B.B. (1978) The Domestic Context of American Foreign Policy. San Francisco: W.H. Freeman.

KHOURI, F.J. (1968) The Arab-Israeli Dilemma. Syracuse, NY: Syracuse Univ. Press.

LIPSET, S.M. (1978) "Further commentary on American attitudes." Public Opinion 1: 16–17.

— — —(1978a) "The polls on the Middle East." Middle East Rev. 11: 24–30.

— — —and W. SCHNEIDER (1977a) "Carter vs. Israel: what the polls reveal." Commentary 64 (November): 21–29.

— — —(1977b) "Polls for the White House, and the rest of us." Encounter 69 (November): 24–34.

MARX, G. (1967) Protest and Prejudice: A Study of Belief in the Black Community. New York: Harper & Row.

McCLOSKEY, H. (1967) "Personality and attitude correlates of foreign policy orientation," pp. 51–109 in J. Rosenau (ed.) Domestic Sources of Foreign Policy. New York: Free Press.

Miller, A.H. and W.E. MILLER (1975) "Issues, candidates and partisan divisions in the 1972 American presidential election." British J. of Pol. Sci. 5: 393–434.

— — —(1977) "Partisanship and performance: "rational" choice in the 1976 presidential election." Presented at the American Political Science Association Meeting, Washington, DC, September.

MILLER, W.E. and D.E. STOKES (1963) "Constituency influence in Congress." Amer. Pol. Sci. Rev. 57: 45–46.

MUELLER, J.E. (1970) "Presidential popularity from Truman to Johnson." Amer. Pol. Sci. Rev. 64: 18–34.

NADEL, M.V. (1972) "Public policy and public opinions," pp. 159–174 in R. Weissberg and M.V. Nadel (eds.) American Democracy: Theory and Reality. New York: John Wiley.

NINCIC, M and B. RUSSETT (1979) "The effect of similarity and interest on attitudes toward foreign countries." Public Opinion Q. 43: 68–98.

NIE, N.H., S. VERBA, and J.R. PETROCIK (1976) The Changing American Voter. Cambridge, MA: Harvard Univ. Press.

NUTTING, A. (1972) Nasser. New York: E.P. Dutton.

PATCHEN, M. (1972) "Social class and dimension of foreign policy attitudes," pp. 455–473 in D. Nimmo and C. Bonjean (eds.) Political Attitudes and Public Opinion. New York: David McKay.

POMPER, G.M. (1975) Voters' Choice: Varieties of Electoral Behavior. New York: Dodd
Mead.
— — —(1972) "From confusion to clarity: issues and American voters, 1956–1968." Amer.
Pol. Sci. Rev. 66: 415–428.
QUANDT, W.B. (1977) Decade of Decisions: American Policy Toward the Arab-Israeli
Conflict, 1967–1976. Berkeley, CA: Univ. of California Press.
— — —(1973) "Domestic influences on United States foreign policy in the Middle East:
the view from Washington." pp. 263–285 in W.A. Beling (ed.) The Middle East: Quest
for an American Policy. Albany, NY: SUNY Press.
REPASS, D. (1971) "Issue salience and party choices." Amer. Pol. Sci. Rev. 65: 389–400.
ROBINSON, J. (1967) "World affairs information and mass media exposure." Journalism
Q. 44: 23–31.
ROSENAU, J. (1967) "Foreign policy as an issue area," pp. 31–47 in J. Rosenau (ed.)
Domestic Sources of Foreign Policy. New York: Free Press.
ROSENBERG, M.J. (1967) "Attitude change and foreign policy in the cold war era,"
pp. 111–159 in J. Rosenau (ed.) Domestic Sources of Foreign Policy. New York: Free
Press.
— — —(1965) "Images in relation to the policy process," pp. 278–334 in H. Kelman (ed.)
International Behavior. New York: Holt, Rinehart & Winston.
SAFRAN, N. (1978) Israel, the Embattled Ally. Cambridge, MA: Belknap Press of Har-
vard University.
SCHNEIDER, W. (1978) "Internationalism and ideology: foreign policy attitudes of the
American public." Presented to the International Studies Association, Washington,
DC, February.
SCOTT, W.A. (1965) "Psychological and social correlates of international images,"
pp. 71–103 in H. Kelman (ed.) International Behavior. New York: Holt, Rinehart &
Winston.
SELZNICK, G.J. and S. STEINBERG (1969) The Tenacity of Prejudice. New York: Harper
& Row.
SHEEHAN, E.R.F. (1976) The Arabs, Israelis, and Kissinger. New York: Thomas Y. Crowell.
SMITH, D.D. (1972) "Dark areas of ignorance revisited: current knowledge about Asian
affairs," pp. 267–272 in D. Nimmo and C. Bonjean (eds.) Political Attitudes and Public
Opinion. New York: David McKay.
SOUTHERLAND, D. (1978) Mideast jets deal "at hand". Christian Science Monitor May 10.
SPANIER, J. and E. USLANER (1978) How American Foreign Policy is Made. New York:
Praeger.
STOOKEY, R.W. (1975) America and the Arab States: An Uneasy Encounter. New York:
John Wiley.
SULEIMAN, M.W. (1977) American Images of Middle East Peoples: Impact of the High
School. New York: Middle East Studies Assoc.
TRICE, R.H. (1978a) "Foreign policy interest groups, mass public opinion and the Arab-
Israeli dispute." Western Pol. Q. 31: 238–252.
— — —(1978b) "The American elite press and the Arab-Israeli conflict: editorial opinion
in selected U.S. newspapers, 1966–1974." Presented at the International Studies Associa-
tion Meeting, Washington, DC, February.
— — —(1977) "Congress and the Arab-Israeli conflict: support for Israel in the U.S. Senate,
1970–1973." Pol. Sci. Q. 92: 443–463.
TRUMAN, H.S. (1956) Memoirs, Volume Two: Years of Trial and Hope. Garden City,
NJ: Doubleday.
WEISSBERG, R. (1976) Public Opinion and Popular Government. Englewood Cliffs, NJ:
Prentice-Hall.
WILLICK, D.H. (1970) "Foreign affairs and party choice." Amer. J. of Sociology 75:
530–549.

BIBLIOGRAPHY

Select Bibliography on American Views and Reporting on the Arabs

Abourezk, Senator James, *Arabs, the Convenient Scapegoat* (Washington, D.C.: American-Arab Anti-Discrimination Committee, 1980).

Abourezk, Senator James, "The United States and the Middle East," (Interview) *Journal of Palestine Studies*, Vol. IV, No. 1 (Autumn 1974), pp. 3–9.

Abourezk, Senator James, "Winning America's Ear," *Middle East International*, No. 67, (January 1977), pp. 16–18.

"Abscam Shows the Arabs as Victims of an Ugly Racial Stereotype," *The Kansas City Times*, Tuesday, March 4, 1980, p. A–9.

Abu-Helu, Yaqub Abdalla, "Images of the Arabs and of Their Conflict with Israel Held by American Public Secondary School Social Studies Teachers" (Ph.D. dissertation, Stanford University, 1978). 312 pp.

Abu-Laban, Sharon M., "Stereotypes of Middle East Peoples: An Analysis of Church School Curricula," in Abu-Laban, Baha and Faith T. Zeadey, eds., *Arabs in America: Myths and Realities* (Wilmette, Ill.: Medina University Press International, 1975), pp. 149–169.

Adams, William C., ed., *Television Coverage of the Middle East* (Norwood, N.J.: ABLEX Publishing Corporation, 1981). 167 pp.

Adams, William and Phillip Heyl, "From Cairo to Kabul with the Networks, 1972–1980," in Adams, William, ed., *Television Coverage of the Middle East* (Norwood, N.J.: ABLEX Publishing Corporation, 1981), pp. 1–39.

Agha, Olfat Hassan, *The Role of Mass Communications in Inter-State Conflict: The Arab-Israeli War of October 1973* (Cairo, Egypt: The American University in Cairo, 1978). 88 pp. in English, 4 pp. in

Arabic. (The Cairo Papers in Social Science, Monograph 3).

Agha, Olfat Hassan, "The Role of Mass Communication in Interstate Conflict: The Arab Israeli War of October 6, 1973," *Gazette*, Vol. 24, No. 3 (1978), pp. 181–95.

Ahmed, Leila, *Edward Lane: A Study of His Life and Work and of British Ideas of the Middle East in the 19th Century* (London: Longman, 1978). 232 pp.

Alami, Adawia, "Misconceptions in the Treatment of the Arab World in Selected American Textbooks for Children" (M.A. Thesis, Kent State University, 1957). 165 pp.

Alami, Adawia, "The Treatment of the Arab World in Selected American Textbooks for Children," in *Essays on the American Public Opinion and the Palestine Problem* (Beirut, Lebanon: Palestine Research Center, 1969), pp. 119–183.

Al-Azmeh, Aziz, *Ibn Khaldun in Modern Scholarship: A Study in Orientalism* (London: Third World Center for Research and Publication, 1981). 330 pp.

Al-Azmeh, Aziz, "The Articulation of Orientalism," *Arab Studies Quarterly*, Vol. 3, No. 4 (Fall 1981), pp. 384–402.

Algar, Hamid, "The Problems of Orientalists," *Al-Ittihad*, Vol. 7, No. 1 (March 1970), pp. 14–18.

Almaney, Adnan, "International and Foreign Affairs on Network Television News," *Journal of Broadcasting*, Vol. 14 (Winter, 1970), pp. 499–509.

Al-Qazzaz, Ayad, "Image Formation and Textbooks," in Ghareeb, Edmund, ed., *Split Vision: Portrayal of Arabs in the American Media* (Washington, D.C.: American-Arab Affairs Council, 1983), pp. 369–380.

Al-Qazzaz, Ayad, "Images of the Arab in American Social Science Textbooks," in Abu-Laban, Baha and Faith T. Zeadey, eds., *Arabs in America: Myths and Realities* (Wilmette, Ill.: Medina University Press International, 1975), pp. 113–132.

Al-Qazzaz, Ayad, "Textbooks and Teachers: Conveyors of Knowledge and Agents of Socialization," in Friedlander, Jonathan, ed., *The Middle East: The Image and the Reality* (Los Angeles, CA: The Regents of the University of California, 1980), pp. 79–85.

Alter, Robert, "Rhetoric & the Arab Mind," *Commentary*, Vol. 46, No. 4 (October 1968), pp. 61–65.

"The American Media and the Palestine Problem," (Interviews with journalists Peter Jennings, Ronald Koven, James McCartney, Lee

Eggerstrom and Marilyn Robinson), *Journal of Palestine Studies*, Vol. 5, Nos. 1 & 2 (Autumn 1975/Winter 1976), pp. 127–149.

The Arab Image in the Western Mass Media (London: Outline Books, 1980), 280 pp.

"Arabs, Israelis and Americans," *The Cambridge Report* Vol. 4 (Summer 1975), pp. 140–194.

Aruri, Naseer H., "The Middle East on the U.S. Campus," *The Link*, Vol. 18, No. 2 (May-June 1985), pp. 1–14.

Asi, Morad Osman, "Arabs, Israelis and U.S. Television Networks: A Content Analysis of How ABC, CBS, and NBC Reported the News Between 1970–1979" (Ph.D. dissertation, Ohio University, 1981). 177 pp.

Asi, Morad, "Arabs, Israelis, and TV News: A Time-Series Content Analysis," in Adams, William, ed., *Television Coverage of the Middle East* (Norwood, N.J.: ABLEX Publishing Corporation, 1981), pp. 67–75.

Aswad, Barbara, "Biases and Inaccuracies in Textbooks: Depictions of the Arab World," in Abraham, Sameer Y. and Nabeel Abraham, eds., *The Arab World and Arab-Americans: Understanding a Neglected Minority* (Detroit, Michigan: Center for Urban Studies, Wayne State University, 1981), pp. 73–79.

Bagnied, Magda Ahmed and Steven Schneider, "Sadat Goes to Jerusalem: Televised Images, Themes, and Agenda," in Adams, William, ed., *Television Coverage of the Middle East* (Norwood, N.J.: ABLEX Publishing Corporation, 1981), pp. 53–66.

Bagnied, Magda Ahmed, "U.S. Television Network Coverage of Sadat's Peace Initiative" (Ph.D. dissertation, University of Cairo, Mass Communication, 1982). 302 pp.

Baha el-Din, Ahmad, "World Media and the Arabs: An Arab Perspective," in Jabara, Abdeen, and Janice Terry, eds., *The Arab World: From Nationalism to Revolution* (Wilmette, Ill.: Medina University Press International, 1971), pp. 77–85.

Batroukha, Mohammed Ezzedin, "The Editorial Attitudes of the *New York Times* and the *Christian Science Monitor* Toward the Arab-Israeli Dispute (January 1, 1955–June 30, 1956): A Content Analysis Study" (Ph.D. dissertation, Syracuse University, 1961). 433 pp.

Beit-Hallahmi, Benjamin, "Some Psychosocial and Cultural Factors in the Arab-Israeli Conflict: A Review of the Literature," *Journal of Conflict Resolution*, Vol. 16, no. 2 (June, 1972), pp. 269–280.

Belkaoui, Janice Monti, "Image Creation in the Prestige Press: A Case

Study of Arab and Israeli Images" (M.A. thesis, Carleton University, Sociology and Anthropology, 1976).

Belkaoui, Janice Monti, "Images of Arabs and Israelis in the Prestige Press, 1966–74," *Journalism Quarterly*, Vol. 55, No. 4 (Winter 1978), pp. 732–38, 799.

Bell, Steve, "American Journalism: Heritage, Practices, Constraints, and Middle East Reportage," in Hudson, Michael C. and Ronald G. Wolfe, eds., *The American Media and the Arabs* (Washington, D.C.: Center for Contemporary Arab Studies, Georgetown University, 1980), pp. 51–58.

Bolling, Landrum R., ed., *Reporters Under Fire: US Media Coverage of Conflicts in Lebanon and Central America* (Boulder, CO: Westview Press, 1985). 155 pp.

Bradley, Douglass, "Was Truth the First Casualty?: American Media and the Fall of Tal Zaatar," *Arab Studies Quarterly*, Vol. 4, No. 3 (Summer 1982), pp. 200–210.

Brownell, Will, "Hollywood's Primal Arab," *Arab Perspectives*, Vol. 1, No. 4 (July 1980), pp. 5–11.

Caradon, Lord, "Images and Realities of the Middle East Conflict," in Hudson, Michael C. and Ronald G. Wolfe, eds., *The American Media and the Arabs* (Washington, D.C.: Center for Contemporary Arab Studies, Georgetown University, 1980), pp. 79–83.

Chafets, Ze'ev, *Double Vision: How America's Press Distorts America's View of the Middle East* (New York: Morrow, 1984). 349 pp.

Childs, Marquis, "It was Sadat's Show from Start to Finish," *The Washington Post*, November 29, 1977, p. A–19.

Childers, Erskine B., *The Road to Suez: A Study of Western-Arab Relations* (London: Macgibbon & Kee, 1962). Ch. II "The Western Image of the Arab," pp. 36–61.

Cleveland, R., "Some 'Middle East Experts' More Dangerous than Non-Professionals," *The Arab World*, vol. 14, No. 12 (December 1948), pp. 10–14.

Cleveland, Ray L., "The Palestinians and the Diminution of Historical Legitimacy," in Perry, Glenn E., ed., *Palestine: Continuing Dispossession* (Belmont, MA: Association of Arab-American University Graduates, 1986), pp. 95–117.

Cockburn, Alexander, "International Terrorism and Double Standards," *The Wall Street Journal*, April 15, 1982, p. 27.

Cooley, John K., "The News from the Mideast: A Working Approach," *The Middle East Journal*, Vol. 35, No. 4 (Autumn 1981), pp. 465–480.

Corbon, Father Jean, *Western Public Opinion and the Palestine Conflict* (Beirut, Lebanon: Fifth of June Society, 1969). 18 pp.

Cox, Harvey, "Understanding Islam: No More Holy Wars," *Atlantic*, January, 1981, pp. 73–80.

Crow, Ralph, "Is There Bias?: What the American Press Printed About the Qibya Incident," *Middle East Forum*, 32 (March, 1957), pp. 12–14.

Curtiss, Richard H., *A Changing Image: American Perceptions of the Arab-Israeli Dispute* (Washington, D.C.: American Educational Trust, 1982). 216 pp. Second edition, 1986.

Damon, George H. Jr., with the assistance of Laurence D. Michalak, "A Survey of Political Cartoons Dealing with the Middle East," in Ghareeb, Edmund, ed., *Split Vision: Portrayal of Arabs in the American Media* (Washington, D.C.: American-Arab Affairs Council, 1983), pp. 143–153.

Daniel, Norman, *Islam and the West: The Making of an Image* (Edinburgh: The University Press, 1966). 448 pp.

Daugherty, David and Michael Warden, "Prestige Press Editorial Treatment of the Mideast During 11 Crisis Years," *Journalism Quarterly*, Vol. 56 (Winter 1979), pp. 776–782.

De Boer, Connie, "The Polls: Attitudes Toward the Arab-Israeli Conflict," *Public Opinion Quarterly*, Vol 47, No. 1 (Spring 1983), pp. 121–131.

Dehmer, Alan, *Unholy Alliance: Christian Fundamentalism and the Israeli State* (Washington, D.C.: American-Arab Anti-Discrimination Committee, 1984). 22 pp. (ADC Issues, 16).

Diamond, Edwin and Paula Cassidy, "Arabs vs Israelis: Has Television Taken Sides?" *TV Guide*, January 6, 1979, pp. 6–8, 10.

Dohse, Michael Arthur, "American Periodicals and the Palestine Triangle, April 1936 to February 1947" (Ph.D. dissertation: Mississippi State University, 1966). 270 pp.

Domestic Communications Aspects of the Middle East Crisis (Washington, D.C.: American Institute for Political Communication, 1967). 8 pp.

Drummond, William J. and Augustine Zycher, "Arafat's Press Agents," *Harper's*, 252 (March, 1976), pp. 24–30.

Dunsmore, Barrie, "Television Hard News and the Middle East," in Hudson, Michael C. and Ronald G. Wolfe, eds., *The American Media and the Arabs* (Washington, D.C.: Center for Contemporary Arab Studies, Georgetown University, 1980), pp. 73–76.

Ehle, Carl Frederick, Jr., "Prolegomena to Christian Zionism in America: The Views of Increase Mather and William E. Blackstone Concerning the Doctrine of the Restoration of Israel" (Ph.D. dissertation, New York University, Religion, History, 1977). 375 pp.

Erskine, Hazel, "The Polls: Western Partisanship in the Middle East," *Public Opinion Quarterly*, Vol. XXXIII, No. 4 (Winter, 1969–70), pp. 627–40.

Essays on the American Public Opinion and the Palestine Problem (Beirut, Lebanon: Palestine Research Center, 1969). 192 pp.

Faris, Nabih, "The United States' Image of the Near East," *Middle East Forum*, Vol. 36 (February 1960).

Farmer, Leslie, "All We Know Is What We Read in the Papers," *The Middle East Newsletter*, (Beirut, Lebanon), Vol. II, No. 2 (February 1968), pp. 1–5.

Farsoun, Karen, Samih Farsoun, and Alex Ajay, "Mid-East Perspectives From the American Left," *Journal of Palestine Studies*, Vol. IV, No. 1 (Autumn, 1974), pp. 94–119.

Feaver, Douglas B., "Envoy Says Post's Israel Commentary Is Among the Most Negative," *The Washington Post*, November 10, 1982, p. A3.

Feith, Douglas J., "Israel, the Post, and the Shaft," *Middle East Review*, Vol. 12 (Summer, 1980), pp. 62–66.

Feldman, Harold, "Children of the Desert: Notes on Arab National Character," *Psychoanalytic Review*, Vol 45, No. 3 (Fall 1958), pp. 40–50.

Findley, Paul, *They Dare to Speak Out: People and Institutions Confront Israel's Lobby* (Westport, Conn.: Lawrence Hill, 1985). 362 pp.

Fink, Reuben, ed., *America and Palestine: The Attitude of Official America and the American People Toward the Rebuilding of Palestine as a Free Democratic Jewish Common-Wealth* (New York: Arno Press, 1977). (Reprint of the 1944 edition, published by Harald Square Press, New York). 522 pp.

Forrest, A.C., "Myths about the Middle East," *The Middle East Newsletter*, Vol. III, No. 3 (April 1969), pp. 3–7.

Friedlander, Jonathan, ed., *The Middle East: The Image and the Reality* (Los Angeles, CA: The Regents of the University of California, 1980). 150 pp.

Friedman, Jane, "Has T.V. Tilted Against Israel?" *Panorama*, (December 1980), pp. 40–43.

Geyer, Georgie Anne (Interviewed) in Ghareeb, Edmund, ed., *Split Vision: The Portrayal of Arabs in the American Media* (Washington, D.C.:

American-Arab Affairs Council, 1983), pp. 67–76.

Geyer, Georgie, Anne, "The American Correspondent in the Arab World," in Hudson, Michael C. and Ronald G. Wolfe, eds., *The American Media and the Arabs* (Washington, D.C.: Center for Contemporary Arab Studies, Georgetown University, 1980), pp. 65–72.

Ghareeb, Edmund, "The American Media and the Palestinian Problem," *Journal of Palestine Studies*, Vol. 5 (Fall-Winter 1976), pp. 127–149.

Ghareeb, Edmund, "The Media and U.S. Perceptions of the Middle East," *American-Arab Affairs*, No. 2 (Fall 1982), pp. 69–78.

Ghareeb, Edmund, ed., *Split Vision: The Portrayal of Arabs in the American Media* (Washington, D.C.: American-Arab Affairs Council, 1983). 402 pp.

Glubb, Faris, "Who is Misreporting?" *Middle East International*, No. 173 (April 23, 1982), p. 7.

Gordon, Avishag H., "The Middle East October 1973 War as Reported by the American Networks," *International Problems*, Vol. 14 (Fall 1975), pp. 76–85.

Graham, Helga, *Arabian Time Machine* (London: Heinemann, 1978). (Part Seven: "Two Views of Arabs in the West," pp. 309–330).

Granberg-Michaelson, Wesley, *The Evangelical Right and Israel: What Place for the Arabs?* (ADC Issues, 8). 10 pp.

Greenfield, Meg, "Our Misperceptions of Islam," *Washington Post*, March 21, 1979, p. A–23.

Greider, William, "Acceptable Villains Make Our Troubles so Manageable," *Washington Post*, July 15, 1979, pp. E1, E4.

Griswold, William J., "Images of the Middle East," *Rocky Mountain Social Science Journal*, Vol. 11, No. 1 (January, 1974), pp. 25–36.

Griswold, William J., *The Image of the Middle East in Secondary School Textbooks* (New York: Middle East Studies Association of North America, 1975). 101 pp.

Gruen, George E., "Arab Petropower and American Public Opinion," *Middle East Review*, Vol. 7 (Winter 1975–76), pp. 33–39.

H., H., "The Middle East Crisis of 1967 and the New York Times," in *Essays on the American Public Opinion and the Palestine Problem* (Beirut, Lebanon: Palestine Research Center, 1969), pp. 35–87.

Hadar, Leon T., "Behind *The New York Times'* Middle East Coverage," *Middle East Review*, Vol. 12 (Summer 1980), pp. 56–61.

Haiek, Joseph R., ed., *Arab American Almanac* (Los Angeles, CA: The News Circle Publishing Co., 1984). 322 pp.

Hallaj, Muhammad, "Palestine: The Suppression of an Idea," *The Link*, Vol. 15, No. 1 (January-March 1982), 15 pp.

Hallaj, Muhammad, "From Time Immemorial: The Resurrection of a Myth," *The Link*, Vol. 18, No. 1 (January-March 1985), pp. 1–14.

Hammons, Terry Brooks, " 'A Wild Ass of a Man': American Images of Arabs in 1948" (Ph.D. dissertation, University of Oklahoma, 1978). 174 pp.

Hatem, Muhammad Abdel-Kader, *Information and the Arab Cause* (London: Longmans, 1974). 320 pp.

Havandjian, Nishan Rafi, "National Differences in the Press Coverage of the Lebanese Civil War" (Ph.D. dissertation, University of Texas, Austin, 1979). 252 pp.

Heggoy, Alf Andrew, ed., *Through Foreign Eyes: Western Attitudes Toward North Africa* (Washington, D.C.: University Press of America, 1982). 194 pp.

Heisey, Ray D., "The Rhetoric of the Arab-Israeli Conflict," *Quarterly Journal of Speech*, (Februay 1970), pp. 12–21.

Hershman, Robert, and Henry L. Griggs, Jr., "American Television News and the Middle East," *The Middle East Journal*, Vol. 35, No. 4 (Autumn, 1981), pp. 481–491.

Hertzberg, Arthur et al., *A Commentary Report: American Reactions to the Six Day War* (New York: Commentary, 1967). 30 pp.

Hester, Al, "Five Years of Foreign News on U.S. Television Evening Newscasts," *Gazette*, Vol. 24 (Spring 1978), pp. 86–95.

Hester, Al, "Middle-Eastern News on U.S. TV," *Communications and Development Review*, Vol. 1, Nos. 2 and 3 (Summer/Autumn 1977), pp. 25–26.

Hornblower, Margot, "Experts Bemoan America's Distorted Idea of Nature of Islam," *Washington Post*, December 11, 1979, p. A–10.

Howard, Harry N., "The Instant Potboilers and the 'Blitzkreig' War," *Issues*, Vol. 21 (Autumn 1967), pp. 48–52.

Hudson, Michael C. and Ronald G. Wolfe, eds., *The American Media and the Arabs* (Washington, D.C.: Center for Contemporary Arab Studies, Georgetown University, 1980). 105 pp.

Hudson, Michael C., "The Media and the Arabs: Room for Improvement," in Hudson, Michael C. and Ronald G. Wolfe, eds., *The American Media and the Arabs* (Washington, D.C.: Center for Contemporary Arab Studies, Georgetown University, 1980), pp. 91–103.

Hussain, Asaf, Robert Olson, and Jamil Qureshi, eds., *Orientalism,*

Islam, and Islamists (Brattleboro, VT: Amana Books, Inc., 1984). 300 pp.

Ingram, O. Kelly, "Christian Zionism," *The Link*, Vol. 16, No. 4 (November 1983), pp. 1–13.

Jabara, Abdeen, "The American Left and the June Conflict," in Abu-Lughod, Ibrahim, ed., *The Arab-Israeli Confrontation of June 1967: An Arab Perspective* (Evanston, Ill.: Northwestern University Press, 1970), pp. 169–190.

Jacobs, Deborah, "Teaching the Arab World: Evaluating Textbooks," *The Social Studies*, Vol. 72, No. 4 (July/August, 1981), pp. 150–153.

Jarrar, Samir A., "Images of the Arabs in United States Secondary School Social Studies Textbooks: A Content Analysis and a Unit Development" (Ph.D. dissertation, Florida State University, 1976). 217 pp.

Kaitz, Merrill, "Sadat's Visit in America's Press," *Moment*, Vol. 3 (January/February 1978), pp. 63–65.

Kanafani, Ghassan, "Bridging the Gap in East-West Communications," *The Middle East Newsletter*, (May/June 1972), Vol. 4, No. 3, pp. 4–5.

Karl, Patricia A., "In the Middle of the Middle East: The Media and U.S. Foreign Policy," in Ghareeb, Edmund, ed., *Split Vision: Portrayal of Arabs in the American Media* (Washington, D.C.: American-Arab Affairs Council, 1983), pp 283–298.

Kays, Doreen, *Frogs and Scorpions: Egypt, Sadat and the Media* (London: Frederick Muller, 1984). 271 pp.

Kearney, Helen McCready, "American Images of the Middle East, 1824–1924: A Century of Antipathy" (Ph.D. dissertation, University of Rochester, 1976). 558 pp.

Kempster, Norman and Ronald J. Ostrow, *The Arab Influence* (A series of articles reprinted from the *Los Angeles Times*, November 22–27, 1978). 24 pp.

Kennedy, Leonard Milton, "The Treatment of Moslem Nations, India, and Israel in Social Studies Textbooks Used in Elementary and Junior High Schools of the United States" (Ed.D. dissertation, Washington State University, 1960). 161 pp.

Kenworth, L.S., "Murals of the Middle East in Our Minds," *Social Education*, Vol. 25, No. 1 (January 1961), pp. 41–46, 50.

Kern, Montague, *Television and Middle East Diplomacy: President Carter's Fall 1977 Peace Initiative* (Washington, D.C.: Center for Contemporary Arab Studies, Georgetown University, 1983). 50 pp.

Khalidi, Walid, "Arabs and the West," *Middle East Forum* (December 1957).

Khalifa, Muhammad, *The Sublime Quran and Orientalism* (London: Longman Group, 1983). 262 pp.

Knee, Stuart E., "American Arabs and Palestine," *Patterns of Prejudice*, Vol. 11, No. 6 (November/December 1977), pp. 25–31, 34.

Ladd, Everett Carl Jr. and Seymour Martin Lipset, "War-Shy Professors Divided over Middle East," *The Chronicle of Higher Education*, December 1, 1975, pp. 1, 2.

Laqueur, Walter, "Israel, the Arabs, and World Opinion," *Commentary*, Vol. 44 (August 1967), pp. 49–59.

Lendenmann, G. Neal, "Arab Stereotyping in Contemporary American Political Cartoons," in Ghareeb, Edmund, ed., *Split Vision: Portrayal of Arabs in the American Media* (Washington, D.C.: American-Arab Affairs Council, 1983), pp. 345–353.

Leuchtenburg, William E., "The American Perception of the Arab World," in Atiyeh, George N., ed., *Arab and American Cultures* (Washington, D.C.: American Enterprise Institute for Public Policy Research, 1977), pp. 15–25.

Levine, Samuel H., "Changing Concepts of Palestine in American Literature to 1867" (Ph.D. dissertation, New York University, 1953). 322 pp.

Lewis, Bernard, "The Question of Orientalism," *The New York Review of Books*, Vol. 29, No. 11, (June 24, 1982), pp. 49–56.

Lichter, S. Robert, "Media Support for Israel: A Survey of Leading Journalists," in Adams, William, ed., *Television Coverage of the Middle East* (Norwood, N.J.: ABLEX Publishing Corporation, 1981), pp. 40–52.

Lilienthal, Alfred M., *What Price Israel?* (Chicago, IL.: Henry Regnery, 1953), pp. 121–147, 255–256.

Lilienthal, Alfred M., *There Goes the Middle East* (New York: Devin-Adair, 1958), pp. 54–73, 88–114, 203–252.

Lilienthal, Alfred M., *The Other Side of the Coin* (New York: The Devin-Adair Company, 1965). (Especially Chapters 5, 6, & 7, pp. 89–163, and pp. 368–379.

Lilienthal, Alfred M., *The Zionist Connection II* (New Brunswick, N.J.: North American, 1982). (Especially Parts II & III, pp. 103–532.

Lipset, Seymour Martin, "Further Commentary on American Attitudes," *Public Opinion*, Vol. 1, No. 2 (May/June 1978), pp. 16–17.

Lipset, Seymour Martin, "The Polls on the Middle East," *Middle East Review*, Vol. XI, No. 1 (Fall 1978), pp. 24–30.

Lipset, Seymour Martin and William Schneider, "Polls for the White

House, and the Rest of Us," *Encounter*, Vol. XLIX, No. 5 (November 1977), pp. 24–26, 29–34.

Lipset, Seymour Martin and William Schneider, "Carter vs. Israel — What the Polls Reveal," *Commentary*, Vol. 64, No. 5 (November 1977), pp. 21–29.

Little, Donald B, "Three Arab Critiques of Orientalism," *The Muslim World*, Vol. LXIX, No. 2 (April 1979), pp. 110–131.

Magee, Judith Helen, "Images of Arabs and Israelis in the Denver Press" (Ph.D. dissertation, University of Colorado, Boulder, Anthropology, Cultural, 1977). 215 pp.

Makari, George J., "On Seeing Arabs," *Arab Studies Quarterly*, Vol. 7, No. 1, pp. 58–66.

Massad, Winifred W., "Analysis of the Treatment of the Middle Eastern Arab States in Selected United States High School World History Textbooks" (Ph.D. dissertation, Miami University, Education, 1976). 130 pp.

Mathews, John, "U.S. Educators Aren't Laughing at Those Arab Jokes," *Washington Star*, January 7, 1976, pp. A1, A17.

Menconi, Evelyn A., "Studying the Arab World: Overcoming Textbook Deficiencies," *Audiovisual Instruction*, Vol. 21, No. 2 (February 1976), pp. 20–21.

Menconi, Evelyn A., "An Analysis of Teachers' Perceptions of the Arab World" (Ed.D. dissertation, Boston University, School of Education, 1981). 185 pp.

Mensch, Eugene Michael II, "American Images of Arabs: A Data-Based Analysis" (M.A. thesis, Naval Postgraduate School, 1978). 189 pp.

Metwalli, Ahmed Mohamed, "The Lure of the Levant, The American Literary Experience in Egypt and the Holy Land: A Study in the Literature of Travel, 1800–1865" (Ph.D. dissertation, State University of New York, Albany, Language and Literature, 1971). 399 pp.

Michalak, Laurence and Ameur Ben Arab, "Conflicting Images: Films on Arabs vs Films by Arabs," *International Development Review*, Vol. 2 (1972), pp. 31–33.

Michalak, Laurence, *Cruel and Unusual: Negative Images of Arabs in American Popular Culture* (Washington, D.C.: American-Arab Anti-Discrimination Committee, 1984?), 22 pp. (A.D.C. Issue Paper, 15).

Miller, Jake C., "Black Viewpoints on the Mid-East Conflict," *Journal of Palestine Studies*, Vol. X, No. 2 (Winter 1981), pp. 37–49.

Mishra, V.M., "News from the Middle East in Five U.S. Media,"

Journalism Quarterly, Vol. 56 (Summer 1979), pp. 374–378.

Mortimer, Edward, "Islam and the Western Journalist," *The Middle East Journal*, Vol. 35, No. 4 (Autumn, 1981), pp. 492–505.

Moughrabi, Fouad, "The Arab Basic Personality: A Critical Survey of the Literature," *International Journal of Middle East Studies,*, Vol. 9 (1978), pp. 99–112.

Moughrabi, Fouad, "A Political Technology of the Soul," *Arab Studies Quarterly*, Vol. 3, No. 1 (Winter 1981), pp. 66–88.

Moughrabi, Fouad, "American Public Opinion and the Palestine Question," *Journal of Palestine Studies*, Vol. 15, No. 2 (Winter 1986), pp. 56–75.

Mouly, Ruth W., *U.S.-Arab Relations: The Evangelical Dimension* (Washington, D.C.: National Council on U.S.-Arab Relations, 1985). 46 pp.

Mousa, Issam Suleiman, *The Arab Image in the U.S. Press* (New York: Peter Lang Publishing Inc., 1984). 187 pp.

"Myths About the Middle East," (Editorial), *The Nation*, Vol. 233, No. 19 (December 15, 1981), pp. 593–597.

Maclean, John, "The U.S. Press and the Middle East (II),"in Richardson, Lucy E., ed., *The Middle East: Press Perspectives and National Policies* (Washington, D.C.: Center for Middle East Policy, 1983), pp. 24–25.

Nabti, Michel George, "Coverage of the Arab World in American Secondary School World Studies Textbooks: A Content Analysis" (Ph.D. dissertation, Stanford University, 1981), 340 pp.

Naim, Samir, "Towards a Demystification of Arab Social Reality: A Critique of Anthropological and Political Writings on Arab Society," *Review of Middle East Studies*, Vol. 3 (1978), pp. 48–63.

Nasir, Sari Jamil, "The Image of the Arab in American Popular Cultures" (Ph.D. dissertation, University of Illinois, Social Psychology, 1962). 187 pp.

Nasir, Sari Jamil, "The Arab World in U.S. Movie Titles," *Journalism Quarterly*, Vol. 40 (Fall 1963), pp. 351–352.

"Nation-wide Public Opinion Survey of US Attitudes on the Middle East," *Journal of Palestine Studies*, Vol. 14, No. 4 (Summer 1985), pp. 117–121.

Nes, David, "American Public Opinion and Israel," *Middle East International*, No. 48 (June 1975), pp. 12–14.

Newsom, David, "The Arabs and U.S. Public Opinion: Is There Hope?" *American-Arab Affairs*, No. 2 (Fall 1982), pp. 61–68.

Nielson, Howard C., "Examining U.S. Perceptions and Attitudes Toward the Middle East," *American-Arab Affairs*, No. 10 (Fall 1984), pp. 9–14.

Otero, G.G., *Teaching About Perception: The Arabs* (Denver, CO: University of Denver Center for Teaching International Relations, 1978). 129 pp.

Othman, Jihad Mahmoud, "A Critique of International Materials for Near Eastern Studies" (D.A. dissertation, University of Washington, Seattle, 1981). 151 pp.

Owen, Jean, "The Polls and Newspaper Appraisal of the Suez Crisis," *Public Opinion Quarterly*, Vol. 21, No. 3 (Fall 1957), pp. 350–354.

Oxtoby, Willard G., "The War of Words: A Look at the Literature in America and the Middle East" (Mimeographed) (New Haven: New Haven Committee on the Middle East Crisis, 1968), pp. 31–36.

Oxtoby, Willard G., "Western Perceptions of Islam and the Arabs," in Hudson, Michael C. and Ronald G. Wolfe, eds., *The American Media and the Arabs* (Washington, D.C.: Center for Contemporary Arab Studies, Georgetown University, 1980), pp. 3–12.

Padelford, Edward A., "The Regional American Press: An Analysis of Its Reporting and Commentary on the Arab-Israeli Situation" (Ph.D. dissertation, American University, 1979). 347 pp.

Pearson, Robert Paul, "Through Middle Eastern Eyes: The Development of Curriculum Materials on the Middle East" (Ph.D. dissertation, University of Massachusetts, Education, 1973). 343 pp.

Peck, Malcolm C., "Teaching Materials and Sources of Information on the Middle East for Secondary School Teachers," *Social Education*, Vol. 40, No. 2 (February 1976), pp. 93–95.

Peretz, Don, "Arabs vs Israelis: Fiction and Fact," *Issues*, Vol. 13 (Fall 1959), pp. 1–14.

Peretz, Don, "Reporting Lebanon the 'Christian' Way," *Middle East Insight*, Vol. 2, No. 4 (September 1982), pp. 46–52.

Perry, Glenn, "Treatment of the Middle East in American High School Textbooks," *Journal of Palestine Studies*, Vol. 4, No. 3 (Spring, 1975), pp. 46–58.

Perry, Glenn, E., "The Reality and Distorting Lenses," in Perry Glenn E., ed., *Palestine: Continuing Dispossession (Belmont, MA: Association of Arab-American University Graduates, 1986), pp. 3–14.*

Pershern, Katherine B., "Images of the Middle East and Vietnam: The Relationship of Religious Affiliation and Political Cynicism" (M.A. thesis, University of Wyoming, Laramie, Political Science, 1974).

110 pp.

Peters, Rudolph, "The Mysteries of the Oriental Mind: Some Remarks on the Development of Western Stereotypes of Arabs," in El-Sheikh, Ibrahim A., C. Aart van de Koppel, eds., *The Challenge of the Middle East* (Amsterdam, the Netherlands: Institute for Modern Near Eastern Studies, University of Amsterdam, 1982). pp. 73–90, 195–198.

Pierce, Patricia Dawes, "Deciphering Egypt: Four Studies in the American Sublime" (Ph.D. dissertation, Yale University, 1980). 178 pp.

Piety, Harold A., "Zionist Bias in American Editorial Pages," in Ghareeb, Edmund, ed., *Split Vision: Portrayal of Arabs in the American Media* (Washingon, D.C.: Institute of Middle Eastern and North African Affairs, 1977), pp. 135–152.

Piety, Harold A., "Bias on American Editorial Pages," in Ghareeb, Edmund, ed., *Split Vision: Portrayal of Arabs in the American Media* (Washington, D.C.: American-Arab Affairs Council, 1983), pp. 125–142.

Protinsky, Ruth Anne, "An Analysis of the Treatment of Middle Eastern Arabs in Virginia Elementary Social Studies Textbooks" (Ph.D. dissertation, Virginia Polytechnic Institute and State University, Education, 1979). 152 pp.

Pruett, Gordon E., "The Escape From the Seraglio: Anti-Orientalist Trends in Modern Religious Studies," *Arab Studies Quarterly*, Vol. 2, No. 4 (Fall 1981), pp. 291–317.

Richardson, Lucy E., ed., *The Middle East: Press Perspectives and National Policies* (Washington, D.C.: Center for Middle East Policy, 1983). 40 pp.

Roeh, Itzhak, "Israel in Lebanon: Language and Images of Storytelling," in Adams, William, ed., *Television Coverage of the Middle East* (Norwood: N.J.: ABLEX Publishing Corporation, 1981), pp. 76–88.

Rubenberg, Cheryl A., "Pro-Israeli Influence on the Media and U.S. Middle East Policy," *Mideast Monitor* Vol. 2, No. 2 (March 1985), pp. 1–4.

Rubin, Barry, "The Media and the Middle East," *Middle East Review*, Vol. 7 (Winter, 1975–76), pp. 28–32.

Sahwell, Aziz S., *Exodus: A Distortion of Truth* (New York: Arab Information Center, 1960). 34 pp.

Said, Abdul Aziz and Alain Sportiche, "Requirements for a Stable Peace: Arab and Israeli Images," in Allen, Harry S. and Ivan Volgyes, eds., *Israel, the Middle East, and U.S. Interests* (New York: Praeger, 1983), pp. 18–25.

Said, Edward [W.], "The Arab Portrayed," in Abu-Lughod, Ibrahim, ed., *The Arab-Israeli Confrontation of June 1967: An Arab Perspective* (Evanston, Ill.: Northwestern University Press, 1970), pp. 1–9.

Said, Edward W., "Orientalism and the October War: The Shattered Myths," in Abu-Laban, Baha and Faith T. Zeadey, eds., *Arabs in America: Myths and Realities* (Wilmette, Ill.: Medina University Press International, 1975), pp. 83–112.

Said, Edward W., *Orientalism* (New York: Pantheon Books, 1978). 368 pp.

Said, Edward W., *Covering Islam: How the Media and the Experts Determine How We See the Rest of the World* (New York: Pantheon Books, 1981). 186 pp.

Said, Edward W., "Orientalism Reconsidered," *Race and Class*, Vol. XXVII, 2 (1985), pp. 1–15.

Salt, Jeremy, "Fact and Fiction in the Middle Eastern Novels of Leon Uris," *Journal of Palestine Studies*, Vol. 14, No. 3 (Spring 1985), pp. 54–63.

Sam'o, Elias, "The Arab-Israeli Conflict as Reported by the Kalb Brothers," in Abu-Laban, Baha and Faith T. Zeadey, eds., *Arabs in America: Myths and Realities* (Wilmette, Ill.: Medina University Press International, 1975), pp. 45–52.

Sandbank, Kenneth, "Literary Representation and Social Legitimation: J.L. Burckhardt's Approach to 'The Orient'," *International Journal of Middle East Studies*, Vol. 13, No. 4 (1981), pp. 497–511.

Sayegh, Fayez A., *Zionist Propaganda in the United States: An Analysis*, edited by Arlene F. Sayegh and Samir Abed-Rabbo (Pleasantville, New York: The Fayez A Sayegh Foundation, 1983). 53 pp.

Schneider, Steven M., "A Content Analysis of Sadat's 1977 Visit to Israel," in Cole, Richard L., ed., *Introduction to Political Inquiry* (New York: Macmillan Publishing Co., 1980), pp. 245–259.

Sedki, George Y[ounan], "The Treatment of Arabs in World History Books Used by Senior High Schools of the City and County of Saint Louis, Missouri, 1974–75" (Ph.D. dissertation, St. Louis University, 1976). 408 pp.

Shaheen, Jack G., "American Television: Arabs in Dehumanizing Roles," in Hudson, Michael C. and Ronald G. Wolfe, eds., *The American Media and the Arabs* (Washington, D.C.: Center for Contemporary Arab Studies, Georgetown University, 1980), pp. 39–44.

Shaheen, Jack G., "The Arab Stereotype on Television," *The Link*, Vol. 13, No. 2 (April/May 1980). 13 pp.

Shaheen, Jack G., "Images of Saudis and Palestinians: A Review of Major Documentaries," in Adams, William, ed., *Television Coverage of the Middle East* (Norwood, N.J.: ABLEX Publishing Corporation, 1981), pp. 89–105.

Shaheen, Jack G., "The Arab Image in American Mass Media," *American-Arab Affairs*, No. 2 (Fall 1982), pp. 89–96.

Shaheen, Jack G., *The T, V. Arab* (Bowling Green, Ohio: Bowling Green State University Popular Press, 1984). 146 pp.

Shouby, E., "The Influence of the Arabic Language on the Psychology of the Arabs," *Middle East Journal*, Vol. 5, No. 3 (Summer, 1951), pp. 284–302.

Simonson, Solomon, "An Analysis of Arab and Israeli Propaganda," *Vital Speeches,*, Vol. 34 (June 1, 1968), pp. 494–497.

Slade, Shelley, "The Image of the Arab in America: Analysis of a Poll on American Attitudes," *The Middle East Journal*, Vol. 35, No. 2 (Spring 1981), pp. 143–162.

Smith, Terence, "The U.S. Press and the Middle East (I)," in Richardson, Lucy E., ed., *The Middle East: Press Perspectives and National Policies* (Washington, D.C.: The Center for Middle East Policy, 1983), pp. 18–23.

Spragens, William, "Camp David and the Networks: Coverage of the 1978 Summit," in Adams, William C., ed., *Television Coverage of International Affairs*, Vol. II. (Norwood, N.J.: ABLEX Publishing Company, 1982).

Sreebny, Daniel, "American Correspondents in the Middle East: Perceptions and Problems," *Journalism Quarterly*, 56 (Summer 1979), pp. 368–388.

Stevens, Richard P., "Zionism Re-examined: U.S. Tool or Israeli Lobby?" in Pennar, Margaret, ed., *The Middle East: Five Perspectives* (North Dartmouth, MA: Association of Arab-American University Graduates, 1973), pp. 29–32. (AAUG Information Paper, 7)

Stevens, Richard P., "The Palestinian Issue and Western Public Opinion." The Second United Nations Seminar on the Question of Palestine, 25–29 August, 1980, Vienna, pp. 398–403 of Proceedings.

Stock, Raymond, "Prestige Press at War: The New York Times and Le Monde in Lebanon, August 1–September 26, 1982," *The Middle East Journal*, Vol. 39, No. 3 (Summer 1985), pp. 317–340.

Stork, Joe, "The American New Left and Palestine," *Journal of Palestine Studies*, Vol. II, No. 1 (Autumn 1972), pp. 64–69.

Suleiman, Michael W., "An Evaluation of Middle East News Coverage in Seven American Newsmagazines, July-December 1956" (M.A. thesis, University of Wisconsin, Madison, Political Science, 1961). 125 pp.

Suleiman, Michael W., "American Mass Media and the June Conflict," in Abu-Lughod, Ibrahim, ed., *The Arab-Israeli Confrontation of June, 1967: An Arab Perspective* (Evanston, Ill.: Northwestern University Press, 1970), pp. 138–54.

Suleiman, Michael W., "The Middle East in American High School Curricula, A Kansas Case Study," *Middle East Studies Association Bulletin*, Vol. 8, No. 2 (1974), pp. 8–19.

Suleiman, Michael W., "National Stereotypes as Weapons in the Arab-Israeli Conflict," *Journal of Palestine Studies*, Vol. III, No. 3, (Spring 1974), pp. 109–121.

Suleiman, Michael W., "Perceptions of the Middle East in American Newsmagazines," in Abu-Laban, Baha and Faith T. Zeadey, eds., *Arabs in America: Myths and Realities* (Wilmette, Ill.: Medina University Press International, 1975), pp. 28–44.

Suleiman, Michael W., *American Images of Middle East Peoples: Impact of the High School* (New York: Middle East Studies Association of North America, Inc., 1977). 72 pp.

Suleiman, Michael W., "American Public Support of Middle Eastern Countries: 1939–1979," in Hudson, Michael C. and Ronald G. Wolfe, eds., *The American Media and the Arabs* (Washington, D.C.: Center for Contemporary Arab Studies, Georgetown University, 1980), pp. 13–36.

Suleiman, Michael W., "The Effect of American Perspectives of Arabs on Middle East Issues," in Ghareeb, Edmund, ed., *Split Vision: Portrayal of Arabs in the American Media* (Washington, D.C.: American-Arab Affairs Council, 1983), pp. 337–344.

Suleiman, Michael W., "The Arab Information Effort in North America: An Assessment," *Arab Studies Quarterly*, Vol. 8 No. 3 (July 1986).

Suleiman, Michael W., "World Public Opinion and the Question of Palestine," in Perry, Glenn E., ed., *Palestine: Continuing Dispossession* (Belmont, MA: Association of Arab-American University Graduates, Inc., 1986), pp. 49–93.

Terry, Janice J., "A Content Analysis of American Newspapers," in Jabara, Abdeen and Janice Terry, eds., *The Arab World: From*

Nationalism to Revolution (Wilmette, Ill: Medina Universtiy Press International, 1971), pp. 94–113.

Terry, Janice J., "The Western Press and the October War: A Content Analysis," in Abu-Laban, Baha and Faith T. Zeadey, eds., *Arabs in America: Myths and Realities* (Wilmette, Ill.: Medina University Press International, 1975), pp. 3–27.

Terry, Janice J., "Zionist Attitudes Toward Arabs," *Journal of Palestine Studies*, Vol. 6 (Autumn, 1976), pp. 67–78.

Terry, Janice J., *Mistaken Identity: Arab Stereotypes in Popular Writing* (Washington, D.C.: American-Arab Affairs Council, 1985). 135 pp.

Terry, Janice J. and Gordon Mendenhall, "1973 U.S. Press Coverage on the Middle East," *Journal of Palestine Studies*, Vol. 4 (Autumn 1974), pp. 120–133.

Thimmesch, Nick, "Arabs: The Latest Scapegoats," *Washington Post*, February 9. 1979, p. A17.

Thimmesch, Nick, "American Media Perspectives on the Arab World," in Hudson, Michael C. and Ronald G. Wolfe, eds., *The American Media and the Arabs* (Washington, D.C.: Center for Contemporary Arab Studies, Georgetown, University, 1980), pp. 59–62.

Thimmesch, Nick, "The Media and the Middle East," *American-Arab Affairs*, No. 2 (Fall 1982), pp. 79–88.

Tibawi, A.L., "English-speaking Orientalists: A Critique of Their Approach to Islam and Arab Nationalism," *The Muslim World*, Vol. 53, Nos. 3 & 4 (July and October, 1963), pp. 185–204; 298–313.

Tibawi, A.L., "Second Critique of English-speaking Orientalists and Their Approach to Islam and the Arabs," *The Islamic Quarterly*, Vol. 23, No. 1 (January-March 1979), pp. 4–8.

Tibawi, A.L., "On the Orientalists Again," *The Muslim World*, Vol. 70, No. 1 (January 1980), pp. 56–61.

Trice, Robert H., "The American Elite Press and the Arab-Israeli Conflict," *The Middle East Journal*, Vol. 33, No. 3 (Summer 1979), pp. 304–325.

Tyrrell, R. Emmett Jr., "Chimera in the Middle East," *Harper's* , (November 1976), pp. 35–37.

Tyrrell, R. Emmett Jr., "News or Soap Opera?" *Washington Post*, January 26, 1981, pp. A–17.

Wagner, Charles H., "Elite American Newspaper Opinion and the Middle East: Commitment Versus Isolation," in Beling, Willard A., ed., *The Middle East: Quest for American Policy* (Albany, N.Y.:

SUNY Press, 1973), pp. 306–344.

Weisman, John, "Blind Spot in the Middle East: Why You Don't See More Palestinians on TV," Part I, *TV Guide*, October 24, 1981, pp. 6–8, 10,12, 14. Part II, *ibid.*, October 31–November 6, 1981, pp. 10–12, 14. (Part II is entitled: "Blind Spot in the Middle East: Why the Palestinians Are Losing the Propaganda War").

Wilson, Ernest J. III, "Orientalism: A Black Perspective," *Journal of Palestine Studies*, Vol. X, No. 2 (Winter, 1981), pp. 59–69.

Wingerter, Rex B., "The Palestine-Israel Conflict in the U.S. Courtroom," *The Link*, Vol. 18, No. 3 (September 1985), pp. 1–13.

Wright, Claudia, "U.S. Coverage of the Middle East," *Mideast Monitor*, Vol. 2, No. 1 (January 1985), pp. 1–4.

Young, Lewis, "American Blacks and the Arab-Israeli Conflict," *Journal of Palestine Studies*, Vol. II, No. 1 (Autumn, 1972), pp. 70–85.

Zamil, Abdulrahman Abdulla, "The Effectiveness and Credibility of Arab Propaganda in the United States" (Ph.D. dissertation, University of Southern California, 1973). 299 pp.

Zaremba, Alan Jay, "An Exploratory Analysis of National Perceptions of the Arab-Israeli Conflict as Represented Through World Newspapers: An International Communications Study" (Ph.D. dissertation, State University of New York, Buffalo, 1977). 294 pp.

Ziadeh, Farhat J. and H. Allen Colvin, *An Evaluation of the Treatment of Egypt in American Primary and Secondary School Literature* (Final Report, ERIC Document, Reproduction Service No. Ed. 128291, 1976). 130 pp.

INDEX

Abdel-Nasser, Gamal, 2, 3, 4, 6, 37, 38, 41, 42, 47, 48, 50, 66, 98, 185, 186, 187, 198

Abscam, 149

Algeria (Algerians), 33, 79

America (Americans), 55, 57, 69, 73, 114, 130, 132, 133, 152, 162, 163, 164, 170, 175, 186, 187, 191, 192, 198, 207, 210; and United States of America (U.S.A.), 15, 44, 59, 116, 118, 178, 183, 184, 185

American Aid, 46, 132, 134, 137, 164, 192, 199, 200, 201, 202

American-Arab relations, 57, 76, 145, 168, 176, 185, 187, 188, 199

American Correspondents, 16, 32, 33, 38, 47, 69

American Interests, 18, 58, 60, 116, 135, 146, 171, 184, 188, 189, 191, 192

American Institute of Public Opinion, *see* Gallup

American-Israeli relations, 116, 118, 119, 138, 192, 198, 200, 210

American Missionaries, 9, 10, 191

American News Media, 12, 16, 19–23, 26–34, 38, 41–45, 47–49, 51, 52, 60–68, 71, 76, 78, 80, 82, 134, 137, 146, 147, 151–153, 178, 184, 199, 200

American Public Opinion, 1, 2, 6, 9, 34, 52, 60, 67, 69, 70, 74, 76, 77, 80, 81, 87, 93–108, 113–127, 130, 131, 134–138, 145–148, 152–154, 171, 183–185, 193, 195, 197–200, 202, 203, 205–207, 209, 210

American World History and social science courses, 80; and schools, 87; and teachers, 81, 89, 90, 93–106, 108, 109; and textbooks, 79, 88, 91, 92, 203

Anglo-American Committee, 128, 130

Arab-American Dialogue, 186–188

Arab-Americans, *see* Arabs in America

Arab Information Effort, 161–167, 169–174, 178, 179

Arab-Israeli Conflict, *see* Palestine-Israeli Conflict

Arab League, *see* League of Arab States

Arab Nationalist Movement, 6; and Arab Nationalism, 3, 4, 37,